Modern Spain 1875 - 1980

Raymond Carr

Modern Spain 1875 – 1980

Oxford New York Toronto Melbourne

OXFORD UNIVERSITY PRESS

1980

Oxford University Press, Walton Street, Oxford OX2 6DP

London Glasgow New York Toronto
Delhi Bombay Calcutta Madras Karachi
Kuala Lumpur Singapore Hong Kong Tokyo
Nairobi Dar es Salaam Cape Town
Melbourne Wellington
and associate companies in
Beirut Berlin Ibadan Mexico City

British Library Cataloguing in Publication Data

Carr, Raymond
Modern Spain
1. Spain–Politics and government–20th century
2. Spain–Politics and government–19th century
I. Title
946.08   DP233   80–40638

ISBN 0 19 215828 7
ISBN 0 19 289090 5 Pbk

Phototypeset in Great Britain by
Filmtype Services Limited,
Scarborough, England

Printed in Great Britain by
Cox & Wyman Ltd,
Reading, Berks.

Preface

This book embodies some sections of my work published over the last twenty years. That work has been immensely enriched (and in many cases corrected) by the extraordinary renaissance of Spanish historiography and the renewal of interest in modern Spanish history on the part of scholars outside Spain. In the bibliography at p. 182, which concentrates on more recent studies, I have tried to spell out the large debt I owe to other historians.

The relative proportions of the book reflect my hope of drawing on the more recent work of Spanish historians and social scientists. Since for the later periods—particularly the Second Republic and the Civil War—the Spanish contribution has been absorbed by English colleagues, and since the history of those years is more familiar to English readers, I have dealt in greater detail with the period 1875–1930.

The concentration on what might be considered orthodox political history implies no denial of the importance of structural factors. I have chosen so to concentrate because I believe that the fundamental problem of Spain in this period was a political problem: the search for a political system which could enjoy legitimacy, that long-term, generalized acceptance which provides stable governments—other than those maintained by force. The various political regimes failed to capture the allegiance and overcome the political apathy of the 'neutral mass'—indeed they thrived on apathy and perpetuated it. The sudden political mobilization of the Second Republic of 1931 brought to the surface conflicts which the previous political systems had buried and which the Republic itself could not master. Spain relapsed into forty years of 'iron surgery'.

The Spain of the 1970s is less fraught with violent social conflict than the Spain of the Second Republic. The new democratic state possesses a legitimacy denied to all previous regimes. It confronts some of the same problems as its democratic neighbours: inflation; unemployment; a falling off of investment; political apathy; terrorism. As always, the regional problems that complicate political life are more acute in Spain than elsewhere: they constitute the most difficult fence to face.

ST. ANTONY'S COLLEGE, OXFORD
December 1979

R.C.

Contents

Chronology

Main Political Events 1868–1979

The September Revolution

1868	September	Liberal military rebellion overthrows Isabella II and forms Provisional Government.
1869		Democratic constitution.
1873		First (Federal) Republic. Cantonalist revolt and Carlist war.
1874	4 January	General Pavia overthrows Federal Republicans; Conservative Republic of General Serrano.
	December	*Pronunciamiento* of General Martínez Campos restores Bourbon monarchy with Isabella's son, Alfonso XII.

1875–98 Era of The 'Turno Pacífico'

	Alternation of Liberal Conservative (led by Cánovas del Castillo) and Liberal (led by Sagasta) parties based on electoral management (*caciquismo*).
1898	The Disaster. Defeat by U.S. and loss of remnants of colonial empire (Cuba, Puerto Rico, and Philippines).

1898–1923 Decay of Two-Party System

1899	Silvela–Polavieja ministry. Failure of first essay in Conservative political regeneration from above.
1901	Foundation of Lliga Regionalista with programme of Catalan autonomy dominated by F. Cambó as representative of Catalan bourgeoisie.
1903	Death of Sagasta. Liberal party begins to split into factions.

1900 on	Lerroux wins over working-class vote in Barcelona for Republicans; opposes Lliga.
1906	Solidaridad Catalana: electoral coalition from Republicans to Conservative Catalans. Ousts *turno* parties in Barcelona.
1907–9	Ministry of Antonio Maura: failure of second attempt at Conservative 'revolution from above' and of co-operation between Cambó and Maura to solve Catalan issue.
1909	Tragic Week in Barcelona: Maura dismissed by Alfonso XIII and Conservative party splits between supporters of Maura and Dato.
1910–12	Ministry of J. Canalejas: Liberal–democratic regenerationism. Canalejas assassinated 1912.
1914–18	European Great War.
1917	a) Military Juntas (junior officer revolt).
	b) Catalan and left-wing protest movement culminates in Assembly Movement against political establishment.
	c) August: general strike suppressed by army.
	d) November: Cambó deserts Assembly Movement.
1918	Maura's National Government: includes Cambó and reformist Liberal Alba.
1919	Intensification of labour struggles in Barcelona. Canadiense strike. CNT and employers in gang warfare.
1921	Disastrous defeat at Anual in Morocco; opens up debate on political responsibilities.
1923	Ministry of Liberal García Prieto with reformist programme.
September	*Pronunciamiento* of Primo de Rivera overthrows parliamentary system.

1923–30 Dictatorship of General Primo De Rivera

1925	'Crowning victory' at Alhucemas in Morocco.
1926	Civil Directory.
1927–9	Failure of Primo to legitimize his rule by a constitution drawn up by National Assembly.

1930–1 Collapse of The Monarchy

1930	January (to April 1931)	Government of General Berenguer.
	17 August	Pact of San Sebastian unites Republican and Catalan left against the monarchy.
	12 December	Military revolt at Jaca.
1931	February–April	Government of Admiral Aznar.
	April	Municipal elections. Monarchist candidates defeated in large towns; Catalan left (Esquerra) defeats Lliga in Catalonia. King Alfonso XIII leaves Spain.

1931–6 Second Republic

1. Republic of the Republicans

1931		Provisional Government under conservative Catholic Alcalá Zamora. Generalidad (i.e. limited self-government) granted to Catalonia.
	May	'Burning of churches'.
	28 June	Election to constituent Cortes: constitution promulgated 9 December.
	14 October	Conservatives Alcalá Zamora and Miguel Maura resign over religious issue. Azaña ministry: coalition of left Republicans and Socialists.
1932	10 August	*Pronunciamiento* of General Sanjurjo.
	September	Cortes pass Law of Agrarian Reform and the Catalan Autonomy Statute.
1933	19 November	General election: Azaña coalition defeated. Victory of Lerroux's Radicals and Gil Robles' Catholic CEDA.

2. Republic of the Right: 1933–6 The Two 'Black Years'

1933–4		Governments of Lerroux's conservative Republicans supported by CEDA.
1934	1 October	Three CEDA ministers enter government.
	6 October	Revolt in Asturias and Catalonia.
1935		Formation of Popular Front (i.e. electoral coalition based on left Republicans and Socialists).
1936	15 February	Electoral victory of Popular Front.

3. February–July 1936 Republic of the Popular Front

1936	February	Azaña government (left Republicans *without* Socialists).
	10 May	Azaña resigns and becomes President. Government of Casares Quiroga (12 May).

1936–9 The Civil War

1936	17 July	Army rising in Morocco: spreads to Spain 18 July.
	July–August	'Spontaneous revolution' of collectivization.
	4 September	Ministry of Largo Caballero brings Socialists into government.
	4 November	CNT join Largo's government.
	8 November	Franco fails to take Madrid. Arrival of International Brigades.
	29 November	Franco becomes Head of State and Head of Government.
1937		Nationalist offensive held at Jarama (February) and Guadalajara (March).
	19 April	Franco amalgamates Falange and Carlists 'from above'.
	April	Franco's northern offensive. Guernica bombed 26 April.
	3–8 May	Revolt of POUM in Barcelona.
	17 May	Fall of Largo Caballero and government of Negrín.
	19 June	Bilbao falls.
	7–26 July	Battle of Brunete.
1938	15 April	Nationalists reach Mediterranean and divide Republican zone.
	July–November	Battle of the Ebro.
	December	Collapse of Republican armies in Catalonia.
1939	5 March	Anti-Communist *coup* of Colonel Casado.
	7–11 March	Communist revolt in Madrid.
	1 April	Surrender of Republican armies.

1939–75 Francoism

1942	3 September	Serrano Suñer dismissed.
1943	17 March	Cortes opens.

1945	19 March	Don Juan's Lausanne Manifesto against Franco.
	17 July	Spaniards' Charter (*Fuero de los Españoles*) promulgated.
1953	27 August	Concordat with Vatican signed.
	20 September	Base agreement between U.S.A. and Spain signed.
1956	February	Student troubles; dismissal of Ruiz Giménez and Fernández Cuesta.
1957	25 February	Franco forms sixth government, including the technocrats of Opus Dei.
1958	17 May	Principles of National Movement presented to Cortes.
1959	22 July	Stabilization Plan announced.
1962	9 February	Spain requests negotiations with EEC.
	April–June	Workers' and students' agitation; State of Emergency in Basque Provinces and Asturias.
1963	28 December	First Development Plan.
1966	22 November	Organic Law of State presented to Cortes.
1967	21 September	Admiral Carrero Blanco appointed Deputy Head of Government.
1969	22 July	Franco presents Juan Carlos as his successor.
1970	3–28 December	Burgos trial of ETA.
1973	20 December	Carrero Blanco assassinated.
	29 December	Arias Navarro appointed Prime Minister.
1974	12 February	Arias announces 'opening' of the regime.
	9 July	Franco taken seriously ill.
	29 July	Opposition forms Democratic Junta.
	23 December	New Law of Political Associations.
1975	June	Moderate opposition forms the Platform of Democratic Convergence.
	20 November	Franco dies.
	22 November	Juan Carlos crowned king.
	13 December	Arias forms new government including reformists Fraga, Areilza, Garrigues.
1976	28 January	Arias presents his programme to Cortes.
	26 March	Opposition unites in Democratic Co-ordination.
	3 July	Adolfo Suárez appointed Prime Minister.
	16 November	Cortes approves Law of Political Reform, which re-establishes democracy in Spain.
1977	9 April	Suárez legalizes Spanish Communist party.

	15 June	First democratic elections since 1936 held.
	29 September	The Generalidad (self-government of Catalonia) re-established.
	25–27 October	Government and opposition sign the Pact of Moncloa.
	30 December	Pre-autonomy given to the Basque Provinces.
1979		Cortes passes constitution.

Glossary of Political Terms and Organizations

ACNP (Asociación Católica Nacional de Propagandistas): Catholic lay organization founded in 1904, dedicated to penetrating the political and intellectual élite.

AP (Alianza Popular): conservative right-wing party founded in the autumn of 1976 by former Franco ministers led by M. Fraga Iribarne.

caciquismo: the system of electoral corruption and management, run by local bosses, which supported the *turno pacífico* (q.v.).

Carlists: classic right-wing Catholic party in Spain. Rejected the 'liberal' monarchy of Alfonso XIII in favour of the claims of the descendants of Don Carlos (1785–1855). Majority of its activists concentrated in Navarre where its militia (the *requetés*) was recruited. Fused with the Falange in April 1937.

CEDA (Confederación Española de Derechas Autónomas): nationwide confederation of Catholic right-wing parties led by Gil Robles, founded March 1933. It had a 'left' which professed social-Catholic doctrine but was essentially a party of the conservative right committed to the corporate state.

CNT (Confederación Nacional del Trabajo): anarcho-syndicalist trades union founded 1910. Believed in 'direct action' against employers, rejecting political action and electoral participation. CNT strength lay in Catalonia (particularly Barcelona), in the Levante and Aragon, and appealed to the rural proletariat of Andalusia.

collectivization: various forms of workers' control during the 'spontaneous revolution' of 1936.

CC.OO (Comisiones Obreras—Workers' Commissions): illegal trade unions formed by Communists, Catholics, and left-wing Marxists. Appeared in late 1950s. Legalized in 1977. Now a Communist-led trade union.

desamortación: sale of Church (1836) and municipal (1855) lands to private owners.

ETA (Euzkadi Ta Askatasuna): clandestine revolutionary organization formed in 1967 by those who considered the PNV (q.v.) too moderate. Responsible for terrorism, including the assassination of Admiral Carrero Blanco (December 1973).

Falange Española: grouping of authoritarian nationalist parties under the leadership of José Antonio Primo de Rivera, son of the dictator. The nearest approach to a fascist party in Spain. Grew rapidly in early months of the Civil War and in April 1937 fused by Franco with the Carlists to form the FET de las JONS—the only political 'party' in Franco's Spain.

Generalidad: the Autonomous Government of Catalonia set up by the Statute of 1932.

ID (Izquierda Democrática): Christian Democrat group led by Ruíz Giménez.

Junta Democrática: coalition of parties of the illegal anti-Francoist opposition, formed July 1974 with the Communists as the leading force. Neither PSOE nor Christian Democrats joined in.

Liberal party: left of *turno pacífico*. Formed by Sagasta and after his death (1903) split into factions.

Liberal Conservative party: right of *turno pacífico*. Led by Cánovas and after 1909 split between factions led by Maura and Dato.

Lliga Regionalista: conservative autonomist party in Catalonia. Dominated by Cambó.

Mauristas: supporters of Antonio Maura's Conservative 'revolution from above'.

Movimiento Nacional: amalgam of all the different groups which supported Franco in 1936. It filled the role of the single party in totalitarian regimes.

Opus Dei: lay brotherhood of committed Catholics, aimed at influencing university and political life. Nursery of the technocrats of the 1960s. Fell from influence in 1973.

OS (Organización Sindical): the 'vertical' Francoist syndicates.

PCE (Partido Comunista de España): Spanish Communist party. Santiago Carrillo was its Secretary General 1960.

PNV (Partido Nacionalista Vasco): the Basque Catholic Nationalist party; ultimate aim full autonomy for the Basque Provinces. Accepted the lay Republic and joined the Popular Front government because that Republic granted the Basque Provinces of Vizcaya and Guipúzcoa autonomy in October 1936.

Plataforma de Convergencia Democrática: coalition of various parties of the anti-Francoist opposition, created in 1975.

Popular Front: electoral coalition of left Republicans, Socialists, and Communists; won election of February 1936.

POUM (Partido Obrero de Unificación Marxista): revolutionary Marxist party founded September 1935 from the former Trotskyist left Communist party of Andrés Nin and Joaquín Maurín's bloc of workers and peasants. As opposed to the CNT, the POUM held that the workers must seize *political* power.

pronunciamiento: an officers' *coup d'état*, the conventional military rebellion of Spain.

PSOE (Partido Socialista Obrero Español): the Socialist party of Spain founded 1879.

PSP: an independent Socialist group launched in 1968 by Professor Tierno Galván. In 1978 united with PSOE.

PSUC (Partido Socialista Unificado de Cataluña): formed in July 1936 by the fusion of the Catalan Communist party and the Catalan branch of the PSOE. Affiliated to Third International; Communist influence in the party grew steadily.

Radical Republican party: led by Alejandro Lerroux in early 1900s. Aimed at gaining working-class support in Barcelona. Rival of the Lliga (see above); became main party of conservative Republicans by 1931.

Reformist Republicans: moderate Republican party ready to accept a democratic monarchy committed to reform.

reparto: distribution of large land holdings to small proprietors.

turno pacífico: the rigged alternation in power of the Liberal and Liberal Conservative parties.

UCD (Unión Centro Democrático): electoral coalition formed in 1977 under the leadership of Prime Minister Adolfo Suárez. After its success in 1977 election, became a unified political party.

UGT (Unión General de Trabajadores): the Socialist trade union. Main strengths in Madrid, and the Asturias mining and the Basque industrial zones.

UP (Unión Patriótica): the political movement created to support the dictatorship of General Primo de Rivera.

TWENTIETH-CENTURY SPAIN

Provincial capitals: Seville ●
Former provinces: NAVARRE

0   100   200 km

1 Revolution and Restoration 1868–1875: The Liberal Heritage

The word 'liberal', as part of our political vocabulary, comes from Spain. It was first used to describe a group of radical patriots, cooped up in Cadiz as refugees from the French invasion of 1808. In 1812 they drew up a constitution which, by enshrining the revolutionary doctrine of the sovereignty of the people, destroyed the basis of the old monarchy; it was to become the model for advanced democrats from St. Petersburg to Naples. In 1890, when the franchise was still restricted in Britain, universal male suffrage was established in Spain.

Much of modern Spanish history is explained by the tensions caused by the imposition of 'advanced' liberal institutions on an economically and socially 'backward' and conservative society: when universal suffrage was introduced at least 85 per cent of the population got its living from the land. The Carlists, strong among the peasant farmers of the Basque Provinces, attempted by two civil wars to destroy liberalism and all its works in order to return to a 'traditional' Catholic society. The conservatives in the liberal camp (when this is defined as composed of those who rejected a Carlist theocracy) were the *Moderados* or Moderates. Relying on the army and the favour of the crown, the Moderates were in power for long periods in the mid-nineteenth century; they rejected a constitution based on the sovereignty of the people and succeeded in perverting liberal institutions, making them the instruments of a narrow political oligarchy based on an amalgam of rural proprietors and the *haute bourgeoisie*. These relapses into conservatism and reaction were punctuated by liberal revolutions. These revolutions—in the sense of a change in the political landscape rather than a social transformation—consisted of two elements: a *pronunciamiento*, an officers' revolt, combined with an urban rising mounted by respectable middle-class Progressives and the lower-middle and working-class democrats who were prepared to man the barricades. This revolutionary alliance was unstable and soon disintegrated. Generals distrusted civilian co-operation and the middle-class revolutionaries fell out with their Jacobin allies.

The last of these revolutions was the 'Glorious Revolution' of September 1868—the most important of nineteenth-century revolutions—which influenced the whole history of Spain from 1875 to 1923. It took the form of a classic *pronunciamiento*.

Why did radical political change in Spain come as a result of the intervention of the army in politics? In a sense the answer is simple. In nations where civil society is weak—for instance in the developing societies of the Third World—the army possesses, not merely a monopoly of physical force, but a disciplined cohesion and *esprit de corps* which no other social group can rival.

In Spain, however, it was the structure of politics that was decisive in fostering a race of political generals: the generals were called in by politicians in search of support. The powers of Isabella II, who was queen from 1833 to 1868, were strikingly similar to those of George III. For it was the crown that appointed a cabinet and gave it the all-important decree of dissolution which allowed the Minister of the Interior to 'make' a parliamentary majority. In her later years Isabella favoured the conservative, hard-line Moderates. She excluded the Progressives from office, thus denying them the all-important decree of dissolution. Since they could not win an election under their own steam without the influence of a Progressive Minister of the Interior, the Progressives had no alternative but to turn to their sympathizers among the generals in order to catapult the party into power by a *pronunciamiento*. Thus the *pronunciamiento* replaced elections as a mechanism for political change.

The political-military revolution of September 1868 which sent Isabella II packing off to France and the hospitality of Napoleon III was the work of 'excluded' Progressives—their 'sword' was General Prim, son of a chemist—and the more conservative Liberal Unionists under General Serrano, once a favourite of Isabella but now likewise excluded by the Queen from the fruits of office. This political united front was called the 'September coalition'. It hoped to install a liberal constitutional monarchy on the English or Belgian pattern.

This it failed to do. The Progressives fell out with their democratic allies in the towns. The coalition found great difficulty in agreeing on a new king—their attempt to enlist a Hohenzollern candidate sparked off the Franco-Prussian War. When they did find a king—Amadeo of Savoy—their squabbles forced him to abdicate. In 1873 Spain became *faute de mieux* a republic and a *federal* republic at that. 'Cantonalist' revolts, in which radical democrats took over the government, broke out in the great southern cities like Cartagena. The unity of Spain seemed in peril. So did its traditional structure: churches were burnt; in Alcoy there was a workers' rising supposedly connected with the influence of the First International. Army discipline collapsed, with soldiers ripping off their officers' epaulettes and dancing on them. In January 1874 General Pavia marched into the Cortes (Parliament) and the Republic governed—if that is the word—by Federal Republicans was replaced by a conservative, unitary Republic under General Serrano.

Confronted with a Carlist war in the north and the disaffection of conservatives in general—particularly in the army and among the Madrid aristocracy, which refused to attend his wife's receptions—Serrano's imitation of the conservative French Republic of MacMahon looked an insecure temporary affair. This insecurity was sensed by the ablest politician of nineteenth-century Spain: Antonio Cánovas del Castillo (1828–97). For him the only hope of a stable political system, protecting the conservative interests outraged by disorder, lay in the restoration of the Bourbon dynasty in the person of Isabella's son, Alfonso XII, a cadet at Sandhurst.

Cánovas detested the intervention of the army in politics. The main aim of the constitutional monarchy of the Restoration, based on the constitution of 1876 which was largely his creation, was to make the *pronunciamiento* a political impossibility. Cánovas hoped to restore Alfonso XII by a 'movement of opinion'. But the generals, to his expressed disapproval, jumped the gun and restored Alfonso by a garrison revolt. At seven o'clock in the morning of 29 December 1875 Martínez Campos, an ambitious, impatient brigadier, led his troops outside the town of Sagunto and, after 'electrifying' them by his oratory, 'declared' for Alfonso XII 'in the name of the army and the nation'. The rest of the army followed his lead and the Restoration, amid the general indifference of the mass of Spaniards, became a *fait accompli*.

Though Cánovas did not realize it, neither the *coup* of General Pavia which toppled the Federal Republic nor the *pronunciamiento* of Martínez Campos was an officers' rebellion in the old style. Whereas up to and including 1868 the generals had acted as the 'swords' of parties, both Pavia and Martínez Campos professed to be acting from higher motives. Pavia saw himself as the saviour of a society threatened by a federal republic presiding over a process of anarchy and social dissolution that was undermining the discipline of the army itself. It was Pavia's officers' duty 'as soldiers *and citizens* to save society and the nation'. General Jovellar, the first full general to support Martínez Campos, professed to be 'preventing the reproduction of anarchy'; the Captain General of Madrid, who went over to the rebels, professed to be acting to preserve 'order' and to keep the army united. He knew his garrison favoured Alfonso and therefore led them from behind to prevent a conflict between officers who supported the Republican government and those who were Alfonsists. Thus the army was acting on principles which were to remain fundamental to its subsequent political action. It was its duty to save the fatherland (the *patria*—an emotive word) from dissolution at the hands of bad governments; in other words to preserve 'order'. The army must act to save itself as an institution when it was attacked by civilians in its conception of 'honour' or in its material interests. Finally, commanders must maintain what was called 'the harmony of the military family'.

II

The one Progressive measure, accepted by the Moderates, that was to have a profound effect on nineteenth-century Spain was the attack on corporate property rights in the name of economic individualism. The two great holders of corporate landed property were the Church and the municipalities, for municipalities were not just towns but included the surrounding countryside. Moreover the institution of entail—the *mayorazgo*—turned the estates of the landed aristocracy into perpetual family possessions. Church land, municipal commons, and entailed estates could not come on to the market to the profit of individuals who might wish to possess them.

A near-bankrupt monarchy had sold Church lands for state bonds at the end of the eighteenth century. It was a combination of economic principle and shortage of ready cash to pay the army fighting against the Carlists (1833–9) that led the liberal governments of the 1830s to put the mass of ecclesiastical property on the open market. It may have been the intention of the advanced liberals who began these sales to create a substantial class of peasant farmers who would support liberalism as French peasants had supported the Revolution. The mechanism of the land sales made such a policy unworkable; sold for cash or depreciated government bonds, the Church lands fell into the hands of those who could put up the money: local 'powerful ones' (*poderosos*), existing landowners, some speculators, and in some regions more modest proprietors. The same fate befell the municipal lands sold after 1855.

These sales (collectively known as the *desamortación*) represented a revolution, involving as they did the transfer of perhaps a third in value of all landed property in Spain. Radical critics of these sales have been over-optimistic in thinking the *desamortación* might have been carried out in a way that could have created a class of small farmers and both increased production and solved the social problems of rural underemployment. Ever since the mid-nineteenth century the *desamortación* has been presented as the great lost opportunity for a genuine agrarian revolution which would have underpinned an industrial revolution. It must be doubted whether a regime of peasant farmers could have performed this role. Nevertheless there can be little doubt that the liberal land revolution worsened the condition of the rural poor.

Only if we remember this process of proletarianization can we understand the alliance of the rural poor with the enemies of liberalism, from reactionary Carlists to revolutionary anarchists. The illegal sale of municipal commons after 1855 caused outbreaks of peasant violence in Galicia and elsewhere; men living near the subsistence level lost the right to pasture a few animals and to gather wood—in a charcoal economy an important privilege.

In Andalusia, the classical land of great estates or latifundia with absentee proprietors, the landowning system was strengthened after the mid-century by a process of concentration which worsened the lot of the small proprietor: in Seville Church lands were farmed by 6,000 families; after the sales they fell into the hands of 400 families.[1] Where the number of minute tenancies multiplied the holdings decreased in size.[2] This created a typical pattern: the coexistence of latifundia and minifundia—a recipe for rural misery. It was the growth of a primitive rural capitalism that fed the rural *jacquerie* of the south-west and explains the spread of anarchism: in 1892 the sherry town of Jerez was invaded and 'those who wear hats' beaten up by small producers driven to the wall by the great firms and by landless labourers. Artisans were striving to restore a 'traditional society'.[3] The consistent cry of the landless labourers, swept into anarchism, was for a *reparto*, the distribution of the latifundia lands to the landless: the thirst of a depressed and marginal class for social justice.

Apart from an addiction to free trade, mid-century liberalism was characterized by a dogmatic administrative centralism based on the French system; until the 1860s France was both the dominant literary influence and the preferred political and economic model.

In the 1830s, as in 1812, liberal legislators split Spain up into uniform provinces, each with its Provincial Deputation and a Civil Governor appointed by the central government. Beneath them came uniform municipalities, each governed by a council that was in the hands of the local 'powerful ones', with a mayor appointed from above. Uniformity meant that the administrative structure of a great city like Madrid or Barcelona was the same as that of a rural township, and that regions like Catalonia, with a tradition of local government rooted in a long history, were divided administratively into 'artificial' provinces. In 1876 liberals

[1] See A. Lazo, *La desamortización de las tierras de la Iglesia en la provincia de Sevilla 1835–45* (1970), 110 ff.

[2] See A.M. Bernal, *La propiedad de la tierra y las luchas agrarias Andaluzas* (1974), 59 ff.

[3] See T. Kaplan, 'The Social Base of Nineteenth-Century Anarchism in Jerez de la Frontera', *Journal of Interdisciplinary History* vi (1975), 47–70.

destroyed the last remnants of Basque medieval liberties with the slogan 'Centralization is liberty' and on the grounds that localism was a form of reaction supported by the Carlists. By completing the centralizing mission of the absolute monarchy, nineteenth-century liberals created for liberal parliamentarianism a regional problem it was to prove incapable of solving.

III

The 'Glorious Revolution' of September 1868 was the culmination of the democratic tradition represented by the Progressive party. As a military *pronunciamiento* combined with a revolutionary take-over by improvised committees in the towns, the legitimacy of the First Republic's governments—unlike those of the Second Republic of 1931—was always in question. The politicians of the September coalition failed in their efforts to create a stable institutional system and to master the extremes of left and right. The professors and lawyers who presided over the First Republic could not control 'the puerile impatience' of local enthusiasts who wished to impose an extremist federal constitution 'from below', and the Republic collapsed in the anarchy of the cantonalist revolt. Serrano could not find the 'crowning victory' against the Carlists in the north which he believed would save his title to rule as a man of order.

The immediate legacy, therefore, of the September revolution was a conservative reaction which underwrote the stability of the monarchical Restoration settlement. Juan La Cierva, a future Minister of the Interior, remembered the murder of the local stationmaster, the carts and carriages of refugees. Churches had been destroyed and conservatives, as always in revolutionary epochs, lamented the sudden spread of pornography, gambling, and irreligion as the inevitable consequences of democracy. The desire for a peaceful life after 'anarchy' meant a return to the Church as the guarantor of the social order and the suppression of workers' associations—illegal until 1881—as a threat to property.

The immediate political failure of the revolution and the conservative reaction it engendered obscure its fundamental importance. The constitution of 1869 was a democratic one, based on universal suffrage and the protection of individual rights and liberties. By guaranteeing freedom of religion it challenged assumptions of the Catholic monarchy. To republican democrats the revolution was a religious revolution, a freeing of the human spirit. For Catholics, to grant freedom of conscience was to give error the privileges of truth.

The September revolution failed as an experiment in liberal parliamentarianism because the individual rights enshrined in the constitution of

1869 were used by urban democrats to set up revolutionary town committees, a threat to the professional politicians and soldiers who had exiled Isabella II in order to grasp political power for themselves. Imagining themselves threatened by a social revolution, the oligarchs reasserted the authority of the government, abandoning the 'principles of September', suppressing the workers' right of association, rigging elections and censoring the press. Already in 1870 the liberal philosopher-educationalist Francisco Giner lapsed into pessimism: 'It [the revolution] affirmed principles in laws and abandoned them in practice, it proclaimed liberty and exercised tyranny . . . it disclaimed the proletarians and terrorized the rich; it humiliated free-thinkers and outraged the Church; it won the antipathy of liberals and conservatives alike, of the élite and the vulgar.' In spite of this apparent failure, the Conde de Romanones (see p. 78), later to lead the Liberal party under Alfonso XIII, claimed that the so-called conquests of the revolution had transfigured Spanish society and could 'never never', in the long run, be reversed. By this he did not mean that the class balance had been shifted—this would have been patently false—but that the nature of men's claims on the state had been modernized. Piecemeal, the liberal conquests—universal suffrage, freedom of association—crept back into the statute book even if the laws that embodied them were suspended or circumvented so that they appeared as little more than the rhetoric of a political élite. It was the liberal attempts to restore the religious freedom of 1869 that were to divide society. Religion remained a prism through which all political and social conflict was refracted.

IV

As long as the moral atmosphere was dominated by the fear of a relapse into political chaos and social revolution, the institutions of constitutional monarchy remained inviolable for all but Republicans and Carlists. These institutions were the expression of the political philosophy of one man, Cánovas del Castillo.

Like so many of the political oligarchs, Cánovas was a self-made provincial. Physically tough and a great eater, he slept only six hours a night. His eminence was that of a hard worker in a lazy society. Unprepossessing in appearance—with his squint, nervous tic, and appalling clothes, he looked like 'a subaltern on half-pay'—he possessed intellectual powers that were an essential part of his political capital in his campaign to capture intellectuals for the monarchy.

Cánovas had come to abhor revolutionary upheavals, above all those precipitated by military malcontents (he expressed his distaste by working in the Simancas archives during revolutions). His sole aim was to make another September revolution a political impossibility. This he could achieve by preventing the emergence of another September coalition composed of politicians excluded from office by a partial crown, and driven to manipulating popular discontents and appealing to generals. The politicians were to be kept happy by the chance of office and the generals were to become the grandees of the regime and not its arbiters. The Restoration was to have 'neither victors nor vanquished'; the constitution of 1876 should embrace 'all Spaniards without distinction'. The constitution of the restored monarchy, Cánovas explained to the British Minister, 'should be formed upon principles as liberal as the condition of the country would allow'. All who accepted the monarchy of Alfonso XII, as enshrined in the constitution of 1876, could play a part in political life: it was 'exclusiveness' which had driven his mother over the frontier.

The exponents of exclusiveness were the old allies of Isabella: the Moderates. They wanted a rigid conservative regime based on enforced religious unity. As soon as he was able, Cánovas ditched them. He refused to allow Isabella to return to Spain and destroyed her supporters in the election of 1876. So rooted was his conviction that the religious liberty, won in 1869, could not be radically reversed that he refused to sit at table with a bishop who advocated a return to enforced religious unity; to the Papal Nuncio he was, as a believer in religious freedom, 'not frankly opposed to the principles of the Revolution'. The constitution of 1876, while it declared Catholicism the religion of state, allowed the private practice of other faiths.

Having held off the intransigence of the Moderates, Cánovas' next task was to win over the men on the left of the September coalition—chiefly the remnants of the old Progressives. They must be led to accept the monarchy and the constitution of 1876. If they did, then they could expect power and a chance to implement their political programme: the 'liberal conquests' of 1869—the jury system and universal male suffrage. By 1881 Práxedes Mateo Sagasta (1827–1903), the strong man of the old Progressives and the leader of what was to become the Liberal party, accepted office under the crown. The Cánovite system was now complete. His own Conservative party and the Liberals could alternate in power, as they did until 1898, and the professional politicians would be satisfied. This alternation of the dynastic parties (i.e. those who accepted the monarchy) was called the '*turno pacífico*' and it replaced the *pronunciamiento* as the instrument of political change.

It must not be imagined that these rotating parties were organized parties in the modern sense of the word, each with a programme appealing to an electorate to vote it into power. They were artificial constructs from above, held together by the distribution of government patronage and dependent for their majorities in the Cortes on electoral management by the Minister of the Interior. Once the Prime Minister and his Minister of the Interior had been granted a decree of dissolution by the King they could, as we have seen, 'make' an election and count on a comfortable majority in the Cortes.

This made the King a central piece in the constitutional mechanism. Ultimately it was to expose Alfonso XIII to the charge of manipulating that mechanism in his own interests. The King not only appointed ministries; he also dismissed them. *Any* ministry to whom the King gave a decree of dissolution could rely on a substantial majority; it was up to the King to judge when a ministry, in the political jargon of the time, was 'exhausted' and it was time for another set of impatient politicians to be allowed to hold office. The importance of the prerogatives of the crown were fully apparent to Lord Granville, the British Minister in 1882: 'as the crown can constitutionally at any moment place this machine [the electoral machine driven by the Minister of the Interior] into the hands it likes, the all-important role assigned to the prerogative at once becomes manifest.' No one was more aware of this than Sagasta: he accepted the constitution of 1876 and abandoned the old Progressive dogma of the sovereignty of the people because only by accepting the role of the King as the maker of ministries could he achieve office.

In making his judgement the King could not rely on the size of a 'false' majority created by fine electoral tuning rather than by the wishes of an electorate; he had to judge, not on numbers, but on the more nebulous concept of 'weight'. He should, in the words of the Liberal leader Segismundo Moret (1838–1913) 'sense the wind before the hurricane', before the discontents of a section of the political class led them to 'threaten' the monarchy. In the early years of the Restoration there was still a fear that factious politicians might tempt a discontented general into another *pronunciamiento*; in 1883 a maverick general, Villacampa, set off a futile Republican barracks revolt in Badajoz. Later there was the danger that the 'outs' of the moment might approach the anti-dynastic parties to cajole the crown into granting them office by the threat of revolution; or that a faction, denied what it imagined to be its fair share of power, might attempt to break up the dynastic parties, thus making the *turno*, which depended on the existence of two strong 'parties of government', an impossibility.

Once the two parties created and sustained by Cánovas and Sagasta began to disintegrate, the stability of the whole system was in peril. Thus Alfonso XIII, when he came of age in 1902, was compelled to intervene in politics by selecting one of the faction leaders as Prime Minister, only to be accused by those whom he did not favour of being an intriguer, a 'traditional obstacle' given to personal political intrigues in the style of his grandmother.

V

It is often asserted, by liberal critics who wish to explain the failure of liberalism in Spain and by Marxists eager to point out the inevitable hypocrisy of bourgeois politics, that the parties of the *turno* represented nothing but the interests of professional politicians who manned them. This is a half-truth. Undoubtedly there were only minor differences in the social extraction and social contacts of those politicians; but Liberals and Conservatives did represent different tendencies, a different political style. The Conservatives would not have introduced universal male suffrage as the Liberals did in 1890; the Liberals, however divided and hesitant in their approaches to the problem, did believe that the political and social influence of the Church should be cut back. Most Liberals—especially under Moret, an enthusiast for English models and representative of a commercial town, Cadiz—remained free-traders after the Conservatives had been converted to protectionism. It is true that there were Liberals who were protectionists and less than zealous anti-clericals, and that ideologies and programmes counted for little. But the history of modern Spain would have been different if both parties had been, as many have argued, virtually identical, taking up issues purely as a move in a closed game of party politics.

The two parties of the *turno* were nevertheless artificial in the sense that they were created from above—unlike a British Conservative leader, Cánovas' main concern was the existence of a strong Liberal party—and in that they were groupings of the clienteles of leaders of sub-factions. There was no powerful national party organization (party matters were arranged in Madrid by meetings of party notables) and locally the party organization was in the hands, as we shall see, of local bosses. Hence there was no party discipline and, increasingly, throughout the Restoration, the major parties were constantly threatened by faction and disintegration.

The division of the spoils at the local level was the heart of what was known as *caciquismo*, that is the electoral manipulation through caciques, or political bosses, employed by each of the dynastic parties in order to secure for itself a comfortable majority in the Cortes while giving a decent proportion of seats to the opposition in order to keep them in the game. At the same time, the non-dynastic parties, who did not accept the monarchy and the constitution of 1876, had to be denied any significant electoral successes. To the contemporary opponents of the Restoration system and its modern critics alike, *caciquismo* summed up the political and moral defects of the Restoration monarchy. Popularized by Costa (see p. 52), it was one of those rare terminological inventions that condemn a whole regime in a single word.

The system—and its variations were infinite—in broadest terms worked as follows: once granted the royal decree of dissolution, the Prime Minister and his Minister of the Interior would work out a list of his followers who needed seats; as factions multiplied this distribution became increasingly difficult. The Minister of the Interior's office filled with hopeful petitioners. He then had to come to terms, not merely with the demands of his own 'flock'—Sagasta was nicknamed the 'Old Shepherd'—but also with the claims of the outgoing dynastic party leader for a 'decent' show of members. Once the list was drawn up, the chosen candidates had to be imposed on the constituencies.

This next step entailed local negotiations, usually conducted by the Civil Governor of the province as the representative of the party in office. It was at this stage that the cacique proper emerged: he was the man who could deliver the votes, whether those of a province or a great city or of a tiny municipality. There was therefore a hierarchy of caciques, each with his portion of influence.

The cacique could only attain influence by having command of the local administration and judicial apparatus. He created his clientele by handing out jobs—from night watchman to judge—and by favouring his client in matters such as passing incorrect tax returns, letting a son off conscription, settling in his 'friend's' favour a property dispute, or seeing that he got a grant of the municipal commons. To do this it was essential to control the municipalities and judgeships. Hence every electoral contest was preceded by a massive change of mayors and local judges.

The aim of the whole system was to accomplish this as peacefully as possible by a series of 'pacts' or local deals: Liberal municipal councils would resign in favour of Conservatives. If not, then local administration was so corrupt and lax that the Civil Governor could find an excuse to sack any mayor or councillor who proved obstinate. Once the municipalities were docile, then the electoral results could be faked and the chosen deputy elected. This process was known as the *encasillado*[4].

All this meant that the electoral contest—if that is the term—took place in the negotiations *before* the elections, negotiations which remained the stuff of electoral politics until 1923. Election results were

---

[4] J. Tusell, *Oligarquía y caciquismo en Andalucía 1890–1923* (1976), 23 ff.

therefore often published in the press before polling day. Usually the opposition candidates, after a show of fight that preserved their *bona fides* for the next time round, withdrew and there was no contest. The bitterest struggles took place, not between opposing parties, but between rival factions of the same party.

Increasingly the whole system came to rest on the rural vote of backward regions like Galicia and eastern Andalusia. Here the votes of an illiterate, apathetic electorate ground down by poverty could be manipulated and falsified at will. This accounts for the otherwise inexplicable fact that rural areas returned 80 per cent polls while the cities showed a strikingly lower participation. Increasingly the city votes were what were called '*votos verdad*', true votes, which often represented opposition to the dynastic parties and their managers. The dynastic parties sought to avoid defeat by gerrymandering, i.e. arranging constituency boundaries so that rural areas, where votes could be manipulated, were attached to towns where they could not. Later the city vote became a threat to the whole system. In Madrid the Republicans scored a breakthrough in 1893 and again in 1903. In 1919 Granada 'revolted' against its 'bad cacique' and elected a Socialist. Dynastic parties abandoned Valencia city as a constituency not worth the trouble of contesting;[5] in the city of Barcelona the dynastic caciques were beaten out of the game after 1900.

This division between a manageable rural vote and an increasingly independent urban vote was a reflection of the social and economic structure of Spain. Philosophically-minded historians use the concept of 'two Spains'; the notion of a contest between the Spain of progress and free thought which looked to Europe and the inward-looking Spain of traditionalist Catholic values. Thus in the eighteenth century, the men of 'light' (*luces*), influenced by the rationalism of European enlightenment, are seen as struggling against reactionaries to whom the Inquisition was an essential institution and free thought a danger to society. That this division existed no one can deny. But besides the 'two Spains' of competing ideologies and value systems there are the two Spains of rural poverty, ignorance, and illiteracy and the more volatile Spain of the larger towns. Those who were excluded from political life by the manipulation of the rural vote claimed that the victory of Republicans or Socialists in the cities represented a moral condemnation of the regime by the only enlightened sector of the electorate. Thus, in April 1931, the urban vote sealed the fate of the monarchy.

Critics of *caciquismo*, from Republicans like Guzmersindo de Azcárate (1840–1917) to the Conservative leader Antonio Maura (see p. 73), saw

---

[5] See L. Aguiló Lúcia, *Sociología electoral valenciana 1903–23* (1976), ch. I and II.

that the system rested on two pillars: the apathy of the electorate and the extreme centralization of an administration whose mayors were government servants who could be dismissed at will rather than the chosen representatives of their fellow citizens. 'Most Spaniards', argued Romero Robledo, the political manager of Cánovite Conservatism, 'do not have sufficient culture or intelligence to understand public interest when they deposit their voting slip in the urn.' 'While there are civil governors and mayors at the disposition of the government,' Cánovas himself confessed, 'the morality of elections must remain a myth.' If apathy could be cured only by a long process of civic education, the reform of local administration, bringing it closer to the citizen, would both hasten this education *and* prevent the manipulation of local government for electoral ends. Local life had been killed by centralizing liberalism. Azcárate became an enthusiast for English local government, as opposed to the French 'statism' slavishly copied by Spanish liberals.

Increasingly the criticism of *caciquismo* by Costa and others became common coinage. Already in the 1880s the farmers of Castile, hit by low wheat prices, had thundered against a system whereby they were represented in the Cortes by deputies installed from Madrid and indifferent to their demand for protectionist policies. They clamoured for regeneration and renovation. Parliamentary government in Spain was, to Costa, a farce. Democratic institutions, based after 1890 on universal suffrage, were perverted by a selfish oligarchy so that the electorate became 'a tribe of eunuchs subjected by a tribe of footpads'.

Caciquismo can be seen as a consequence of the imposition of democratic institutions upon an underdeveloped economy and what José Ortega y Gasset (1883–1955) called an 'anaemic society'. Old and rooted social formations and habits, the clientelism of local élites, broke down and through the new political structures. (When the Liberals introduced the modern jury system in 1888 it merely fell into the hands of the local notables of small towns.) Electoral corruption can be presented as a *rite de passage* presiding over the transition from a traditional society to a fully democratic state. But it was also the defence mechanism employed by a governing élite to postpone the proper use of democratic institutions by a mass electorate to press social demands—to prolong in fact the restricted property franchise retained by Cánovas but abolished in law in 1890.

An electorate such as that described by Romero Robledo could only understand particular, private benefits. This the cacique could provide in return for a vote. The caciques and professional politicians were rarely corrupt in the venal personal sense. Borbolla had controlled the Seville liberal vote for years; but he died with a modest fortune. Moreover, the so-called 'good caciques' did not merely deliver the vote; they stood between the state and the citizen in the matter of favours to be extracted from a mysterious and paper-riddled bureaucracy. The Pidal family, who controlled rural Asturias, were notorious for their dexterity in obtaining exemptions from military service; Asturias 'owed to *caciquismo* [of the Pidals] a veritable luxury of roads'. Moret was called in the Cadiz press the 'paternal benefactor' of the city. La Cierva, the great cacique of Murcia, got a university for his capital. The successors of Cánovas as Conservative Prime Ministers, Silvela (see p. 65) and Maura took up the cry against *caciquismo*. They professed to favour 'sincere' elections (i.e. the neutrality of the government which presided over an election) and a reform of local government that would destroy corruption at its roots. They issued instructions to their Civil Governors forbidding intervention in local politics, and Maura's law in 1907 attacked abuses; but these moves made little impression on electoral mores. As a local cacique boasted, he could drive a coach and horses through the law.

Reformers saw *caciquismo* as an administrative malady, not a social disease; destroy the overcentralized administrative superstructure on which it thrived and the evil would vanish. There were strong reasons for a reform of local government. A reformed local administration might accommodate regional demands. Neither municipalities nor provinces had incomes adequate for their functions. The basic local government law of 1877 had been buried under a host of governmental regulations. But the main drive to reform was to secure a 'ground clearance of *caciquismo*' and open the way to 'sincere' elections. Yet repeated projects for local government reform came to nothing; 'sincere' elections only occurred where management failed.

Increasingly management did fail and the more dilapidated *caciquismo* became in the twentieth century, the more force and persuasion had to be used to make it work—for instance, straight purchase of votes seems to have increased. Hence the more vocal criticism of what Ortega y Gasset, in a famous phrase, was to call 'old politics'. Intellectuals created the categories of a 'real' Spain of the people and an 'official' Spain of the politicians, a new version of the theory of the two Spains. Politics were, on this analysis, an autonomous activity, with politicians moving in a world of their own out of touch with the 'live forces' of society. This was, in part, an exaggeration. The system could not have survived had it been so unresponsive to important economic and social pressure groups as its critics maintained. Castilian parties *did* come to represent the interests of the wheat farmers; the deputies of Granada *did* represent the powerful sugar interests. The monarchist caciques of Barcelona *did* represent dominant economic interest groups. The Catalan Lliga (see p. 64) claimed that *caciquismo* 'blanketed' Catalan demands. All the Lliga did was to break the old cacique network and substitute for it what its opponents considered to be a *caciquismo* of businessmen.

What is true is that a system which could make no claims to be representative in the democratic sense was less capable of resisting the organized pressure of powerful 'oligarchic' interests. This was particularly evident in the claims of sectoral interests for tariff protection when no one of these interests was sufficiently powerful to impose its terms on the rest. Spain therefore came to have 'protection all round' with the highest tariff barriers in Europe. This was the end-process of conceding to the demands of pressure group after pressure group, regardless of any concern for the rising costs of production and the competitiveness of Spanish exports.

This is not to say that Spanish politicians and political managers were merely the corrupt servants of an oligarchy. They were less personally corrupt than French politicians, nor were their connections with the business world more intimate than those of British or French politicians. It was less that politicians were a caste apart, separated from the 'real needs' of the country, than that the party structure reflected the incoherence of what Maura called 'the shapelessness of Spanish society'. Inevitably, as the two-party structure which had provided alternating Conservative and Liberal governments, equipped with safe majorities, became increasingly enfeebled and as the parties themselves split into factions, so attention centred more and more on the making and unmaking of ministries. If the distinction between the two major parties was discernible, those between the competing factions within the parties seemed only to represent the personal ambitions of faction leaders.[6] Politics could be represented as a trivial occupation on which no decent man should waste his time, as a series of meaningless ministerial crises, staged by the factions and manipulated by the king, consummated in equally meaningless elections.

We cannot understand the fate of parliamentary democracy in Spain without remembering this legacy of the Restoration. Even under the Second Republic of 1931, with the advent of mass politics and the decline of the apathy without which the 'old politics' could not have functioned as a system, repeated ministerial crises gave the impression that the President of the Republic was re-enacting the role of Alfonso XIII.

---

[6] M. Artola, *Partidos y programas políticos 1808–1936* (1974), i, 360.

2 The Economy 1875–1914: Stagnation and Progress

On the eve of the Great War of 1914–18 half the active population was employed in agriculture. Spain was a rural country, a country of landlords, peasants, and agricultural labourers. Land remained, in the words of a modern historian, 'the most important instrument of social domination'.[1] This moulded its society and conditioned its politics.

To English observers the salient feature of rural Spain was its extreme diversity. This was due partly to climate and soil, partly to the historic structure of landholding. There was the divide between the 'Mediterranean' south with its wines, olives, and citrus fruits, and the north where a Welsh farmer would feel at home. There was the great division between irrigated lands, mostly on the periphery, capable of three crops a year, and the arid *secano* of the interior where the cultivator might scrape a cash crop only once every three years. Galicia had an 'Irish' rainfall; the land round Almería in eastern Andalusia was a quasi-desert. In Andalusia, La Mancha, and Extremadura the medieval Christian reconquest from the Moors had combined with the land sales of the nineteenth century to make these regions the classic home of the latifundia—the extensively cultivated great estates of absentee landowners. In the Basque Provinces the smallholder, in spite of pressure on the land and the inroads of industry, seemed to foreigners still to live a life of Homeric simplicity; at the western extreme of the northern coast, the Galician peasant scratching a poor existence out of his handkerchief plot reminded English visitors of Irish wretchedness.

The civil servants of the eighteenth century who had sought, like their heirs in the Second Republic of 1931–6, to reform what one of them termed this 'bizarre' structure, believed that the main stumbling block in the way of prosperity and social justice alike was the coexistence of latifundia and minifundia—great extensively cultivated estates and dwarf farms divided into minute plots.

In Andalusia the whitewashed *cortijos*, where the mules were stabled and the work force housed during harvest time, dominated the landscape

[1] M. Martínez Cuadrado, *La burguesía conservadora* (1973), 62 ff.

like feudal castles. Whether the estate was farmed by its owner or let out to a rich tenant (the *labrador*), the land, apart from a handful of permanent workers, was worked by gangs of seasonal labourers—the *braceros* who, unemployed for half the year, starved in the agro-towns. They were the most wretched agricultural labourers of Western Europe.

Latifundia (and they existed in other regions of Spain—Aragon and New Castile) were attacked on two grounds. They were wastefully and extensively farmed; given the great pool of cheap labour that waited in the town squares to be given jobs, there was little incentive to modernize. A vast estate, using techniques which had scarcely changed since Roman times, still yielded an adequate income to allow its absentee owner to live a life of conspicuous consumption in the provincial capital, if he was a local *señorito*, or in Biarritz or Madrid if he was a great aristocrat.

Galicia, a land of gorse and granite, stood at the other extreme. A peculiar form of tenure, the *foro*, combined with a growing population, had produced a peasantry cultivating millions of minute plots. The grinding poverty of a subsistence economy was reflected in a high rate of illegitimacy and the export of men as seasonal labourers. Under their 'kings' 30,000 labourers went south for the harvest in the 1890s. I still saw them, with their sickles wrapped in sacks, hanging about railway stations in the late 1940s. Besides seasonal immigration there was permanent or semi-permanent emigration to Latin America—especially Argentina, where the *gallegos* were waiters and taxi-drivers—and to other parts of Spain where the Galician wet-nurse or domestic servant was a stock theatrical character. Those who remained fought a bitter battle of arson, boycott, and cattle-maiming against landlords who sought to turn the traditional *foro*, which had given the peasant relative security of tenure, into a rent contract. But Galician misery was created not by an iniquitous form of land tenure (the redemption of the *foros* was carried through in the 1920s) but by the pressure of population on a limited amount of poor land. Galicia, unlike Andalusia, had no landless proletariat but a proletariat of minuscule farmers. Perhaps only the potato averted a total failure of the land to feed its inhabitants.

The heartland of Spain was the bleak tableland of Castile where the villages, their streets dusty in summer and lanes of mud in winter, could scarcely be distinguished from the flat and dreary landscape that surrounded them. The wool trade had once made Castile rich; in the nineteenth century it declined vertiginously, leaving the Castilian towns inhabited by a bourgeoisie of large farmers, mill owners and government servants, and, in the countryside, a conservative peasantry dependent on cereals or vines.

Though there were large estates and substantial farms round Salamanca and elsewhere, the blight of Castilian agriculture was the dwarf farm divided into scattered, minute walled plots which demanded a great deal of labour. Tenancies were bewildering in their complexity and the Castilian small peasant was often also a labourer on a larger farm. The curse of Castile was usury, and this explains the success of Catholic co-operatives and unions which provided credit, in the early twentieth century, at better rates than the local mill owner or landlord. As in Galicia, emigration was a necessity. In 1905 the 300 inhabitants of the village of Boado offered themselves to the President of Argentina *en masse*. There was a 'patriotic' protest. The villagers replied, 'Patriotism consists in eating and giving one's children something to eat.'[2]

The more stable and prosperous rural societies were to be found on the periphery. We will examine briefly three: Catalonia, the Levante, and the Basque Provinces.

Not all of Catalonia was the home of a prosperous peasantry. Arthur Young found the mountain regions 'all poor and miserable' and it was from these pockets of poverty that Catalan industry first drew its cheap labour. The agricultural riches of Catalonia lay in the wheat plains and vineyards of the centre and the rich cultures of the coastal plains. In the strict hierarchy of the Catalan countryside the substantial farmers, supported by secure tenancies, almost ranked as a petty nobility, their prosperity reflected in their solidly built farm houses.

It was the profits of these regions—particularly from the export of wine and spirits to Spanish America—that provided the capital for the beginnings of a textile industry in the eighteenth century. The loss of these markets lamed industry and agriculture alike, but when phylloxera struck the French vineyards in the 1860s 'black jack' was exported to be bottled in France. Catalan growers enjoyed an unexampled prosperity which was to last until the early 1890s. But when phylloxera invaded Spain the collapse was complete, and the modern tourist can observe the results in the deserted terraces around the beaches of the Costa Brava.

It was this collapse which destroyed the supposedly 'idyllic' social peace of the Catalan vine-growing districts. In fact the traditional form of tenure called *rabassa morta* had caused conflict since the eighteenth century. The cultivator believed that his lease, which lasted for the life of the vine, gave him permanent ownership. Landlords sought to turn *rabassa morta* into a simple crop-sharing tenancy.

What had been a struggle over a complicated and confused traditional tenancy became a bitter war when, with the coming of phylloxera, the peasants had to substitute the short-lived, expensive American vine for the native stock. To Costa, Catalonian vineyards witnessed an Irish struggle.[3] The *rabassaires* organized a union in 1893 and fought the landlords with strikes and boycotts. This was to turn a conservative peasantry, starting with a struggle to retain their traditional rights, into a reservoir of support for the Catalan Republican left.

Nor was it only the vineyards that were facing a crisis. The import of foreign wheat to supply the modern steam mills of Barcelona brought disaster to the wheat district. Once again, the less fortunate emigrated to the industrial areas: in ten years Tarragona, stricken by phylloxera, lost 10,000 inhabitants.[4]

Prosperity there was in other areas. Around Figueras and on the Costa Brava was the most important cork industry in the world, employing 30,000 workers in 1900. While Tarragona, a provincial capital, had only 14 telephones, the small cork town of Palamós boasted 170. The demands of Barcelona sustained a profitable, specialized, flexible market-garden economy. Thus in the Maresme (the area around Mataró) early potatoes and flowers replaced oranges and vines.

No greater contrast can be imagined than that between the irrigated *huertas* of the Levante and the *secano* of Castile: tedious to the eye, the *huertas* of Valencia and Murcia, with their garden crops, supported the highest rural densities in Europe. A large farm was two acres. On the edge of the Valencian *huertas* orange groves supplied what was becoming Spain's most important export: growth was prodigious (12.5 per cent a year). It can be argued that it was the export of citrus fruits that supplied the foreign capital for the import of capital goods which in turn allowed a modest industrial growth. The 'Spanish Switzerland'—the Basque Provinces of Guipúzcoa and Vizcaya—suffered no such radical agrarian changes. Not until the twentieth century did population increase force an uneconomic division of farms; in the 1930s sons of farmers began to leave the symbol of this stable society, the *caserío* or family farm, for the high wages of the nearby factories of Bilbao.[5]

II

These examples can only give an impression of the diversity of Spanish agriculture: it was reflected in the landscape. The rural workers of the south huddled into large villages or small towns, miles from their work place in a countryside without inhabitants. In the Basque country and Galicia the farms were so dispersed that the whole countryside appeared

[3] See A. Balcells, *El problema agrari a Catalunya 1890–1936* (1968), 39.
[4] J. Romero Maura, *La Rosa de fuego* (1974), 47.
[5] See Miren Etxezarreta, *El caserío vasco* (1976).

one large, scattered village. No region was homogeneous: the Basque Provinces of Alava merged into the Castilian plateau; even in Castile a river valley could suddenly change the *secano* into a fertile oasis. In Andalusia the rich commercial crops of the Campiña de Cordoba, the garden products of the irrigated *vega* of Granada, or the sophisticated vineyards that produced sherry and brandy contrasted with large areas of mountain pasture given over to sheep and esparto grass. Even in Andalusia, besides the great estates, there were pockets where property was evenly divided and where small farmers faced a struggle for subsistence as hard as that of the Castilian peasant.

The result of this rural diversity was that some regions stagnated or declined while others prospered; some regions, throughout the century, showed signs of progress and investment in new crops—sugar beet and cotton for instance—or a capacity to meet changes in the market: thus Jerez compensated for the decline of sherry by the manufacture of cheap brandy. It was the onset of what is now called 'the crisis of traditional agriculture' that gave most concern. It affected, above all, the granary of Spain, the cereal monocultures and the vineyards of Castile.

The agriculture crisis of the 1880s resulted from the incapacity of traditional agriculture—the Mediterranean triad of wheat, wine, and olives—to meet new market conditions. This was a result of poverty, conservatism, and the lack of alternative crops. Wine and olives had an export market; wheat (its yields the lowest in Western Europe and its costs of production high) relied on the domestic market. When in the 1880s the markets of peripheral Spain were invaded by foreign imports Castilian wheat farmers organized themselves to press for protection and, given their political weight, they won increasingly prohibitive tariffs from 1891 onwards. Forty years of protection made Spain self-sufficient in cereals as a consequence of a new increase in the area sown to wheat.

Seen in purely economic terms, this was a barren achievement. It combined with high transport costs and food taxes to deny cheap food to the industry of the periphery; but industry did not care, since it had been equally successful in the cry for protection. It kept down to wheat areas (for instance the rich Campiña de Cordoba) better suited to other crops, and the prospect of guaranteed prices reinforced the innate conservatism of the Castilian farmer. Nevertheless the reasons for cereal protection were socially compelling. Without support, either in the form of protection or—as happened after the Civil War—guaranteed purchase and prices, the Castilian farmer would have been driven to the wall and the heartland of Spain reduced to a near-wasteland inhabited by a rebellious peasantry—though it was the substantial farmer who profited most from protection while the marginal cultivator was forced to emigrate.

The desire to get immediate returns had not only sustained the wheat acreage (it had declined in the 1870s to grow once more in the 1890s); combined with the demand for charcoal—until very late extensively used for domestic cooking and heating—and building, it further denuded the already sadly diminished forest cover of Spain. Between 1866 and 1932 perhaps half the woods left standing by mid-century speculators were cut down. Without adequate cover, the soil of Spain blew away or was washed away by torrential winter rains; denuded watersheds, unable to absorb water in the higher reaches, produced disastrous floods or dried up in river courses in summer. Useful rivers, for irrigation and, later, for hydro-electric schemes, were a corollary of useful forests.

From the eighteenth century deforestation had been denounced as the historic crime of Spanish agriculture. It became an obsession with the *fin de siècle* reformers; Costa's 'hydraulic policy' became the main plank of his programme for the revival of Spanish agriculture. Since Jovellanos (1744-1811) liberals had maintained that private enterprise could be relied on to replenish Spanish forests. But trees give slow returns compared to cash crops. Only the state could undertake the task of reversing a secular trend and, in spite of the efforts in 1902 of Costa's disciple, Gasset, to legislate into existence a 'hydraulic plan', it was left to a paternalist dictator, Primo de Rivera, to begin to implement the policy of Costa in the 1920s.

Critics inveighed against the conservatism of Spanish farmers and their addiction to traditional techniques. Many of the urban prophets of modernization failed to realize that apart from the fact that many of these techniques were well-adapted to natural conditions, the small farmer could not modernize because he lacked the capital when his liquid resources were taken up by taxation and when credit at reasonable rates (in Castile usurers charged 20 per cent) was denied him; he stuck to the *noria*—the water wheel with its pots turned by a mule—because he could not afford a pump.

Castilian history had seen a long battle between pastoral farmers and agriculturalists. Whereas in the sixteenth century it was the great sheep owners' guild—the Mesta—that won out, by the nineteenth century the terms of the conflict had been reversed. This caused a serious imbalance. There was too little manure. Neither a country with a permanent balance of payments deficit, nor the poor farmer, could afford artificial fertilizer. There was also too little meat. This was to become, in the 1960s when the dietary habits of a more affluent society changed, a serious bottleneck, and the import of meat a serious drain on scarce foreign exchange.

Spanish agriculture, apart from the privileged regions, remained a poor performer. 'Rudimentary techniques', argues Nicolás Sánchez

Albornoz, 'which demanded minimal capital investment and an abundant supply of labour persisted intact from time immemorial and kept the productivity of labour low.'[6] Supplying local markets and caught in a vicious circle, Spanish agriculture could not supply capital for industrial investment in the way that, in the eighteenth century, Catalan rural savings combined with the profits of agricultural exports to finance the textile industry. Moreover, industry, once the empire had gone, had to find its outlet in an impoverished rural domestic market with a limited capacity to purchase factory products. This dependence continued into the 1950s. 'A year of good harvests', runs the report of the Banco de Bilbao for 1948, 'is a year of prosperity for industry.'

III

Spanish economic historians, in recent years, have been much concerned with Spain's failure to industrialize during a century when other western European nations achieved some sort of industrial take-off. The title of Jordi Nadal's recent book is indicative of this concern: 'The Failure of the Industrial Revolution in Spain 1814–1913'. This failure is attributed to a variety of factors: the absence of a 'real' agricultural revolution as the necessary condition for industrialization; the poverty of the Spanish state after the loss of the American colonies; 'mistaken' investment in railways rather than 'proper' investment in industry; the alienation of Spain's mineral resources to foreigners. All these are seen as the 'mistakes' of a liberal state. Others adopt simpler answers: lack of cheap coal; a geography that made the creation, by an adequate system of transport, of a national market costly and difficult; the lack of entrepreneurial spirit in a traditional Catholic society.

Before attempting to sort out these variables let us examine the structure and performance of Spanish industry 1870–1914.

The striking feature is the persistence, in most of Spain, of artisan concerns supplying a local market and the concentration of industry in selected areas: the Basque Provinces (above all in Vizcaya), Catalonia (above all in the province of Barcelona), and, to a lesser extent, in Asturias and around Saragossa. Such polarized concentration is common to most economies—particularly developing economies. These developed areas drain the poorer areas of men and capital, just as the industry of northern Italy left the south a pool of poverty and underemployment.

Barcelona and its surrounding countryside—by 1900 two-thirds of the Catalan work force was concentrated within thirty kilometres of the

[6] N. Sánchez Albornoz, *España hace un siglo: una economía dual* (1968), 8.

capital—had by the end of the eighteenth century become a second Lancashire. The cotton industry was based on the prosperity of Catalan agriculture and exports to the Spanish-American empire. The Napoleonic wars and the loss of empire inflicted a severe wound. Nevertheless it was still, in 1870, the most important industrial area in Spain and by 1860 it used half the installed steam power in the country. With Biscay it was the only region with a market mentality and an industrial proletariat.

In the 1850s a woollen industry—concentrated round Sabadell and Tarrasa—was added to cotton, and factory-produced woollens were to strike a crippling blow at the widely dispersed artisan concerns. Catalan industrialists were conscious of the dangers of this 'lop-sided' structure based on textiles; consumer goods are not necessarily a 'leading sector' and it is the production of capital goods that is the mark of an advanced industrial society. But the attempt to break through into a modern, diversified industrialized economy was slow and painful. The biggest metallurgical concern, La Maquinista Terrestre y Marítima, only slowly got beyond textile machinery, small ships, and marine engines.

After the loss of Cuba in 1898 Catalan industry was confined to and dependent on the purchasing power of the domestic market. Hence, as we shall see, the Catalan industrialists' support for agricultural protection which would at least preserve, if not enhance, that purchasing power. English manufacturers wanted cheap food; Catalan industrialists preferred a safe home market.

Given the low purchasing power of a poor domestic market, the expansion of Catalan industry was limited—as were its resources for modernization. Apart from a few modern giants, created in the 1890s, the textile industry was dominated by conservative small firms—what was later to be called 'industrial minifundism'. It was, compared to its British rivals, a high-cost industry—in spite of cheap labour—and its lack of competitive edge made it dependent on high tariff protection.

Nothing is more remarkable, in Catalan protectionist literature, than the insistence on figures which showed Catalan 'inferiority': factories equipped with half the average number of spindles for the rest of Europe; output per man less than half that of the U.S.A. To modernize 'our poor and feeble' industry in order to make it competitive would, it was held, fling half the cotton operatives out of work. However justifiable on humanitarian and social grounds this was scarcely the argument of a resolute entrepreneurial class.

There was no acute crisis but the continual malaise of over-production, small profit margins, periods of unemployment. Some saw in the cut-throat competition of small factories the 'atavistic individualism' of the Catalan artisan which so annoyed the advocates of big business and economies of scale. It was difficult for the larger cotton concerns to rationalize and modernize as they had done in the '90s. They met dwindling profits by firm resistance to wage demands and by laying off hands.

Although Catalonia remained the greatest industrial complex in Spain, by the 1870s a second centre was developing in the Basque Provinces, home of an old, conservative iron industry. Like the Catalans, Basques had what a Basque writer, Maeztu (1875–1936), called 'the sense of reverence for money'. The great Basque industrialists and bankers were the financial pillars of the Catholic revival: but they were, in their businesses, modernizers and sensitive to the economic climate of Europe.

Basque prosperity was based on the iron mines of Vizcaya. It was the liberal mining laws of the September revolution combined with the demands of the Bessemer process for the low-phosphorus-content 'red ore' of Biscay that encouraged foreign investment, particularly British, in Vizcayan mines. The open cast mines were near the sea and there was an abundant supply of cheap labour. In 1889 5 million tons were exported to South Wales.

As we shall see, this investment was viewed as 'colonial exploitation'. But it was the revenues paid to the mine proprietors—and the return freights of cheap coke—that provided the money and cheap fuel to modernize the technically backward Basque iron industry (the first coke blast furnace in 1865; the first Bessemer converter 1885). By the end of the century there was a shipbuilding and a heavy metallurgical industry (the first locomotive built in 1884). Above all the Restoration saw the establishment of the great Vizcayan mixed banks, together with the railway companies, the first modern corporations in Spain. They were to play a vital role in injecting savings into industrial growth. Catalonia, for all its reputation for enterprise, failed to develop a comparable private banking system, perhaps because the tradition of the family enterprise was too deeply rooted in Catalan *seny* (or common sense) for the flourishing of corporate enterprise. While the big Basque and Madrid banks survived economic crises, the smaller Catalan concerns went under.

No other region developed industrial complexes comparable to those of Vizcaya and Catalonia. For a time, before the Basque boom, it looked as if a metallurgical industry would grow up round the Asturian coal mines; but the blast furnaces moved to the iron mines and the availability of cheap Welsh coke. Even more dramatic was the collapse of the nascent industrialism of southern Andalusia, its furnaces dependent on charcoal. In 1844 Malaga produced 72 per cent of Spanish iron; in 1868 a mere 5 per cent.

Elsewhere industry remained an artisan concern supplying local markets. The small textile workshops of Castile and Aragon were gradually priced out of existence by cheaper Catalan products. There was no considerable industrial development in Madrid until the twentieth century: it remained an administrative, political, and financial capital, a city of consumers and luxury trades attacked by Catalans as 'artificial' and 'parasitical'. Castilian towns remained administrative, military, and ecclesiastical centres dominated by farming interests; the 2,000 employees of the Valladolid railway workshops were the only modern proletariat in Castile. Cordoba and Seville were agricultural capitals (in 1906 La Cierva could not find a typewriter in Seville). The sugar beet industry brought some large concerns to Aragon and Granada. But these were islands of modern industry in what we would now characterize as an underdeveloped economy, less prosperous than its former colony Argentina which appeared to the rural poor, who could find little employment in Spanish industry, as a land of opportunity. A national market developed slowly. For much of the nineteenth century the economy remained, in Fontana's words, 'an aggregation of isolated rural cells, with no significant traffic between them', a collection of local self-sufficient 'monopolies'.[7] Thus only after 1900 did the setting up of branches of the big banks in the provinces create a unified financial market.[8]

IV

How are we to account for this faltering development? Was Spain a 'late starter' or was she a case of a country whose incipient mid-century industrialization had been frustrated by structural impediments and mistaken policies?

One answer is that industrial 'take-offs' (as can be argued in the case of the English model) are dependent on the purchasing power of the rural market. A poor agriculture means a poor industry. Spanish agriculture was poor, the argument continues, because the agricultural modernization and prosperity was blocked by the survival of the *ancien régime* in the countryside. The liberal land settlement was a 'revolution from above', Prussian-style, which increased the concentration of property in fewer hands and inhibited the emergence of a prosperous rural community of middle farmers with the purchasing power to buy industrial products. 'Deprived of an authentic agrarian revolution,' Nadal argues, 'most of

[7] J. Fontana, 'La primera etapa de la formació del mercat nacional a Espanya', in *Homenatje a Jaime Vicens Vives*, ii, 17, 18, 33.

[8] J.L. García Delgado, *Orígenes y desarrallo del capitalismo español* (1975), 95.

Spain could not catch the train of the industrial revolution.' Though the preservation or creation of small proprietors may be socially or politically desirable, and though it may be argued that an agrarian revolution may increase the purchasing power of the domestic market for cheap industrial products such as textiles, the whole history of agricultural progress, conceived in terms of increased production, has been one of concentration. In any case a reparto was inconceivable within the framework of liberalism. For liberals private property, as opposed to corporate property, was sacrosanct. Jovellanos, though eloquent on the defects of the latifundia, drew the line at expropriation; only the forces of the market, by driving out the inefficient cultivator, could increase production.

Was the chronic poverty of the Spanish exchequer responsible for the failure of Spain to measure up to its European rivals? After the loss of the American colonies, the state ran deep into debt.[9] Because no government was up to the task of reforming an inequitable and unproductive tax system, the state was dependent on loans. This encouraged the purchase of government stock to the detriment of productive investment, just as the *desamortación* of the mid-century is blamed by critics for siphoning scarce savings into 'unproductive' land purchases. These same critics assert that the main, almost sole, concern of the Bank of Spain, when it was the dominant financial institution, was to provide the government with funds rather than to finance productive enterprise. Not until 1900 did it embark on investment in industry. It is argued that the government raised money abroad and that this foreign indebtedness weakened Spain's capacity to import capital goods and raw materials. Above all, the poverty of the state prevented it from assuming a promotional role in a backward economy. It could not even fulfil the educational needs of a modern society, much less provide the necessary social infrastructure for development. Cambó (see p. 36), as the leader of the bourgeoisie of a 'backward' economy, in 1918 put forward an ambitious programme of state intervention; it was the poverty of the state, combined with the vicissitudes of party politics, that brought his plans to nothing.

One thing the state did help to provide: a railway system. Construction, which had slowed down after the crisis of 1866, picked up again in 1877. Yet the way this system was financed and built is considered one of the 'lost opportunities' of the nineteenth century. Dependent on foreign creditors, the argument runs, the state gave concessions which allowed the companies to import all railway material; hence the Spanish steel industry continued to languish until the protectionist legislation of the later nineteenth century gave it a chance to benefit from backward

<hr>

[9] For this see J. Fontana, *La quiebra de la monarquía absoluta* (1971).

linkages. Moreover, for a long period, too much investment went into railways at the expense of native industry. In Spain investment in railways during the railway boom was seven times that in industry, whereas in Britain it accounted for some 30 per cent.[10]

This argument of what might have been rests on two fallacies. Firstly the railways were built by foreign—largely French—money because there was no attractive Spanish alternative to the foreign investor until the development of mining and public utilities. Without foreign capital Spain would have got her railways much later and their undoubted contribution towards economic development, in a country where canals were a physical impossibility, would have been delayed; it has been calculated that by 1878 the social savings on railways equalled total exports and by 1900 rail transport was half the price of road transport. It has been argued that the generous concessions to import rails and other railway goods free of customs duties inhibited the growth of the native iron industry; but the domestic iron industry could not have filled the gap in providing railway equipment in the early stages, as its costs were far too high. Later, it can be argued with more conviction, the lack of tariff protection did enfeeble the processes of backward linkages and the expansion of the metallurgical sector through the demands of the railway companies.[11]

The Liberals of the mid-century, it is argued, not only handed over the railways to foreign concerns: the law of 1868, a direct result of the difficulties of the Treasury, opened up Spanish mines to foreign investment. Certainly foreign investment produced dramatic results where Spanish capital had not developed resources: in ten years foreign capital and British engineers quadrupled the output of the Río Tinto mines, making Spain the greatest copper producer in Europe, employing 9,000 workers by 1889. This created a series of foreign enclaves where foreign concerns behaved as quasi-sovereign states, exploiting Spain as a colony, and where decisions were made in Cardiff or Glasgow whither the profits flowed back. At the Tharsis mines, 'in their sun helmets and white jackets, mounted upon horses in which they took great pride, these Scotsmen in their hill empire evoke the idea of a Raj not very different from that of India.'[12] Like Latin American nations, Spain had become an export economy supplying raw materials to the developed West; only one-tenth of Vizcayan ore went to local blast furnaces.

[10] This argument has been put forward with great ingenuity in G. Tortella Casares, *Los orígenes del capitalismo español* (1973). For a general view see his 'An Interpretation of Economic Stagnation in Nineteenth-Century Spain' in *Historia Ibérica* no.1 (1973), 121–32.

[11] For railways see R. Anis, 'Relaciones entre el ferrocarril y la economía española (1865–1935)', in *Los ferrocarriles en España 1844–1943* (1978), ii, 356 ff.

[12] Quoted S.G. Checkland, *The Mines of Tharsis* (1967), 177.

These developments fostered economic nationalism, not only in economic historians, but among Spanish industrialists. Up to the late 1880s the modicum of free trade introduced by the Liberals in 1869 seemed to yield results; these were the years of the 'cotton euphoria' and the growth of a wool industry that was the third largest in Europe. As prosperity turned to depression in the late '80s Catalan industrialists and Basque ironmasters pressed for protection; so did the stricken wheat farmers of Castile. In 1891 the Spanish state, giving in to the demands of pressure group after pressure group, embarked on a wave of protectionism. The arguments for protective tariffs were pressed by Catalan and later by Basque industrialists with a unique fervour. Protection, they argued, was not the selfish demand of a region or a class: it was a *national* demand. The farmers of Castile needed protection as much as the Catalan textile magnates and Basque industrialists. Agriculture and industry were complementary: Catalans could buy Castilian wheat only if Castilians bought Catalan textiles—though in fact it was probably Catalans and Basques themselves who provided the main domestic market for consumer goods. The protectionist argument was accepted ultimately by all but a handful of doctrinaire liberals. 'Political economy must accept the concept of the *patria* and subordinate itself to it. The *patria* is an association of and for the mutual aid of consumers and producers in order to create a life of its own as an individual family is created.' The metaphysics of autarky were thus stated by Cánovas in the '90s: another Conservative, Maura, gave it further extension by the legislation of 1907 which forced national products on all industries connected with the state—railways and public works in particular. Thus Spain preferred an expensive home-made navy to cheaper ships bought abroad.

Autarky was to become the ideal of two dictators: Primo de Rivera and Franco in his early years. It proved, in the long run, a false philosophy, however valuable state aid could be in establishing 'missing' industries. It forced excessive, piecemeal intervention that was self-defeating and resulted in a succession of bottlenecks; it tended to protect existing industry rather than to encourage new developments; it cut Spain off from the world in general and the European economy in particular without which she could not survive. The industrial revolution came in the 1960s, not with protectionism and autarky but with a more liberal economy.

At the time Spain's poor performance was attributed by Spaniards less to a historical development that had created a great gap between rich and poor, or to structural causes in general (though the land sales had been criticized by radicals since the 1850s), than to some inherent racial vice. This was the period when the Latin races were compared unfavourably with the Anglo-Saxons as lacking practical sense and enterprise, as given to conspicuous consumption rather than efficient production. Maeztu complained that Spaniards lacked the Anglo-Saxon love of money; Ortega that a Spaniard bought a car not to travel in, but to equip with a chauffeur as a status symbol; later Américo Castro remarked that Spaniards had produced great art but never a comfortable chair. This breast-beating is a feature of the national pessimism that lies behind the regenerationist movement of the last years of the century. That it was exaggerated was proved by the economic performance of the 1960s.

As long as what, for all the looseness of the term, we may call traditional society is felt to satisfy most human needs, its members have little inclination to 'catch the train of the industrial revolution' and imitate the pace-setters of the West. At least in one respect, however, Spain was edging in to the European model that was the ideal of regenerators. In the eighteenth century Spain was probably underpopulated (7.5 million inhabitants). By 1900, with a population of 18.6 million, its birth rate and expectancy of life were approaching European levels. The eighteenth-century complaint was that the countryside lacked 'hands'; Spain now had too many mouths to feed and Andalusia could still be swept by the 'dear times' of hunger (the last serious famine was in 1898). The safety valve was emigration, since industry could not absorb the rural surplus that agriculture could no longer employ.

V

If in relative terms Spain was a poor performer, the slow move towards an industrial economy was under way. In 1900, for the first time, there were more industrial workers than artisans registered in the census. The metallurgical industry of the Basque Provinces was a modern one with a true industrial proletariat; Basque banks and shipping were dynamic enterprises. Railways were creating a national market, as is shown by the gradual convergence and levelling out of prices over the country—a process that was to be completed by the advent of the car and the lorry in the 1920s. Spain's foreign trade was growing at a faster rate than that of France or Italy, its composition changing over time. The relative weakness of the Spanish economy and the effects of foreign loans were, however, apparent in a chronic balance of payments deficit. With Spain as a supplier of Europe at war between 1914 and 1918 (see pp. 73), Spanish exports boomed and a deficit turned into a healthy surplus. It has been argued that this meant 'the consolidation of capitalism' in Spain. That it meant soaring profits is true; but these came from overtime and the exploitation of under-utilized resources rather than from modernization via new investment. Nevertheless, when imports were cut off by war, the need to find substitutes for these did establish new industries. This was the beginning of an industrial development that, although seriously interrupted by recessions and the setbacks of the Civil War, was to be a continuous process; but it was still a slow process. The industrial revolution, the great exodus from the countryside to the towns, came in the 1960s.

3 Society in Transition 1875–1914

I

In 1921 the *philosophe* Ortega y Gasset published one of his most famous books: *Invertebrate Spain*. The lack of cohesion in Spanish society which Ortega saw as a psychological characteristic was rather a reflection of a compartmentalized, fragmented economy. The 'shapelessness' of Spanish society was a reflection of a particular stage of economic development: the coexistence of separate societies developing at different rates was a characteristic of early industrial development in Europe.

In the fragmented economy of the nineteenth century localism and regionalism, rooted in the historical process by which Spain had been unified, were inevitably strong social forces. It has been frequently observed that a Spaniard's loyalty is—or at least was—inversely proportional to the area of its application, that it is first concentrated on the *patria chica* (the little country) of the village, town, or region. This is an exaggeration; but a Spaniard will still visit his local village, still identify himself as a Catalan, a Basque, a Galician, or an Andalusian. Reformers saw in this local patriotism a means of revivifying local government and, through an awakened sense of grass-roots citizenship, an opening towards political regeneration. 'Adolescent love of the *patria chica*', declared Maura, should mature in the adult citizen into love of country.[1] The existence of local loyalties and local economies meant that greatly differing social structures could coexist, reflected in a persistent provincialism and the small-town mentality described in all the social novels of the period—for instance in Clarín's picture of Oviedo in the greatest work of this depressing genre, *La Regenta* (1884).

II

This society produced a governing class which many historians have described, following Costa, as an oligarchy. In a country where half the active population was in agriculture its core was composed of landed proprietors. The distinguishing feature of Spanish society was that the

---

[1] Quoted J. Tusell, *La reforma de la administración local en España 1900–1936* (1973), 111.

aristocracy and non-noble proprietors combined in a single class. The liberal bourgeoisie mounted no attack on the landed interest; it became part of it, forming a landed élite which assumed its classical form in the south and south-west. There it reached from the tenant who rented a large farm (the *labradores* of Andalusia) to the grandee owner of a vast estate. It was a landed class rather than a relatively homogeneous landed interest in the English sense: the concerns of the owner of olive groves and vineyards were other than those of the proprietor of extensively cultivated fields of wheat; there was little in common between a sherry baron and the proprietor owning hundreds of small fields, often monastic land sold in the *desamortación* and let out to a multiplicity of small farmers.

Most larger landowners were absentees, living either in the local town, in the provincial capital, or in Madrid. This was particularly the case with the higher aristocracy: in the 1930s nearly 70 per cent of grandees had been born in Madrid. Unlike their English equivalents, with no field sports or interest in scientific farming to keep them in the country, they were 'a landed élite by virtue of possession of land rather than by permanent rural residence'.[2] Aristocratic absenteeism, however, represented more than a preference for urban life. A large estate contained widely scattered farms; direct cultivation was impossible and the simple solution to the management problem was to let them out on short leases.

The tip of the élite was the titled aristocracy. It had lost much of its political power in the eighteenth century but its social prestige survived intact and its economic power was still considerable, though the great aristocratic houses sold off some of their *cortijos* to non-noble purchasers in the south-west after 1830.[3] As with the Church, its influence outside court circles was at a low ebb in the 1860s and, like the Church, its influence increased with the conservative reaction that followed the revolutionary upheavals of 1868–74. Cánovas was an habitué of aristocratic salons. The direct political influence of the aristocracy seems to have waned in the reign of Alfonso XIII. Although its recreations were modelled on the more powerful English sporting aristocracy—Alfonso XIII was one of the best shots in Europe—the frivolity of its social life, centring on the court, imitated the less responsible sectors of the French aristocracy.

Conformist, formally religious, the aristocracy could impose its values and the tedious routine of its social life on the upper ranges of society—for instance the *veraneo* (summer retirement from the cities),

---

[2] R. Herr, 'Spain', in D. Spring, ed., *European Landed Élites in the Nineteenth Century* (1977), 103.

[3] Cf. M. Artola, *Los Latifundios* (1978).

originally a court and aristocratic habit, spread downwards with railways and cheaper travel. The whole history of the titled aristocracy in the nineteenth century had been one of accretion through the incorporation of successful soldiers, politicians, financiers, and, later in the century, industrialists. Massive ennoblements doubled the size of the titled aristocracy in the course of the century. Like Edward VII, Alfonso XIII showed a penchant for the company of millionaires. The incipient war between the old nobility and 'the brutal *conquistadores*' of modern industry, which Unamuno detected in the Bilbao of the 1890s, was smothered by the ennoblement of the brutes.

Lower down in the landed élite came the local small-town *poderoso* or powerful one. Often a modernized version of the old *hidalgo*, now caught up in local politics and municipal government, the *poderoso* basked in the satisfactions of acknowledged pre-eminence, in the exercise of influence as cacique. The less benevolent were petty tyrants.

We have discussed the lot of the rural proletariat of landless labourers and the small peasant on a dwarf family farm (pp. 5, 16–18). One point needs emphasis. There was only a small middle sector of substantial farmers; a crude estimate in 1930 counts 96 per cent of all cultivators as small farmers and 3.1 per cent as middle-sized farmers. If we compare Spain and Britain it is the relative absence in the former of the substantial tenant farmer co-operating—sometimes uneasily, it is true—with his landlord in agricultural improvements (the great tenants of Andalusia—the *labradores*—are a case apart) that is most striking; nor was there a middling peasantry as in France. This agricultural community composed largely either of landless labourers or subsistence farmers remained, in most of Spain, submerged in the introspective world of the *pueblo*, the only contact with a wider world provided by the returned conscript, the tax-collector, or the occasional pedlar. Hence the sudden reactions of rural 'ignorance' to the intrusion of the world outside: in 1907 the peasants of Roquetas (Catalonia) agreed to destroy the local meteorological station and kill its director on the grounds that the station brought drought.[4]

The rural population—particularly of the Castilian heartland—was hard hit by the agricultural crisis of the 1880s. Migration was the only escape from rural misery. Overseas emigration went to Latin America, with a peak of 133,994 in the year 1912. More important, in the long run, was migration to Madrid, Barcelona, and the mining districts of the north, especially Bilbao. New arrivals from the overpopulated rural areas, with their fertile families, alone accounted for the rapid growth of

[4] J. Romero Maura, op.cit., 48–9.

cities where the birth rate was low. By 1914 Greater Madrid was growing at the rate of 10,000 a year, and only half of its citizens were native born. The Catalan demographer Vandellós, writing in the 1930s, feared the extinction of the Catalan way of life, swamped under a flood of poor, illiterate immigrants. The influx burst the old city limits: in Madrid the more prosperous were moving out of the old centre into the new *ensanches*, filled out with uniform blocks of flats; the workers came to the *extraradio*, dreary disease-ridden suburbs without water or proper roads. Urban expansion meant new building and street widening (the Gran Vía of Madrid begun in 1905, lined by banks and offices; the Vía Layetana of Barcelona in 1910). The new urbanism struck even provincial cities like Cartagena; it pulled down its remaining medieval walls in the 1890s. All this meant that the building trades provided jobs for the unskilled migrant workers; building labourers became the largest sector of the Madrid working class. Their strike, in June 1936, was the most impressive demonstration of proletarian power the capital had seen.

This demographic shift, which was to assume dramatic proportions in the 1960s, was already noticeable in the later years of the nineteenth century and was to accelerate after 1914, as the following table of percentages of the active population in agriculture and industry shows:

	Agriculture	Industry
1877	70	11
1887	66.5	14.6
1900	66.34	15.99
1910	66.00	15.82
1920	57	22
1930	46	27

But Spain was still a country of small towns, villages, and hamlets: in 1900 half the population lived in communities with under 5,000 inhabitants.

III

Most Spanish towns and even great cities like Cordoba were agricultural and administrative capitals. Artisans, shopkeepers, and their employees formed the bulk of the population. In the late 1870s a third of those paying the industrial tax in Spain were millers or bakers. Civil servants and army officers in the larger towns were, for the most part, birds of passage, gracing the local clubs and forming, with landowners, the provincial town élite. It was to escape from the confines of provincial life that promising sons went to Madrid to get a *título* (the necessary certificate for entry into the civil service) from the university or one of the specialized schools. Nearly all the great politicians of the nineteenth century were men of relatively modest origins born in the provinces and who died in Madrid: most of them were lawyers who had devilled for an established politician. While the immigrants who poured into Barcelona were workers, those who came to Madrid ranged from Galician water-carriers to university intellectuals.

It was the petty bourgeoisie that had provided the radical parties of the mid-century with their militants; it bred a sub-species, a 'bourgeoisie of agitation' composed of struggling journalists. After 1876, apart from a few cities like Barcelona and Valencia, its members shared the general conservative reaction of the '70s. The colonial Disaster of 1898 (see p. 47) gave them a 'sense of identity' as a class which their leaders failed to consolidate.[5] By 1909, and particularly after 1919, they started on a process which was to divide their political and social loyalties. There were conformists to whom descent into the working class remained the ultimate social degradation in a society which set great store by appearances—its key word was 'decency'; others rejected conservative conformity as the obstacle to the emergence of a 'modern' middle class and were prepared to ally with or join the Socialists: this was particularly true of intellectuals and professionals. Azaña, who led the bourgeois left in the Second Republic, was a writer and Secretary of the Ateneo; the Socialists won the allegiance of professors like Besteiro, Fernando de los Ríos, and Jiménez de Asua. It was a division between pessimists and optimists, between those who sought to preserve traditional values and those who looked outward to Europe. Negrín, the last Prime Minister of the Republic, joined the Socialist party because it was a 'European' party. More important quantitatively were lower-middle-class recruits to the party: they swelled the Socialist vote in the Second Republic. On the edge of the working class and sharing its troubles over housing and secure employment, they were often more prone to radical attitudes than the workers themselves.

IV

The only true industrial bourgeoisie and industrial working class was, in 1900, confined to Catalonia and the Basque Provinces. The Catalan *haute bourgeoisie*—textile and shipping magnates, bankers—was dominated by twenty or so families. Though Catalan industry was undergoing a process of concentration—fifteen textile concerns owned 80 per cent of the

[5] M. Martínez Cuadrado, op.cit., 357.

industry by 1900—there were still large numbers of small enterprises. Catalan entrepreneurs were capable of mounting an offensive against the 'parasitic' capital Madrid much in the style of Cobdenite attacks on the British political establishment; but they lacked Cobden's faith in the capacity of their enterprises to prosper under free trade. They were fiercely protectionist, constantly battling for higher tariffs to protect what was no longer an infant industry. The greatest representative of the Catalan *haute bourgeoisie*, Cambó, believed that Catalans remained a nation of shopkeepers whose fear of large enterprises as a means to conquer large markets stemmed from the artisan's desire to be master in his own house; yet Cambó, too, was an advocate of high tariffs. The Catalans' reaction to organized labour was similarly defensive; by 1919 they were determined to destroy it by the lock-out and the army.

If, by 1900, Madrid had become the financial, administrative, and educational capital of Spain (only Madrid University could grant doctorates), Barcelona was a city with an autonomous middle-class civilization, based on commerce and industry, and open to influences from abroad. Like Madrid it knocked down much of its old quarter to make way for tree-lined boulevards and new upper-class residential quarters. The *avant-garde* architecture—in Gaudí, Catalonia produced an architect of genius—expressed the confidence of her millionaires, whereas the new rich in Madrid built conventional palaces. Barcelona staged Ibsen's plays and Wagner's operas as early as any other great city. Its bohemian world nourished the early Picasso. But for all this Barcelona was, in terms of social life and family patterns, conservative and 'respectable': a box at the opera or a seat in the Liceo theatre was the stamp of social success; it was to strike at the temple of bourgeois values that anarchists planted a bomb in the Liceo in 1893. Gaudí built houses for millionaires; but his greatest achievement was his unfinished cathedral.

The general conservatism was a reflection of the paternalism of the Catalan industrialists: their factories were the *casas* (homes) of the employers with the workers as an extended family. Some employers lived up to this ideal, providing everything from toys at Christmas and sickness benefits to cheap housing. They were to foster Catholic unions and adopt the philosophy of social Catholicism as a tactic to solve the social question. But for many paternalism was merely a device to resist organized labour and the attempts of the state to regulate hours and working conditions. The employer's relation with his individual employee was direct; neither a union nor the state should come between them. Hence their determination 'to break the pact' with unions and keep state factory inspectors at a distance. Most employers were harsh masters. Federico Rahola, an enthusiast for the re-Christianization of the working class, attacked his fellow industrialists for neglecting their responsibilities to their workers in the quest for 'gross profits'.[6]

The Basque bourgeoisie was—partly because Basque enterprises were on a larger scale than the Catalan family firm—in entrepreneurial terms more modern, more open, and more possessed with what the Basque Maeztu called the 'sense of money'. As we have seen, Catalan banks were family concerns, whereas the Basque banks became the dominant corporate financial institutions of Spain. It was this expansion beyond the frontiers of the Basque provinces that helps to account for the indifference or hostility of the rich Basque industrialists to Basque nationalism. Catalan industrialists, bred in the narrower world of Catalan industry, patronized the Catalan renaissance and supported the demand for Catalan autonomy. The common interest that bound Basque industrialists to their Catalan colleagues was not regionalism but protectionism, and a determination to resist the demands of organized labour. Both began to organize federations of employers for the battle with labour and to bring pressure on governments for higher tariffs. In 1914 the Spanish Employers' Federation was founded to preserve the 'liberty' of employers in the face of the pressures of trade unions, and to extract economic concessions from Madrid.

V

In 1884 the government sponsored an enquiry into working-class conditions. This was a sign of an increasing concern with the 'social question', a concern that is revealing of attitudes to the working class. Poverty was regarded as a blemish on a fundamentally sound society; the demands of organized labour as an illegitimate interference with the individual freedom of employers and workers alike. Cánovas regarded property rights as sacred and the army as the ultimate bulwark against the 'barbarian invasion of the proletariat'. Most conservatives clung to the view that the 'social problem' derived from the increasing secularization of society which had produced a godless working class. 'If God's authority is not respected' the Jesuit periodical *Razón y Fe* maintained in 1909, 'no authority will be respected.' *Ergo* the working class must be re-Christianized. Re-Christianization usually took the form of a charity naïve in its assumptions: the Fathers of the Hospital of St. Peter recommended music to 'soften' workers and a 'religious culture' as the only sure remedy for strikes.[7] These condescensions were rejected by the socialists as degrading to the workers' dignity. Nothing is more striking

[6] Federico Rahola, *Catecismo de Ciudad mia* (1919), 51.
[7] A. Elorza and M. del Carmen Iglesias, *Burgueses y proletarios* (1973), 400.

than the Spanish working class's rejection of conventional religion; it was seen as hypocrisy (pawnbrokers went to church) and working-class leaders like Pablo Iglesias (see p. 54) were proud of a working-class morality in family and private life which was independent of the 'farce' of organized religion.

Whereas the founder of Catholic trade unionism, Father Vicent (see p. 41), could believe that working-class protest derived from the twin heresies of Protestantism and liberalism and that its cure was Christian resignation, liberals believed in the 'harmony of capital and labour'. It was therefore legitimate for the workers and employers to form their own associations but illegitimate for the state to intervene in the harmonious equilibrium which would emerge from the bargaining process. However, by the end of the century some Conservative politicians had begun to abandon re-Catholicization as a solution to the social question and liberals their fear of state intervention. In 1883 Moret, the Liberal leader whose doctoral thesis had been on the harmony of capital and labour, set up the Commission on Social Reform, which later became the Institute of Social Reform. It was responsible for the preparation of reports on labour conditions which are an invaluable source for historians. The Conservative Dato (see p. 79) began with his Worker's Compensation Act of 1900, a series of laws that was to culminate in the Eight-Hour Day Act of the Liberal Romanones in 1918. As we shall see (p. 89) in the attempts of the politicians to resist the Catalan Employers' Federation's 'battle against unionism', the state was not a mere 'tool of the bourgeoisie', as Pablo Iglesias asserted. But all the legislation was either opposed or sabotaged by the employers as an illegitimate attack on their liberties and an impoverished state lacked the resources to implement any extensive programme of social security, or even pay an efficient factory inspectorate.

VI

Just as the only true bourgeoisie was to be found in Catalonia and the Basque Provinces, it was there and in the mines of Asturias that the industrial proletariat was concentrated. The Vizcayan open-cast mines employed local *fijos*—permanent workers—and temporary immigrants from Castile and Leon, isolated in the countryside, housed in barracks and dependent on the company stores; with the development of metallurgical and shipping industries in the factories and docks of Bilbao, the semi-rural proletariat of the mines was supplemented by a true urban proletariat. In Guipúzcoa industry was more scattered except for the big paper mills. But neither Asturias nor the Basque Provinces had a tradition of association and proletarian militancy as had Barcelona—in 1900 there was no real union in Asturias.

The industrial workers of Catalonia were concentrated in Barcelona itself and the textile factory towns of the Ter and Llobregat valleys. Given the dominance of textiles, a third of the work force of the province of Barcelona was composed of women. Men objected to women's work; but it was a necessity for most families—by 1913 a family with two children needed 5.75 pesetas to survive when the man's average daily wage was 3.85 pesetas. Women were resistant to unionism run by men and the Catholic organizations were concerned less with women factory workers, than with the religious salvation of domestic servants and the victims of small textile sweatshops.

In Barcelona some workers still lived in the crowded streets of the old city centre, cut off from the new quarters of the bourgeoisie by the Paralelo—a street lined with the cheap theatres and cinemas which helped to integrate the 'new proletariat' of immigrants into urban life. Most of the workers lived in the formerly independent municipalities, incorporated into Barcelona city. By 1910 they had become suburbs; without water or drainage and with a Neapolitan mortality rate.

The Madrid working class was concentrated in building, the luxury trades, and in transport; its aristocracy was the printers, early organized in a 'society of resistance' under the leadership of Iglesias. Characteristic of Madrid was the large number of tailors, bootmakers, and women milliners using sewing machines bought on the instalment system. The Public Enquiry of 1884 revealed bad housing conditions where the labouring classes still lived in garret apartments in the old centre, and a mass of suffering at the base of urban life reminiscent of Dickensian England. Increasingly the sufferings of the working class (the death rate in working-class quarters was twice that of the 'respectable' quarters) were removed, both in Barcelona and Madrid, to the suburbs where they were unrelieved by Catholic charity which concentrated on the parishes of the old city centres. The visible symptom of social misery was prostitution, often child prostitution. Socialists regarded descent into prostitution, not as an individual lapse as Catholics tended to do, but as an economic necessity forced on families denied a decent wage.

All the evidence reveals the precarious nature of the working-class family budget. Even the daily struggle to survive (symbolized by clothes and shoes bought by minute instalments) was threatened by the total disaster of the loss of the wage-earner's job in a period of recession. Iglesias calculated that over a third of the 900 printers of Madrid lost their jobs in the early 1880s; there were massive dismissals in Catalonia after 1900 and again after 1919. Those flung out on the streets had no alternative but recourse to usurers (who would loan a peseta for a week at 10 per cent), the municipal or church soup kitchens, or begging. Low as they were, real wages remained stable or even rose after 1900 and this may account for the relatively low level of working-class militancy. It was unemployment (or chronic underemployment in the case of the rural labourers of the south) that was the main preoccupation. The swarm of dignified beggars in the streets of the cities impressed every visitor from England or France.

VII

Every tension in Spanish society was refracted through the prism of the religious issue. The conservative reaction of the 1870s was paralleled by a Catholic revival. The revolution must be extirpated at its root: irreligion. Spain must be re-Catholicized. Re-Catholicism triggered off the anti-clerical response. Both militant Catholicism and anti-clericalism were defensive reactions to a supposed threat. Catholics imagined that society and religion were alike threatened by the advance of a secular army of free-thinkers and masons begotten by liberalism. *Razón y Fe* added Jews (of whom not many were left in Spain) as responsible for the ruin of Spain. The harsh, medieval conservatism of the Spanish Church is perhaps explained by the fact that half of the bishops came from Old Castile. Liberalism was heresy. The parliamentary monarchy was 'intrin-sically evil and perverse', to be rejected *in toto* by the Integrists (see p. 48) and accepted only as a 'lesser evil' by more moderate churchmen until it enforced Catholic unity as a confessional state. To liberals the attempt to re-Catholicize Spain meant handing over the nation to 'the irreconcilable enemy of modern institutions, the recognition of the forces of the past as the directing element in society'. To Catholics the Institute of Free Education (see p. 43) was a step towards a godless Spain; to anti-clericals Spain was already in danger of falling into the hands of Jesuits.

The Catholic revival of the Restoration was an aristocratic and upper-middle-class concern. Its characteristic instrument was the devo-tional or charitable organization run by 'the elegant sanctimonious swarm' of aristocratic ladies. Its patron *par excellence* was the Marqués de Comillas, a Catalan shipping magnate; he financed a workers' pilgrimage to Rome (1894) and allegedly used his influence as a railway director in order to further the aims of the Association of Catholic Fathers by keeping dangerous literature off station bookstalls. The revival was morbidly puritanical and, like many contemporary religious movements, was much concerned with fallen women. Comillas succeeded in getting the dancer La Bella Chiquita banned from the Madrid stage.

Socialists, Republicans, and left-wing Liberals professed to believe that the financial resources of Catholic organizations—the Basque millionaires poured money into Catholic schools and colleges and set up a Jesuit-run university at Deusto—would enable them to compete for the support of the working class by lavish charity, the establishment of schools in working-class quarters, and the organization of Catholic unions. Yet it was the aristocratic leadership of the Catholic revival that paralysed its efforts to regain the loyalty of the working class. Comillas successfully blocked any form of unionism that could make an effective bid for working-class support. He insisted on confessional unions in which the employers be represented. 'Mixed' confessional unions could offer little but charity and Catholic unionism became a strong force only in the Basque country, and in the Catholic, agrarian heartland of Castile and Navarre where it took the form of peasant co-operatives to purchase seed and fertilizers and insure against crop failure. The patronizing attitude of the magnates of the movement was bitterly resented by priests like Fathers Gafo, Gerard and Arboleya who wanted 'free' unionism as the only effective weapon to penetrate the working class. Arboleya came to regard Comillas as 'the insuperable obstacle' to any genuine Christian democratic movement with a wide appeal. Insistence on a profession of Catholicism as the entrance card to a union was as absurd as to demand 'Catholic pubs and Catholic dances'.

The identification of the Catholic revival with upper-class interests intensified the feeling of the urban lower classes and the rural poor of Andalusia that the Church was part and parcel of upper-class life. To Pablo Iglesias, Father Vicent, a Valencian Jesuit and the founder of the Catholic Workers' Circles, was 'a zealous servant of the bourgeoisie'. Thus the working classes of Valencia and Barcelona, in sharp contrast to the popular peasant piety of Castile and Navarre, were attracted to a violent and vulgar brand of anti-clericalism. The working-class mobs who burnt the churches in 1909 believed they were burning the temples of the rich—the *'gent de bé'*—inhabited by Jesuits who used the confessional to provide employers with information about their employees. This resentment was given a crude and ideological structure by men like the Republican journalist Nakens, and Ferrer (see p. 58) whose lay schools were regarded by the Bishop of Barcelona as a more serious threat to morals than the brothel. It found a more respectable representative in the novelist Galdós: his anti-clerical play *Electra* sold 10,000 copies in two days.

Liberal politicians were prepared to appeal to popular anti-clericalism on occasion; but it did not lie at the root of liberal policies. Liberals objected to the influence of the Church on two grounds. They were what, in the eighteenth century, were called regalists—Erastians who believed that the Church should be subject to the laws of the state. They also believed that if the Church retained its monopoly of secondary education, then the future governing élite would be educated in 'seminaries of fanatic youth'. Both issues involved the Regular Orders: the Orders escaped the control of the state and its laws of association and they ran the Church's secondary schools. The aim of liberal legislation, therefore, was to control the growth of the Regular Orders supplied with a new 'proletariat of soutanes' fleeing from 'persecution' in France.

The Liberal governments were weak and their efforts half-hearted, dividing as much as uniting the party; nor did anti-clericalism give the party a mass base. It was the Liberal democrat Canalejas, Prime Minister 1910–12, who finally decided to 'give battle against clericalism' with his 'Law of the Lock'. It was not so much what the law did—it merely limited temporarily the growth of the Orders—as the mere fact that the Spanish state attempted to limit unilaterally the privileges of the Church that released a Catholic reaction of unprecedented violence and intensity. Canalejas was vilified in the aristocratic salons of Madrid and confronted with protests and demonstrations which bordered on civil war in the Basque Provinces; he sent a gunboat and 700 Civil Guards to San Sebastian.[8]

Why, in spite of repeated attempts, did a great Catholic party, committed to the defence of the Church and conservative interests in general, fail to materialize? The answer is that in spite of anti-clerical noises, the Church was not in danger in the Restoration. Alarmed by the mild Liberal legislation, Angel Herrera, an able journalist and editor of *El Debate* (1911), hoped to found a Catholic party that would attract conservative interests; its élite would be bred in the Catholic Association of Propagandists (ACNP), the fighting arm of Catholic Action. The great conservative Catholic party was a failure; nor did the later effort to form a European Christian Democratic party (the PSP founded in 1922) with an 'advanced' social programme get off the ground. Herrera had to wait for the Second Republic's onslaught on the Church—a vastly more dangerous offensive than the mild legislation of Canalejas—in order to rally conservative opinion behind the war cry of 'the Church in Danger'.

A constitutional monarchy whose king dedicated Spain to the Immaculate Conception posed no such threat. But, with all the compromises and hesitations that bedevilled Liberal policies, they were based on a world view that could not be reconciled with that of traditional Catholicism, which saw the restoration of Catholic unity as the only step that would

[8] J. Andrés Gallego, *La política religiosa en España 1889–1913* (1973), 385–6.

legitimize the state. Moret who, as Prime Minister, mounted only the most feeble attack on the Church, had been influenced by the tolerant liberalism of 1868 and by the Institute of Free Education set up in 1875 by professors who had lost their chairs in the reaction of the first days of the Restoration. The Institute was dedicated to the ideal of a non-dogmatic, modern education which should nurture the élite needed to create the intellectual preconditions of a modern democracy. It failed as a free university but succeeded as a school for a bourgeois élite. Its presiding genius was the gentle philosopher Francisco Giner; apolitical to the point of fanaticism, 'presenting no confession as the only one worthy of faith', he insisted that the child should make up his own mind. To Catholics, rather than respect for all faiths, this was hostility to one—their own. 'Neutral' education was an attempt to introduce the morals of the godless French Third Republic. The activities of the Institute, with its modern syllabus (the dogmatic content of Catholic education was matched by its archaic pedagogic methods) and such innovations as walks in the country, sports, and visits to art galleries, were regarded with horror by right-wing Catholics.

The Institute, as a minority concern with direct pupil-teacher relations, could not change the face of Spain. Nor could the state afford to finance a system of secondary education independent of the Church; the grip of the Regular Orders on the secondary education of the affluent classes (*clases acomodadas*) was a result of the poverty of the state and the superior financial resources of the Church. The Regular Orders' capital endowment in buildings, the contributions of the pious rich, the fact that monks and nuns were not paid to teach, meant that Church education was relatively inexpensive. It expanded rapidly in the late nineteenth century (by 1908 there were 40,000 pupils in religious *colegios* as opposed to 14,000 in state secondary schools), moving later into technical education. Associations of ex-pupils maintained the influence of and interest in the schools in later life. To the middle classes, seeking social mobility for their children via a *título* granted by a secondary school, the educational issue was *the* issue in the early twentieth century. It divided that class. To the readers of *Razón y Fe* secular education must lead to revolution and socialism. To the intellectuals and progressives attracted to the Reformist Republicans (see p. 50), only a modern, secular educational system could bring Spain into the modern world.

The narrow intellectual horizons of the Spanish Church could not embrace the best minds. Spanish literature was in 1875 at its lowest ebb. In the literary revival of the last quarter of the century—the so-called 'generation of 1898'—most of the writers were either indifferent or hostile to organized religion. The novels of Galdós show the disastrous personal consequences of bigotry—a thesis refuted by José María de Pereda of whom it might be argued that his defence of Catholicism distorted what talents he possessed. The polymath Menéndez y Pelayo was the only considerable writer who came to the defence, not of clericalism, but of a brand of patriotism that identified Spain with the defence of Catholicism. He elevated second-rate Spanish philosophers to the status of universal geniuses. He became the hero of right-wing Catholicism, revered as an intellectual giant when he was no more than an erudite scholar with a gift for polemical writing.

The only Catholic writer of eminence was Miguel de Unamuno (1864–1936), but his Catholicism was so eccentric and personal—he had, for instance, written for the socialist press—that he was considered by bigots as a heretic. The younger poets and novelists were, with few exceptions, 'European' liberals who continued to be morally repelled by the shams of Restoration politics and bourgeois piety. But the modernist *fin de siècle* writers, in bringing imagination back to literature, rejected the moralism and realism by means of which a previous generation had criticized or supported traditional values ; indeed, the symbolists severed any connection with the real world. The conscious élitism of the modernists was defended by Ortega in his *Deshumanización del arte*: 'difficult' literature was justified precisely because it separated the élite from the mass. Ortega's élitism came to extend beyond literary criticism to a criticism of mass democracy as such. This anti-democratic stance—most radically developed in *The Rebellion of the Masses* (1930)—opened up a perspective that was to drive a whole generation back to social and politically committed literature.[9]

VIII

After the upheavals of the mid-nineteenth century Spanish society did not suffer any radical modifications because the economic infrastructure was changing only slowly. After 1900 the cumulative effects of a slow process of industrialization were already apparent; during the Great War of 1914–18 changes were dramatic and, in the long run, irreversible. Even before the war Barcelona was making cars and aeroplanes.

Between 1900 and 1913 one and a half million people left the countryside for the towns, or for Latin America. The decline of the relative importance of the land is revealed in a rapid drop in the land tax as a proportion of budgetary income: from 40 per cent in 1900 to 14 per cent in 1918. Between 1910 and 1930 the proportion of the active

[9] For a radical presentation of this view see J. Butt, *Writers and Politics in Modern Spain* (1978), 20–5.

population engaged in agriculture dropped by 20 per cent with corresponding increases in industry and the service sector. In the 1920s Barcelona grew from a city of 750,000 to nearly a million. With the emigration to Latin America dropping off, cities like Saragossa and Seville grew from provincial capitals into modern cities. With the depression of the '30s the gates of Latin America closed and opportunities in industry contracted; until the late '50s the rural exodus was stemmed. Demographically there was an interlude of re-ruralization.

The slow growth of industry had altered the character of both the working class and the middle sectors. As far as the middle class is concerned this is reflected in the growth of the number of students in technical schools and universities after 1900. The professional classes probably doubled between 1920 and 1930. The élite were still the civil servants organized in powerful *cuerpos* (corporations) to protect their interests and gain extra privileges. Civil servants regarded their posts as their private property; low pay encouraged absenteeism and double employment. But the structure and values of the 'traditional' middle class were changing; by 1930 the private service sector was double the size of the public sector. These new servants of commerce and industry were, if the periodicals they read is any guide, more optimistic and open-minded, more 'European' than their predecessors. In Barcelona a class of new rich wartime profiteers had sprung up alongside the staid family businesses of the nineteenth century.

It was the increase in the size of the working class that was to be the most important in the long run. In the province of Barcelona it seems to have doubled in the '20s. Madrid changed from a 'parasitic' capital of politicians and government servants into a city of bankers, secretaries, businessmen, workshop and factory hands. By 1930 70 per cent of its active population was classed as workers.

All these changes were to have political manifestations after the political winter of the dictatorship of Primo de Rivera. It was the enlarged working class which was to determine the politics of the Second Republic. Confronted with an organized and powerful working class (as far back as 1918 the *Herald of the Middle Class* complained that the 'middle classes' were 'neglected' because they could not organize as did the workers), the middle classes were to split between those who returned to the mid-nineteenth-century radical alliance with the working class and those who sought safety in a revival of the Catholic conservative party that had been mooted, but never formed, in the years before the dictatorship but which had been unnecessary under it. In the '20s technocrats had flourished with the plans and government agencies of Primo. Recession meant the end of these ambitious plans and the posts that went with them. The Republic was supported by journalists and university professors rather than by engineers. It was the failure of his struggle as a haulage contractor to maintain middle-class respectability that turned Manuel Hedilla, future leader of the Falange, into a counter-revolutionary.

4 Regenerationism and the Critics of the Regime

Eighteen ninety-eight was the year of 'the Disaster'. Spain lost the last remnants of a once-great colonial empire: Cuba, the 'Pearl of the Antilles . . . the richest colony in the whole world', Puerto Rico, and the Philippines. Cuban separatists had revolted in 1895; once joined by the United States there was no chance of victory for the mother country. In May 1898 Admiral Dewey blew the Spanish Pacific fleet out of the water; on 3 July 1898 the Atlantic fleet under Admiral Cervera was destroyed at the cost of one American casualty. Cut off in Cuba by the most complete naval disaster of modern times, the army surrendered; it had lost 2,129 men in action and 53,000 through disease. At the Treaty of Paris, Spain lost her empire at the very time when other powers were staking their claims to colonies.

As the sick and ragged remnants of the army returned to Spain it was the politicians rather than the soldiers and sailors who were held responsible for defeat at the hands of American 'sausage-makers'. Years later General Mola, organizer of the rising of July 1936, was to write, 'What responsibilities should fall on the shoulders of the politicians of that epoch. With their improvisation and negligence they started operations without supplying the troops with the most elemental necessities.'

To its enemies and critics the Disaster proved the 'incapacity' of the 'monarchy of Sagunto' (so called after the town where Martínez Campos had risen to restore Alfonso XII); the only alternative to blaming the political system was to relapse into the racial pessimism which denied to Latin nations the capacity to face the modern world. It is important to realize that the criticism of the constitutional monarchy as corrupt and unrepresentative of the great interests of the nation was not new: the Disaster merely heightened the tone as critics, in search of a wider audience, assumed the grandiloquent title of Regenerators. 'The Regenerator', wrote a satirist, 'a tonic for weak nations. Recommended by the best doctors, apostles and saviours.'

The Republicans rejected monarchy as an illegitimate and outmoded form of government; the Carlists rejected the Alfonsine branch of the dynasty and the liberal institutions it symbolized. The Socialists regarded the monarchy as a reactionary concern which must be turned into a bourgeois democracy as the next step in the historical process that must lead to a socialist society. The anarchists rejected it—or any other state—*in toto*. To the regionalists the apparatus of the dynastic parties strangled local interests. Those whom we may call the radical regenerationists believed that there must be a root-and-branch reform as a preliminary to national revival.

The question to be answered is, Why did these protest movements fail either to overthrow, or radically to reform, a discredited political system? The answer is threefold. The protest movements were fissiparous, divided in tactics and as much rent by personal feuds as the 'corrupt' parties they attacked. Secondly, the political system was more open and flexible than its critics admitted. Finally, apathy and the regionalist issue (see p. 61) inhibited the creation of mass *nationwide* parties of protest.

II

The Carlists remained faithful to the true dynasty, the heirs of Don Carlos who had led them against the liberal armies in the 1830s. Carlism, its dynastic fanaticism apart, was a 'populist' protest against urban liberalism. Carlists were theocratic utopians hankering after a pre-industrial society: Bilbao, with its industries and banks, was the Babylon to be taken and destroyed. Carlism was 'a disintegrating traditional society's outcry against the visible evidence of change and modernity'.[1]

It ceased to be a military threat with the defeat of the Pretender's armies in 1876. But Carlists remained unassimilated and, in their consistent attacks on the established order, were regenerationist after their fashion: regeneration would come from the inevitable collapse of the 'system' and the enthronement of the true dynasty; they were ready to aid the march of history by conspiracy. Fortunately for the Alfonsine monarchy, Carlists were paralysed by internal disputes. Integrists accused the Pretender, the Duke of Madrid, of liberal deviationism and proclaimed the kingship of Christ the King. Orthodox Carlism experienced with a young Galician orator, Vázquez de Mella, the doctrinal overhaul it badly needed, turning from bald dynastic fanaticism to a doctrine of regional revival under a patriarchal 'social' monarchy. Some form of Catholic corporatism was the Carlist recipe for regeneration.

The Integrists, not all of whom came from Carlism, were a small but vociferous faction. Nevertheless, their inflexible Tridentine Catholicism was a threat to the Cánovite ideal of comprehension. Any Catholic who

[1] M. Blinkhorn, *Carlism and Crisis in Spain 1931–39* (1975), 16.

accepted the liberal monarchy even as a 'lesser evil' was a 'half-breed'. The Integrist influence on Spanish Catholicism was disastrous, driving it to the right. Neither the Vatican nor the hierarchy could temper their fanaticism.

Carlism professed to be a national movement; its 'circles' sprang into life to commiserate with or congratulate members of the true dynasty on family occasions. Its only real strength as an anti-liberal movement lay in the Basque Provinces and rural Catalonia. After 1876 Carlism declined, living on memories of the past, only to come to life when the Second Republic mounted its attack on the Catholic unity of Spain.

III

By definition Republicans could not accept the monarchy as a legitimate form of government. Once the prospect of a republic installed by a discontented general receded, all that remained was the mystique and memory of the Republic of 1873. Its surviving dignitaries assumed the mantle of an effortless intellectual and moral superiority. They did not need a programme: Republicanism would triumph in an evil world as a self-evident truth. There was always a conspiratorial wing, fed on the verbiage of bohemian journalists; but a fissiparous movement dominated by professors is unlikely to stage a revolution. Republican newspapers and clubs (*casinos*) changed hands among competing groups and the committee work behind these shifts of allegiance was the occupational disease of local Republican worthies.

After a revival in 1900–3 the future of Republicanism lay in two divergent directions. Alejandro Lerroux (1864–1949) and his Radical Republicans represented the revolutionary tradition based on a working-class alliance. The Reformist Republicans, led by a group of university intellectuals, were evolutionists: the form of the regime, which lay at the heart of historic Republicanism, was less important than the implementation of a practical programme of democratic and social reforms.

Lerroux was the son of an army veterinary surgeon who had made his name in the world of Republican journalism. Denounced as a cynical demagogue (when caught drinking champagne he boasted that he was drinking today what the workers would drink tomorrow), he was the only Republican leader to forge an effective, if temporary, alliance with the working class.[2] His appeal to the Barcelona proletariat lay less in a specific programme than in his recognition of the cultural gap that separated workers from the *gent de bé*—the self-satisfied bourgeoisie of

[2] For a revaluation of Lerroux see J. Romero Maura, op.cit., 270 ff; and Octavio Ruiz Manjón, *El Partido Republicano Radical 1908–1936* (1976), esp. chs. ii-iv.

Barcelona with its contempt for the 'uncultured' workers and those who sought their votes. Lerroux's *Casas del Pueblo*—clubs with modest libraries—sustained a working-class sub-culture, the main ingredient of which was a violent brand of anti-clericalism as the most immediate means of attack on bourgeois values: 'Young barbarians of today', the followers of Lerroux were admonished, 'pillage the decadent civilization of this wretched country, destroy its temples, trample its gods under foot, tear aside the veils of novices and elevate them to the category of mothers.'

Lerroux did not merely appeal to 'the virginity of adolescence, the cruelty of the child' in his young barbarians. He was a machine politician determined to defeat Barcelona *caciquismo* by a rival organization based on voluntary helpers. His stalwarts stood pissing in the room as the votes were counted—a symbol of the defeat of the caciques of the *gent de bé*. From 1901 until the Great War he was to dominate Barcelona politics.

The language of Radical Republicanism (the leader of the party in Valencia once declared that a Browning automatic was the true security for individual rights), its attacks on 'religion, property, and the family' as resting on 'erroneous conceptions and absurd laws', made the party unacceptable to respectable bourgeois committed to Catalanism (see p. 61 ff.). Between 1900 and 1914 Lerroux's Radicals and the bourgeois regionalists fought a bitter electoral battle. But by 1914 Lerroux had lost his working-class support in Barcelona. The Radical Republicans started out on the road to respectability; the 'old lion' was domesticated, ending his career as the messiah of frightened conservatives in the Second Republic.

The remnants of the revolutionary tradition in historic Republicanism offered, in 1914, no serious alternative to the system they denounced. 'I have never believed', wrote the eccentric novelist Pío Baroja, 'that the Republican party will make its revolution. I have never considered it an organ of progress and culture, nor have I been able to convince myself that its leaders are in any way superior to the monarchical caciques who are devouring Spain.'

The Reformist Republicans rejected the revolutionary tradition altogether, scorning its verbal violence. Moderate bourgeois Republicans followed the lead of Azcárate and Melquíades Álvarez into the Reformist Republican party, created as a separate grouping in 1912. The Reformist strength lay in the intellectual quality of its leadership; the party never gained more than twenty seats. It captured the allegiance of the new promotion of intellectuals: Ortega y Gasset joined the party—characteristically only for a short period—and the young Azaña stood as a Reformist candidate. The closest parallel in programme and temper to these reformers was the radical wing of the Liberal party which came to power in England in 1906. Their ideal, from first to last, was democratic parliamentary government *a la inglesa*—with or without a monarchy.[3]

The Reformist vision was a modernized Spain, tolerant, democratically ruled, with up-to-date educational and social legislation. The Reformists were practical men, and from the first they aspired to be 'a party of government'; their Fabian programme had little in common with the habitual catch-phrases of Republican revolutionism. To Melquíades Álvarez Republicanism became more a threat to force the monarchy along the paths of democracy and modernization than an end in itself. If the king recognized himself to be 'the slave of opinion', if he ruled through and by an honestly elected parliament, there was no harm in him. If he did not, then he would meet on his way the 'spectre of a Republic'.

Until 1931 Republicanism constituted a threat to the monarchy, less through its strength as an organized party or its danger as a revolutionary menace than by its constant attacks on every failure, every defeat of the regime, from military disasters in Morocco to the peculations of a small-town mayor in Andalusia. Its political *raison d'être* was as a protest against the 'barbarities of the system', against the electoral corruption which denied it any representation outside the great cities. While Republican strength grew slowly, Republican victories in Madrid, Valencia, and Barcelona alarmed monarchist politicians and 'proved' the Republicans' assertion that they represented enlightenment and numbers against the managed votes of rural idiocy. The sustained propaganda of Republicanism eroded the moral foundations of the monarchy. Azcárate seemed justified in his prophecies: 'I believe that a kind of fatality prevents this dynasty from being able to solve the social and political problems which are arising at the present time; I consider that the only form of government likely to provide the solution is a Republic.'

IV

The career of Joaquín Costa (1846–1911), the greatest figure of the radical regenerationism of the intellectuals, embodies its central weakness. It was easy for intellectuals like Costa to mount a devastating attack on the evils of the 'old' politics; it proved impossible to mobilize a democratic alternative to redress them.

Costa was the son of an Aragonese peasant whose life was a long struggle against poverty and muscular dystrophy. A self-educated poly-

[3] For Reformist Republicans see M. García Venero, *Melquíades Álvarez* (1954).

math and compulsive writer and worker (a seventeen-hour day produced forty books and five hundred articles), he suffered and bitterly resented the rebuffs of a conservative establishment which would not recognize his achievements. He failed to get a professorial chair at Madrid and his best book, 'Agrarian Collectivism in Spain', published in 1898, was rejected by the jury for a literary prize as too 'socialist'. A visit to Paris, financed by the local cacique, convinced him of the backwardness of Spain. All his early writings are obsessed with the search for the historical roots of this backwardness. By 1896 he had worked out a one-man programme for national regeneration.

This programme would replace the trivial politics of the Restoration, dismissed as an empty rhetorical façade sheltering the interests of an oligarchy, by 'practical realizations': new roads; a 'hydraulic policy' which would co-ordinate a vast scheme of irrigation; schools; the establishment of a prosperous peasantry by reversing the Liberals' *desamortación* in favour of a new distribution of the land that once belonged to the Church and the municipalities; the encouragement of co-operation which Costa believed to be rooted in Spanish communal traditions.

This ambitious programme was to be realized by the mobilization of the 'neutral masses', excluded from political life by the electoral machinery of *caciquismo*. Spain must no longer be ruled by 'those who ought to be behind bars, in a lunatic asylum, or on a school bench'. The politicians of the parliamentary regime had achieved nothing but their own survival. 'Politicians to private life, the people to public life.'

It was the post-Disaster atmosphere of 'regenerationism' which induced in Costa the belief that an opportunity for rallying the 'neutral masses' at last existed. In February 1899 he organized his League of Producers and in March 1900 joined forces with the Chambers of Commerce movement of Basilio Paraíso in the National Union of Producers. Whereas Costa represented the agricultural protest, Paraíso, the proprietor of a modest looking-glass factory in Saragossa, channelled the discontents of the middle class. No great landowners supported Costa; the Basque and Catalan industrialists cold-shouldered Paraíso.

The movement failed to make any impact on Spanish politics. It was not merely that the determination of the 'productive classes' to secure tax reductions (by government economies in military and administrative expenditure) was with difficulty reconcilable with Costa's programme of increased expenditure on education and agriculture; the Union of Producers represented divergent interests and pursued contradictory tactics. Costa wanted to turn the Union into a new independent political party which would 'break with the accursed tradition of political parties'.

If the governing parties refused to mend their ways and implement the Union's programme, then it should assume power as a national government; Costa himself for a short period entertained the absurd hope that he would be invited to join a ministry. Paraíso consistently opposed the conversion of his movement into a political party. His chosen weapons were the respectful petition to the crown backed by the threat of a taxpayers' strike. Costa saw that the government would dismiss middle-class regenerationism as a selfish, unpatriotic shopkeepers' protest. The taxpayers' strike was a miserable failure.

This failure is significant because it exposes the weakness of the regenerationism of which Costa was the apostle. It was the victim of a myth: that there was a 'healthy' substratum in Spanish society imprisoned by the orthopaedic apparatus of a corrupt political system. What lay beneath the surface of politics was apathy. Costa finally despaired and his assaults on politics and politicians, and the vocabulary in which he clothed them, became the stock in trade of authoritarian iron surgeons who, far from wishing to modernize Spanish society, were determined to keep it in a straitjacket.

V

By 1914 the Republican protest was becoming increasingly a middle- and lower-middle-class protest. We must now examine the working-class protest.

The fascination of the early history of Spanish labour movements has obscured their insignificance. In the conservative reaction of 1875 all working-class organizations were declared illegal and remained so until 1881, and even after that operated under severe legal constraints. In 1907 Spain was still the only major European country without a working-class deputy in parliament.

The Spanish labour movement was to be weakened, as the Republicans had been, by division and internecine strife; and on the same issue—whether to proceed by revolutionary violence or by legal pacific means. The revolutionary strand was represented by the anarchists and the anarcho-syndicalist union, the CNT, founded in 1910–11; the more gradualist tradition by the Socialist party, the PSOE, founded in 1879 and the Socialist union, the UGT, which followed in 1882. Each movement was to be torn by struggles: between syndicalists prepared to tread the long road to victory by building the CNT into a strong organization and anarchist activists for whom revolution was just around the corner; between the sober bureaucrats of the UGT and young militants prone to the rhetoric of proletarian violence.

Until his death in 1925 the Socialist party and the UGT were dominated by the personality of Pablo Iglesias (b. 1850). Iglesias, the son of a poor washerwoman, turned an old-fashioned printers' craft guild into a militant union. He and his friend Mesa, a Paris journalist, were to imprint the PSOE with the influence of French Marxists and their leader Guesde. From Guesde Iglesias derived his harsh platform oratory and his doctrinaire hostility to bourgeois politicians, especially Republicans. An austere ascetic, controlling his party with his enormous network of correspondence, Iglesias stamped the party with his own brand of proletarian Calvinism.

The programme of the party was set out in 1886: its first point was the possession of power by the working class; its second 'the transformation of the instruments of work into the common property of the nation'. Growth was slow, and painfully achieved. On its left the party was attacked by anarchists who rejected the struggle for *political* power embodied in the party's first point; on its right the urban workers could still be attracted by Republicans like Lerroux, who rejected the over- throw of capitalism as such, appealing to 'a formula of harmony between social interests' which would 'dignify' labour, but who were willing to exploit working-class resentments.

Many of the Socialist leaders, particularly its intellectuals, had been bred in the liberal Republican tradition. It was the socialist fight against the impurities of the system—particularly in municipal government— that attracted intellectuals to the party. It became, in Ortega's phrase, 'an emblem of purity', particularly in municipal government as Lerroux's Radicals became experts in the manipulation of city patronage. Fernando de los Ríos (b. 1879), a professor of public law at Granada, rejected 'materialism', crude class hatred and violent anti-clericalism. An inde- fatigable lecturer to working-class audiences, he believed that the 'moral redemption' of the workers must precede their 'economic redemption'. The use of a Christian vocabulary is typical of his 'humanist socialism'.

The possibility of an electoral alliance with the bourgeois Republicans as the only way to break into political life haunted the Socialists as the party failed to grow. Repeatedly attempted, both locally in municipal councils and as party policy, the alliance inevitably collapsed. La Obra, a workers' society in Granada, could not bridge the gap between near- anarchists and the Republican leader Duarte, a prosperous oculist who 'smoked cigars and rode in a carriage'.[4] In 1909 Iglesias abandoned 'purity' for an electoral 'conjunction' which gave the party its first parliamentary deputy. But it was not until 1918 that the Socialists

[4] For La Obra see A. M. Calero Amor, *Historia del movimiento obrero en Granada 1909–1923* (1973), 143–9.

advanced again; by 1923 there were seven Socialist deputies as against eleven Republicans.

Until 1914 membership of both the UGT and the party fluctuated. Membership swung upwards in the late 1890s only to drop sharply in 1907, rising again until 1913 when the PSOE had 14,729 members. It remained a party of the industrial workers, dominated by the labour aristocracy of Madrid and with its strength in the Asturian mines and in the mines, steel, and shipping concerns of Vizcaya. In the villages of the depressed Old Castile of the 1880s 'centuries of silence' were broken with the formation of 'societies of resistance' under Socialist influence. Opposed by the large farmers as 'an insult to the employing classes', the movement petered out. It was not until the 1930s that the rural labourers flooded into the UGT, infusing the movement with a new radicalism.

The strength and weaknesses of socialism can be illustrated from the labour history of its northern stronghold, Vizcaya. In spite of the existence of large industrial concerns (Altos Hornos de Vizcaya with 7,000 workers in its ironworks was the largest single concern in Spain), the PSOE and the UGT were much weaker than one might expect. Membership fluctuated wildly, swelling during successful strikes and collapsing as suddenly afterwards. Before 1890 there was 'social peace' in Vizcaya; between 1890 and 1923 there was a series of strikes, first in the mines and then in industry. These strikes were characterized by violence. This was a sign of weakness, not of organized strength.

It was the attitude of the employers which conditioned the labour climate of Vizcaya. They set their faces against any recognition of Socialist unions; workers must present their grievances as individuals. The employers' organizations drew up 'Black Lists' of Socialist militants who were refused employment as 'an immoral and criminal element and a grave danger to employers'. They encouraged and subsidized Catholic unionism which rejected the class struggle as a concept and violence as a tactic. The intransigence of the employers' organizations made negotiations with Socialist unions an impossible form of labour relations.

Hence until 1911 strikes in Vizcaya took a peculiar pattern set by the miners in 1890. A 'spontaneous' strike would be taken over by PSOE militants. Violence would be employed against blacklegs and 'public order' threatened. This forced the intervention of the Civil Governor and the military authorities; in turn, the authorities forced a settlement on the employers and workers alike.

Violence, therefore, was a substitute for the organized strength to support a long strike. 'In Bilbao socialism was made in taverns. Union organization was a mere skeleton, with very few members paying dues; the men of action paralysed the life of the region whenever it took their fancy.[5] The violent men found their leader in Facundo Perezagua, whose strident oratory and strong-arm tactics were scarcely distinguishable from those of anarcho-syndicalists committed to direct action and the rejection of any alliance with the bourgeois left. The efforts of the moderates like Indalecio Prieto, whose relations with Republican leaders became increasingly close, to create a disciplined, educated proletariat— Zugazagoitia, Prieto's lieutenant, advised workers to read two hours a day and avoid taverns—were regarded by Perezagua as a means of integrating the workers into a capitalist system which they should have been committed to destroying. In the end, Perezagua deserted socialism for the revolutionary tactics of the Communists.

Prieto was dependent on 'corrupt' deals with monarchist politicians and Republican votes for his Socialist safe seat in Bilbao. 'I am not a man of doctrine,' he wrote in 1920, 'I am a man of realities.'[6] And the reality was power.

The conflict between 'men of realities' like Prieto and men of violence like Perezagua was to characterize the history not merely of Basque socialism but of Spanish socialism. It was the organization men like 'Father' Iglesias who set their mark on the movement. Always confronted with the threat of desertions to the anarcho-syndicalists, Socialists often indulged in language more violent than that of the British socialists whom leaders like Professor Besteiro admired; the movement even lurched into revolutionary action, as in 1917. But they were reformists, union bureaucrats loath to risk in rash enterprises an organization built up with great difficulty. 'Revolutionary gymnastics' could be left to the anarcho-syndicalists. As revisionists (Iglesias wrote a preface to the Spanish translation of Kautsky) they held that a bourgeois democracy (and in Spain this could only mean a republic) was the next step on the road to socialism, and by 1923 they often appeared less as a workers' party than successors to the Republicans as the moral critics of a 'feudal' monarchy doomed by the forces of progress.

VI

Anarchism had been injected into the Spanish labour movement by the arrival in 1868 of Fanelli as a missionary for Bakunin's revolutionary Alliance of Social Democracy, a quasi-secret society within the First International. Without a word of Spanish, Fanelli persuaded a group of Madrid workers to join Bakunin's Alliance; the Spanish members of the

---

[5] Andrés Saborit, quoted in Ignacio Olabarri Gortazar, *Relaciones laborales en Vizcaya 1890–1936* (1978), 91.

[6] J.P. Fusi, *Política obrera en el país vasco* (1975), 483.

International were thus committed to a struggle with the 'authoritarian' Marxists who finally succeeded in expelling Bakunin and his Alliance from the First International. From then on anarchists and socialists were to compete for the loyalty of the Spanish worker. All attempts to unite them in one powerful workers' organization failed, a failure with tragic results for the Spanish labour movement. Rivalry between the two movements was endemic in the geographical distribution of their strength. The anarchist capital was 'the rose of fire'—industrial Barcelona. Its second stronghold was rural Andalusia, and there were outposts in Aragon, the Levante, and Galicia. Madrid was the organizational centre of socialism: its mass support lay in the mines and factories of Vizcaya and Asturias.

How can one account for this persistent division? In particular, how can one explain why it was only in Spain that anarchism, in the form of the anarcho-syndicalism of the CNT, succeeded in becoming a mass movement? That it was the appeal of the libertarian ideas, central to anarchism, to the supposed exaggerated individualism of Spaniards is an argument that will not hold. As Vicens Vives, the Catalan historian, argued, employers get the unions they deserve and it was the exaggerated Victorian individualism of employers, who refused to recognize any of the claims of organized labour, that made reformist unionism seem a useless tactic, leaving revolutionary syndicalism as the only feasible strategy. Whereas socialist unionism tended to appeal to established workers, anarchism was always to attract the *new* recruits to industry, the rural worker caught in a strange impersonal world, and the artisan displaced and pauperized by industrialization. (Sometimes anarchism seems a Spanish edition of Luddism—a protest of the members of a traditional society against the inroads of capitalism.) There was, in Victor Serge's phrase, 'a vast world of irregulars, outcasts, paupers and criminals' attracted to Barcelona and its port; marginal men who could find no outlet but in a craving for violence.

The division between anarchists and socialists remained one of temperament and tactics. There was a type of revolutionary energumen, bred in the ferment of 1869–73, to whom Marxist doctrine and gradualist tactics could make no appeal. To join the socialists was 'to do the goose-step in a Prussian regiment'.

All anarchists, however moderate, used the language of revolution, whether they saw the revolution as the culmination of an organized struggle or as the chance gift of a successful street fight or a terrorist campaign. Iglesias was an eminent Victorian. Socialists regarded the anarcho-syndicalists as a collection of gun-toting vegetarian cranks with whom no alliance could hold against their inveterate proclivity to revolutionary gymnastics and pointless strikes. Society would be transformed by a series of partial victories, not by the anarcho-syndicalist version of a Sorelian revolutionary general strike. The anarcho-syndicalists were aware of the necessity of supporting concrete working-class grievances; but the state of war against the employers was permanent, and 'direct action' precluded the intervention of the bourgeois state by means of which the socialists sought satisfaction through 'small gains' that would gradually, legally (but irreversibly) transform society.

From their very beginnings the various anarchist organizations were divided both on the nature of the future anarchist society and on the means of destroying bourgeois society: libertarian communists were ranged against collectivists, terrorists and professional revolutionaries against union organizers and educators. Repression threw the movement into the hands of the wild men bred by clandestinity. In the 1890s a wave of bomb outrages shocked bourgeois opinion; police barbarity set off the mechanisms of reprisal which accounted for the assassination of three Prime Ministers.

Terrorism was a minority doctrine which ran parallel with another anarchist tradition: self-improvement and rationalist education. Unsuccessful terrorism produced lethargy and in the trough of despair anarchists organized debates on free love, property, the city of the future, and sent their children to Ferrer's Modern Schools.

Francisco Ferrer (1849–1909) had started life as a Republican revolutionary and conspirator. An inveterate womanizer who got through three 'official' companions, he inherited a small fortune from a pupil. Once he was converted to anarchism this allowed him to establish an anarchist extended family and to acquire, as a benevolent philosopher-king, a powerful hold on anarchist circles: he financed schools and periodicals. His activities coincided with the decline of terrorism, when the anarchist classics became the intellectual baggage of the bolder spirits of the Barcelona proletariat.

In their early years the growth of anarchist organizations was erratic: this was particularly true of Andalusia, where the numerical strength of the movement lay until the 1890s. Whereas in a complex industrial society the anarchist utopia is an inconceivable anachronism, in the face-to-face society of the *pueblo*—the agro-towns of Andalusia—once the rich had been eliminated the dream of a libertarian society could be conceived of as a possibility. But anarchism spread rapidly in Andalusia, only partly because Bakunin's gospel coincided with the messianic traditions of primitive society; more importantly anarchist apostles were prepared to adopt as their own the *specific* demands of the Andalusian labourers, even when these were theoretically in conflict with the principles of the movement. These demands had long included the abolition of piece-work, higher wages, and, behind these, the 'indigenous socialism' of the *reparto*—the 'magic word which has electrified the masses' with the cry for a division of the great estates.

At times this rural anarchism organized itself, or rather fell under the influence of small organized groups, and was carried into movements of social protest or strike action. Great cyclical gusts of peasant violence, crop burning, killings of watch dogs, assassinations of rural guards, swept over the south; in the early 1880s a small terrorist group, the Black Hand, convinced the landlords that they were confronted by 'a huge war machine'. Five thousand 'anarchists' were arrested and their trial used to break the movement.[7] With repression and failure the enthusiasts sank into what the historian of Andalusian anarchism called 'Moorish apathy'. But rural anarchism was something more than the primitive protest of the disinherited or a rural form of religious revivalism: nor do the classical areas of the great latifundia correspond neatly with the strongholds of rural anarchism. Anarchism combined a protest against the disintegration of a traditional society, a visionary faith in the moral transformation of the world on 'the day', and a trade union movement committed to specific demands.

With the foundation of its union, the CNT, in 1910–11, the organized strength of anarcho-syndicalism came to rest in Catalonia, above all in Barcelona with its long tradition of workers' associations. Declared illegal in 1912 (apparently on the advice of the Barcelona employers), the CNT was to display extraordinary powers of sudden recruitment compared with the slower growth of the UGT. The CNT consistently inflated its membership figures; nevertheless the claim that the membership of the Catalan CNT rose from 14,000 in 1914 to 700,000 in 1919 signified a remarkable expansion.

The most important divisions within the anarchist movement itself, and above all between anarcho-syndicalists and socialists, centred on the function and nature of the revolution and the role of the workers' union. The enemies of the CNT (and many foreign observers) fastened on the persistence of a pure anarchist tradition. To anarchists bourgeois capitalist society was doomed, not by some ineluctable historical process, the 'objective conditions' of the Marxist analysis, but by its moral decrepitude. With feet of clay it would fall to a revolution which was a spontaneous act of the masses. The Revolution cannot be led from above; it can only be sensed and seized by the gifted leader. Such views easily led to a mystique of violence and a worship of the revolutionary hero-

---

[7] See C.E. Lida, 'Agrarian Anarchism in Andalusia', *International Review of Social History* xiv (1969), 315–52.

superman (many anarchists read Nietzsche). Hence the anarchist canoni-
zation of men like Durutti, bank robber on principle. The attraction of
violence was contradicted by a belief in the redemptive powers of love;
hence the movement's Dostoevskian concern for the redemption of the
criminal—at the same time a useful revolutionary and a man who had
been despised by a society indifferent to his sufferings.

The so-called 'moderates' in the CNT rejected the spontaneous
revolution and terrorism as a tactic. Influenced by French syndicalism,
they followed the anarchist tradition of apoliticism and scorn of
bourgeois politics. This meant in practice abstention from elections to
the cry 'Don't vote'. The ballot box was a device to enslave the workers;
bourgeois democracy could never be a historical stage in the transition to
socialism. 'The Republic is not worth a drop of the workers' blood.' The
tactic of revolutionary syndicalism was direct action: a constant war with
the employers to be waged by strong unions which would produce results
in the form of wage settlements. If their ultimate vision was a new society
based on the great unions without passing through the historical stage of
bourgeois democracy, and if they usually rejected Socialist inclinations
towards any alliance with Republicans, anarchist leaders like Seguí (see
p. 89) were preoccupied with building up union strength for the
day-to-day battle with the employers. In 1918, after a long debate, the
CNT abandoned the old craft unions for the *sindicato único*: the industrial
union. Imperfectly implanted, it was the *sindicatos únicos* who were to
deliver the great labour offensive of 1919 (see p. 89).

The sober organizers of the Socialist party and the UGT despised in
the anarcho-syndicalists what they regarded as a combination of sen-
timentality and infantile revolutionism which opened up opportunities
for spies and *agents provocateurs*. It was not that the anarchists were
averse to organization; indeed they talked of little else at many congresses. Like the extreme federalists of the 1870s, they held that revolution
must come *abajo arriba*, from the bottom to the top; they sought, and
failed, by a highly complex organizational structure, to reconcile the
contrary demands of effective joint action and individual liberty of
choice. While Largo Caballero was giving the Socialist main office paid
secretaries and typewriters, the complicated anarchist organization was
run by temporary, unpaid officials. Anarchist congresses remained
sovereign bodies, without dictated agendas and managing committees;
those of the UGT were firmly controlled by the committees and topics
which embarrassed the leadership kept off the agenda. To the end, every
constituent union of the CNT preserved its sacred right to individual
direct action.

Both Socialists and anarcho-syndicalists played an important part in educating the Spanish proletariat; in the early twentieth century the Socialist *Casas del Pueblo*, with their primitive libraries and lecture courses, replaced the Republican *casinos* as centres of cultural diffusion. The Socialists were determined to give the workers immediate benefits: much of Largo Caballero's early work was devoted to setting up burial societies, sickness insurance, and co-operatives. The anarchists gave the workers the vision of a heavenly city based on harmony and justice. In 1898 an anarchist congress portrayed the society which should issue from the great revolutionary destruction of the past: great apartment houses, lit by electricity, serviced by automatic lifts and rubbish disposers, would house workers who were to be the leisured supervisors of machines: a society where wood was replaced by steel and prisons by 'Houses of Medical Correction', money by tokens, and the state by a bureau of statistics co-ordinating 'harmonious labour'. Some have seen anarchism as a sort of left-wing Carlism, looking back to a lost past. Anarchism was often nearer the world of science fiction and, indeed, such works did have a vogue in anarchist circles.

VII

The protest movements of Catalans, Basques, Galicians, Valencians were similar to other peripheral regionalisms in nineteenth- and twentieth-century Europe. A pre-existing sense of regional or national identity becomes a regionalist movement demanding some form of special treatment—*political* recognition, for instance, of what was called 'the differential factor' of Catalonia, or the restoration of the 'ancient liberties' of the Basque Provinces. A sense of separate cultural identity, distinct from that of the dominant central state of which the regions form a part, is based on a regional language and a unique historical experience. On this sense of cultural and historic identity are grafted economic grievances, a conviction of special regional economic interests, of relative deprivation; a belief that the political and administrative structure of the centralized state discriminates against the regions. The intensity of regional sentiment and the consequent regionalist programmes can vary. 'Catalanism' could range from the cultivation of folklore through administrative devolution to separatism.

Apart from the tensions between the regions and the state, regionalism poses a particular political problem. It weakens the political structure by hindering the development of *nationwide* parties; regional parties resist becoming mere 'branches' (*succursales*, the word for a local branch of a bank) of a party centred on Madrid. The Socialists had to fight the nationalist unions in the Basque Provinces and never succeeded in founding a strong party in Catalonia; during the Second Republic Conservative interests in Catalonia were defended by the Lliga (see p. 64) and in Spain as a whole by the CEDA, while the Catalan left was organized in the Esquerra, distinct from the Spanish Republican left though allied with it. The effect of regionalism in complicating the party system and therefore weakening the political structure cannot be over-emphasized.

Catalanism

The Catalan language was the living centre of Catalanism. The early heroes of Catalan nationalists were poets, philologists, and historians. To Mañe y Flaquer, a supporter of Cánovas and a Conservative regionalist, 'the use of our language' was 'the most eloquent manifestation of our personality. As long as the Catalan language exists every attempt at unification will be an act of tyranny.' It was the aim of the Catalan 'renaissance' of the 1840s and '50s to revive Catalan as the literary tongue it had been in medieval times. The renaissance was a stilted and artificial affair, and it was by bridging the gap between popular, everyday Catalan and the language of the revivalists that the poet Verdaguer, in the words of his follower Joan Maragall (whom Unamuno considered the greatest poet of his age), became the 'master of us all, who *created* our language'. Catalans were fortunate in that Catalan, unlike Basque, was a flexible language that could be used as a vehicle for modern thought.

The Catalan renaissance shared the concern of the European Romantic movement (of which it was a part) with history. Catalans brooded on the memory of their great medieval trading empire and their independent political institutions destroyed by the 'Castilian conquerors' in 1716. Only Catalan civil law escaped the imposition of Castilian unity by the Bourbon monarchy. Nineteenth-century Liberals were as resolute devotees of centralization as the absolute monarchs of the eighteenth century; in 1812 they had divided the historic principality into four uniform provinces modelled on French *départements*; in 1867 they had forbidden the use of Catalan except for minor, comic characters in plays. From this view of their history as a conquered nation Catalans came to view the Spanish national state as a 'Castilian concern'; Castilians conceived of Spain as a unitary state, Catalans as a plurality of 'nations', each with its own history and culture. Castilians were the enemies of Catalan liberties: from Madrid they governed Catalonia as a conquered country. As the most famous of Catalan political generals, Prim, complained, Catalans were treated by Castilians 'as colonists and slaves', victims of the Castilian mania for uniformity in unity, 'a hollow unity, a unity without content', as Unamuno put it, 'unity for the sake of unity'.

The most obvious manifestation of what an earlier generation had described with the colourless phrase 'the differential factor of Catalonia' was the campaign for the protection of the Catalan high-cost textile industry against 'unfair' British competition. Catalan industrialists saw, in the tariff reductions of Figuerola's 1869 budget, a threat to their existence. Though the new tariffs did not 'ruin' Catalan industry—indeed the 1870s were the years of the 'fever of gold'—the prospect of lower tariffs flung the Catalan industrial bourgeoisie into a long and bitter defensive agitation. To Spaniards hostile to Catalan demands, the struggle created the image of a Catalonia determined to press its selfish claims against every national interest. To Catalans 'neglect' of those claims turned defence of interest into the awareness of a Catalan community attached by the fortuitous processes of history to 'something dead', condemning that community to the calculated and contemptuous indifference of the 'Castilian' state. This belief was not altogether without foundation. Moret—the most anti-Catalan of Liberal prime ministers—told the British Ambassador in 1891 that, in return for a few concessions on import duties for raisins and other agricultural products, 'you can get what you want of us.' 'How about Catalonia?' the Ambassador asked. 'Oh,' Moret replied, 'only make good terms with us in the few things we require [i.e. tariff concessions for non-Catalan agricultural products] and we shall know how to silence the manufacturers of that province.' Suspicion of such attitudes produced in Catalonia a sense of outraged virtue.

The 1890s saw the emergence of political Catalanism. Throughout its history, this movement was divided. On the right Bishop Torres i Bages in his 'Catalan Tradition' (1893) defined Catalonia in Thomist terms; Catalonia was 'a true entity, with its own life—*indivisum in se et divisum ab aliis*'. The spirit of Catalonia was conservative; regionalism was therefore a vehicle to preserve a Catholic civilization threatened by the urban civilization of sensual man. Catalanism, in its right-wing manifestations, was close to Carlism, and could count on the support of resolute Integrists like Father Sardá, the hammer of Liberal heretics. The restoration of the monastery of Poblet (1893) was a manifestation, not only of the recovery of the Catalan past, but of the strength of the Catholic revival. To Canon Collel of Ripoll regionalism was 'decidedly catholic'.[8]

To the left, especially to Republicans, the spirit of Catalonia was progressive, positivist, and practical, open to European influence. The

---

[8] J. Massot i Muntaner, *L'església catalana al segle XX* (1975), 20 ff.

problem for Catalanists was to unite these two strands in an irresistible force; this political Catalanism achieved rarely, only to see right and left part again, to tread separate and mutually hostile paths.

To create a party that would have as its 'only banner our love of Catalonia' was the aim of Valentin Almirall (1840–1904). Coming to Catalanism from the left—he was a Federal Republican by origin—Almirall saw that to 'prostitute' Catalanism by associating it with the violence and failures of 1873 would cut it off from bourgeois and peasant support. Almirall's great Catalan party was a failure. It was his disciple Prat de la Riba (1870–1917) who, in his twenties, revived the idea of an all-Catalan party, but a party based on the Conservative right which should act legally and seek satisfaction for Catalan demands 'within Spain'.

If Prat was convinced that only a Conservative party could extract concessions from Madrid, he nevertheless transposed the language of regionalism into that of nationalism. Its strident tone was scarcely calculated to inspire confidence in non-Catalans. Beside the true *patria* of all Catalans the Spanish state was 'one of the great mechanical units formed by violence', holding Catalonia in a slavery as vile as that of the Turks over the Greeks. If 'age-old living together' created bonds with the oppressor state that could not be broken, that state must now be transformed into a federal state of all the 'Iberian nations'. Shorn of its linguistic exaggerations, the programme later outlined in Prat's *Catechism* (1894) had become the essential programme of Catalanism set forth in a series of resolutions known as the Bases of Manresa (1892): home rule for a Catalan-speaking state with posts reserved for born or nationalized Catalans. Prat's aim was to unite all parties behind the Bases and, by taking the movement out of the hands of intellectuals and Republicans, win over the conservative countryside.

The Disaster, which robbed Catalonia of its Cuban market, offered the prospect of a following among the middle classes. Catalanism could implement the strategy of Manresa: enter Spanish politics as a party. The first attempt via the Conservative Polavieja failed (see pp. 71–2); but the coalition which had won a striking electoral victory in 1901 was transformed into the most powerful and effective force Catalanism was to create: the Lliga Regionalista.

The Lliga was a conservative, autocratic concern, bitterly opposed by Lerroux's Radicals. Run in Catalonia by Prat and his friends, its representative in Madrid was Francisco Cambó (1876–1947), a self-made millionaire and born statesman. Both Prat and Cambó were pragmatists who wished to replace the extremism of nationalist nostalgia—the poets, Cambó said, exaggerated the exaggerations of historians—by a concrete, clearly defined programme of regional autonomy, which they could hope to achieve by the day-to-day task of propaganda and political pressure in Madrid. In their hands, the Lliga became a rich and highly organized pressure group with canvassers and card indexes. It organized propaganda tours in which its luminaries sought to win sympathy throughout Spain for the regionalist case.

To the Catalan left the Lliga was doubly suspect: a conservative affair run by businessmen, it was unlikely to compete effectively against Lerroux, who could slate it as an 'Irish' clerical party; and it was an organization of practical men, concerned with results. Its leaders were ready to sacrifice nationalist purity to the Realpolitik of engineering autonomy by negotiation in Madrid.

Cambó's first attempt, in 1904, at a solution within Spain merely split the Lliga and led to the organization of a separate Republican nationalist party hostile to any compromise solution. It was the concession in 1906 by a weak Liberal government of the Law of Jurisdictions—which gave the army the right to judge civilians' attacks on its honour—that opened the way for the organization of the most powerful and all-embracing concentration of forces Catalonia had seen: Solidaridad Catalana. The defence of civil liberties allowed the formation by the Lliga of a Catalan coalition ranging from Republicans to the Carlist right. Its programme was a weakened version of the Manresa autonomy resolutions. In the elections of 1907 it won an overwhelming election victory. With forty-one Solidaridad deputies in the Cortes, Cambó had high hopes of a settlement 'within Spain' that would be 'essentially conservative'.

Cambó's optimism was based on the hope that Maura, the Conservative Prime Minister, could expand his zeal for local government reform into sympathy for regionalist demands. This concealed a misunderstanding, both of Maura and the Catalan left. For Maura the Catalan question was a problem of local government, for Cambó the recognition of a 'personality'. With the modest concessions that Maura, as a defender of the sovereignty of the Spanish state, was prepared to make, Cambó could not hold the left. Solidaridad was defeated at the polls in 1908 and with it any hope of co-operation between Maura and Cambó.

The Lliga was saved by the folly of the Catalan left in allying with the Radical Republican Lerroux. It was under the Lliga, therefore, that Catalonia won its only substantial victory: the Mancomunidad which in 1913 united the *pre-existing* powers of the four provinces in a single body, restoring a geographical replica of the historic principality without any diminution of the sovereign powers of the Spanish nation. Prat, as the first President of the Mancomunidad, pushed its power to the maximum. Catalans prided themselves on their status as progressive 'Europeans'.

The Mancomunidad devoted much of its attention to technical education and the improvement of the road and telephone systems. Above all, it was the greatest instrument for what the Republican nationalist Rovira y Virgili had called 're-nationalization': the revival and protection of Catalan culture as a symbol of the renewed vitality of Catalonia in the 'desert state'. Prat's successor as President was the historian of Catalan art, Puig i Cadafalch.

The Mancomunidad fell far short of autonomy; once the Lliga sought to expand its functions towards autonomy, the old sterile discussions on sovereignty prevented any progress. In 1917 Cambó, in order to achieve autonomy, was prepared to ally with the 'revolution' in the 'Assembly Movement' which embraced Republicans, Socialists, and had contacts with military frondeurs (see p. 86). Cambó was a conservative who played with revolutionary threats but, as a 'man of government' concerned with 'realizations', detested revolution; once his representatives entered the government he deserted the revolution. His was the fate of all moderate home rulers. In Madrid he was accused of a tactical unscrupulousness that hid a project 'to tear the nation to tatters'; the moment he dropped threats of 'concession or else' for co-operation he was called a traitor in Barcelona. Cambó's earnest endeavours to present his campaign for autonomy as part of the vision of a Great Spain, based on vigorous regional governments, could not disarm suspicion. After 1919 the Lliga lost ground: the moderates' failure to achieve results always strengthened the radical nationalists of the left who accepted separatism as the logical result of defeat by the master race.

To Catalan nationalists the Lliga had become 'an appendix of monarchical conservatism'. Its insistence on a solution 'within Spain' had accomplished nothing, while its businessmen's conservatism held little appeal for the Barcelona middle classes or the tenant farmers of the countryside. Catalanism, therefore, turned to the left. The *rapprochement* of Catalanism and Republicanism was the work of the young enthusiasts of Acció Catalâ (1922). Spain, according to Acció, was 'an oppressor country in a state morally inferior to the nation it oppresses'. Cambó was still the most powerful man in Catalonia, but the emotional leader of Catalan nationalism was Francesc Maciá (1859-1933), who came to believe that Cambó's policy of winning 'practical' concessions would be barren and that Catalonia would have to fight for her recognition as a free republic within a federal Republican Spain. He rejected the Lliga's monarchism, its moderation, and its ambivalent nationalism. For Maciá autonomy was not enough. He demanded separate representation for Catalonia at the Peace Conference of 1919.

An army officer who had sacrificed his career to Catalanism, resigning his seat in the Cortes in protest against the 'frivolous futility' of Spain where Catalonia was concerned, Maciá possessed the looks, austerity, and personal simplicity of a nationalist hero—a role which Cambó would have despised because he believed effective power lay with governments, not with ideals. Simplicity in politics means violence, and it was violence which this quiet man Maciá brought to Catalan youth and to Catalan intellectuals weary of the realism of the Lliga. It was the alarm inspired by the separatist violence of the younger Catalan nationalists that helped to turn the older politicians of the Lliga into the passive supporters of an army *coup* in 1923. They paid for this folly with the electoral defeat of the Lliga in 1931. Catalanism deserted its conservative origins and flowed into the rising torrents of the left.

Why had Catalanism achieved so little after forty years of struggle and agitation? Until the 1930s, its class basis was narrow. Even the nationalist left made little impression on the working classes, an increasing number of whom were non-Catalans. At first the workers followed Lerroux, the local arch-enemy of Catalanism, as their messiah; later they were attracted to revolutionary anarcho-syndicalism. To the CNT leader Seguí the nationalists were 'gentlemen who claimed a monopoly of Catalan politics in order to further their class interests, not to achieve the freedom of Catalonia. These Catalans fear nothing so much as the rising up of a Catalonia that is not subject to them.'

Basque, Galician, and Valencian nationalism

Whereas, as Romanones complained, the Catalan question hung like a millstone round ministries in Madrid, the rise of Basque nationalism was a local irritant rather than a national problem. This was because Basque Nationalism was, in its origins, a conservative, peasant movement; though the Basque industrialists were willing to listen to Cambó's pleas for protection, unlike their Catalan colleagues they were monarchists and conservatives, unwilling to finance a nationalist movement which disowned the Spanish state and which regarded those industrialists responsible for the prosperity of Vizcaya as villains who had destroyed the rural simplicity and the peasant economy of Basque society by importing workers from other regions who 'defiled' the purity of the Basque race and provided recruits for a godless 'internationalist' Socialist movement.

While Catalan nationalism could attract the best in Catalan life, Basque nationalism appeared an archaic concern, 'savage' and primitive. It produced no literature even remotely comparable to that of the Catalan renaissance; its cultural achievements remained at the level of ballads, folklore, and the elevation of the 'manly sports' of the region into a mystique. The Basque tongue was rejected as a literary instrument by the greatest Basque writers—Maeztu, Baroja, and Unamuno. Moreover it was steadily on the retreat before Castilian, especially among the middle classes, and it was a sense of diminishing assets—the decline of the Basque language combined with the ravages of industrialism—that drove early Basque nationalism to the extremes of what Unamuno called 'absurd racial virginity'.

This sense of 'degradation' and decline was exacerbated by the Liberal revenge for the Carlist rebellion; in 1876 the remnants of the Basque '*fueros*'—the medieval privileges which had given the Basque Provinces independent institutions—were abolished. 'Foralism', the defence and romanticization of these institutions as a popular democracy, was turned by the prophet of Basque nationalism, Sabino de Arana (b.1865), into a claim for an independent state which he called Euzkadi.

Sabino de Arana was a rural populist. He saw in religion and the Basque language the foundation of a *patria*, the characteristics of a distinct race, its existence threatened by urban liberalism and industrialism. It was the racialism of Basque nationalism, which distinguished it from Catalanism, that influenced the foundation in 1894 of the Basque Nationalist Party (the PNV). Euzkadi (the name coined by Sabino de Arana for the Basque Provinces as a national entity) would be a racialist state with Basque as its official language. The PNV in its early propaganda discouraged marriage to non-Basques: 'Let it [the PNV] purify the race; let it isolate itself from the outside world in character and customs.' Against the *maketas*, poor immigrants from Castile who came to the mines and factories round Bilbao and who were responsible for the dramatic demographic revolution in Vizcaya (the population doubled between 1857 and 1900) which threatened to swamp the Basque race and adulterate its culture and bury its language, the nationalists thundered, calling them 'rotten goods'. Sabino de Arana saw Euzkadi as a theocratic state from which non-Catholics would be excluded. The PNV was fervently Catholic and supported by Basque priests who saw Basque culture as an insulation against liberalism. 'Don't teach your son Castilian, the language of liberalism.'

This fierce programme could scarcely hope for widespread support in a region where the national language was on the decline and where the PNV was confronted with powerful and established political enemies. The Carlists, strong in Navarre, detested its radical separatism. The Socialists, strong in Bilbao, denounced its reactionary Catholicism and its attacks on a working class of *maketas*. Above all the party failed to win the support of the Basque new rich: industrialists could not stomach its resolute ruralism; bankers, great figures in the aristocratic salons of

Madrid, had no sympathies with assaults on the Spanish monarchy. Nevertheless the PNV carried seven deputies to the Cortes of 1918. In the debates of the succeeding years its note of melancholic nostalgia gave added force to the protest of Catalonia.

The PNV was to modify its early reactionary violence; but it could never, as did Catalanism, take a turn to the left. It remained a Catholic Conservative party with a Christian Democrat wing.

Whereas Catalan and Basque regionalisms were the protest movements of developed regions, Galician regionalism is the protest of a deprived region neglected by the central state. The Catalans wanted protection for their industry; Galicians wanted state subsidies for railways which alone could bring prosperity to a backward rural region cut off from the national market. From the 1860s a group of intellectuals had pressed the claims of Galicia only to find them ignored by deputies with no interest in or connection with their constituents, and the funds that were available swallowed up by the corruption of local government and the *douceurs* of caciques to their clients.[9]

All that the Liberal state, perverted by *caciquismo*, had brought to Galicia was crippling taxation, which fell on a semi-destitute peasantry whose condition had been made even more precarious by the great Liberal land sales of the mid-century. The peasants had lost their common rights of pasture and wood-gathering: their blind protest took the form of the burning of tax registers and the houses of local officials and 'powerful ones'. Against the other imposition of centralist Liberalism—conscription—their protest was equally the outcome of despair: self-mutilation and emigration.

The Galician regionalists never gathered the strength of the Catalan protest, partly because in Galicia the domination of the caciques over a disseminated and impoverished rural population was so complete. Though Galician poets produced the first 'social poetry' in Spain, the journalists and intellectuals failed to make an effective alliance with the grievances of peasant proprietors, acutely felt though those grievances were. Nor could they interest the conservative bourgeoisie in regional protest; to the 'respectable classes' Galician was a peasant dialect which no self-respecting citizen would wish to use.

Without the social base that Catalan nationalism had built up, the attempt, in 1906–7, to form a Galician counterpart to Solidaridad Catalana fizzled out, as did the peasant unions which sprang up at the same time.[10] The regionalism of the Lliga Regional Gallega remained a

[9] María Rosa Saurín de la Iglesia, *Apuntes y documentos para una historia de Galicia en el siglo XIX* (1977), 229–309.

[10] For Solidaridad Gallega and the peasant movement see J.A. Durán, *Agrarismo y movilización campesina en el país gallego* (1977), 140–278.

literary protest in the hands of intellectuals, lamenting the loss of Galician menfolk by emigration overseas—again something that the Liberal state tended to regard as part of a self-regulating economy rather than as the mark of destitution. These writers took refuge in the glories of the medieval kingdom and in a misty 'Celticism'—not unconnected with the debate then current about the inferiority of Latins to Germans. At least, as Celts, the Galicians were not Latins. It was not until the 1930s that Galician nationalism became a serious political force. It found its most eloquent voice in the writings of the artist and journalist, Castelão, whose *Sempre en Galiza* is the bible of Galician nationalism.

Valencian regionalism, like Basque regionalism, failed to win the enthusiastic support of the prosperous local agrarian bourgeoisie. Bitterly opposed by the Radical Republicans—led by the writer and journalist Blasco Ibáñez, one of whose widely read realist novels describes the wretchedness of the rural poor of the region—it remained an affair of intellectuals concerned with the cultivation of the local Catalan dialect. Like Catalanism it emerged, in the 1930s, divided between a Republican left and a Catholic right. Andalusian regionalism existed only in the minds of a few eccentrics, to be resurrected in the 1970s by the founding fathers of yet another autonomous region. The flamenco folklore of Andalusia, the staple diet of the Madrid music hall, was presented as a tourist attraction by those great enemies of regional autonomy Generals Primo de Rivera and Franco.

5 Politics 1898–1917: The Failure of Revolution from Above

I

The more intelligent dynastic politicians, enmeshed as they were in the mechanics of the alternating parties of the *turno*, were nevertheless aware of the defects of liberal parliamentarianism in Spain and conscious of the flood of hostile criticism released by the Disaster of 1898. Though there were those who did not want to disturb the system which guaranteed them their seats, others saw in *caciquismo* a cancer which threatened the life of the constitutional monarchy. Only by becoming more genuinely representative could the parliamentary system survive.

The new liberalism and the new conservatism of the late nineteenth century adopted different approaches to the problem of revitalizing politics. The Conservatives concentrated on 'a ground clearance of *caciquismo*', attacking its roots in local corruption by a reform of local government. This would bring the 'people' into government and make possible 'sincere' elections: since Conservative reformers believed that the country was conservative, 'the revolution from above' would ensure their political survival and a stable social order. The reformers on the Liberal side sought to rally popular enthusiasm behind their party with a democratic programme; since a main plank of this programme was an attack on the privileges of the Church, Liberal regenerationists have been dismissed as anti-clerical rabble-rousers desperately seeking to inject new life into a moribund party rather than striving to modernize Spain.

The first essay in Conservative regenerationism came with the Polavieja–Silvela ministry. It came to power (March 1899) in the immediate aftermath of the Disaster when criticism of the political system was running at full tide and when right-wing Catholics like Cardinal Cascajares were echoing the pessimism of Costa. The Cardinal prophesied nothing short of national dissolution unless the old party system was destroyed. 'Only a sword, aided by a civilian, can save us.' The saviour appeared in the form of the 'Christian General', Camilo Polavieja (1838–1914). Polavieja shared the army's resentment of politicians who had let soldiers rot in Cuba; he toyed with the idea of a military dictatorship and set out his regenerationist programme on 1 September 1898 with the habitual appeal 'to the neutral elements of opinion' against the old corrupt parties. Nowhere was 'neutral opinion' more critical of the political system than in Catalonia, where the Catalanist Union picked up Polavieja's reference to administrative decentralization: the Catalanists 'adhered' to Polavieja's programme in return for the promise of some form of autonomy for Catalonia—a 'collaborationist' gesture immediately disowned by 'all or nothing' Catalanists, to whom all Spanish governments were tainted.

If Polavieja hoped for sole power he was discouraged by the Queen Regent (Alfonso XIII was a minor), who wanted to save the system via the normal servants of the crown. Polavieja had to come to terms with the leader of the 'new conservatism', Francisco Silvela (1845–1905), a successful company lawyer. Silvela's ministry included Polavieja as Minister of War, and a representative of the General's Catalan friends, the lawyer Durán y Bas.

The Queen Regent was aware that in calling on Silvela she was not appointing a politician hardened in the practices of the Cánovite *turno*. Silvela made no secret of his detestation of Cánovas' political mores; he had deserted the party leader in 1891, not on some minor issue but on 'a total divergence as to the manner of governing people and things in the Conservative party'. An austere Catholic—he took his Cabinet to mass—his repugnance for the *bas fonds* of Restoration politics was that of a moral aristocrat. They must be purified by a radical reform of local government as a precondition for 'sincere' elections.

Silvela's ministerial regeneration was a failure: regenerationism must be a choice between conflicting remedies. Polavieja, who wanted a costly army, resigned when Villaverde, as Minister of Finance, insisted on rigid economies and a modest profits tax to 'liquidate the Disaster' and pay off a public debt that ate up 60 per cent of the budget. Silvela could never hope to bring his party to support autonomy for Catalonia, and Villaverde's taxation produced a middle-class revolt of shopkeepers in Barcelona and elsewhere. Durán y Bas resigned: 'We shall never understand each other' was his epitaph on the first effort at conciliation between Madrid and Barcelona.

Silvela's second ministry was equally unproductive: Villaverde's economies precluded a respectable navy while, to the Prime Minister, a nation that preferred 'materialism' to national dignity could not be saved. 'You see before you a man who has lost faith and hope.'

Silvela's heir as proponent of Conservative regenerationism, and his successor as leader of the party, was Antonio Maura (1853–1925), a self-made lawyer politician from Majorca. Like Silvela he was a devout Catholic, giving up smoking if his daily examination of his conscience revealed a fault. Like Silvela he was 'austere', believing that private and public morality were coincident. Unlike Silvela, his political nerves were of iron. His political hauteur, his crushing eminence in debate, his determination to put his ideals into legislative form polarized politics. Spanish politics, Lerroux declared, could be reduced to the formula: 'For Maura or against Maura'.

Maura's aim was to revitalize politics by a reform of local government and electoral laws which would 'make effective, sincere, honest and total the political representation and presence of all the forces in Spain in the government of the country'. The underlying assumption was that 'official Spain'—the Spain of the political élite, the Spain of *caciquismo* and corruption—suppressed 'real Spain'; that society was sound and the removal of a deficient political structure would allow 'the neutral mass' to enter politics and revitalize them. This was the regenerationists' great illusion. The 'neutral masses' were, in Ortega's phrase, 'inert,' not the stuff from which national revivals are born.

To his admirers Maura remains the great reformer frustrated by short-sighted politicians. Yet his critics were not without a case. The results of his attack on *caciquismo* via an electoral law to banish corruption were either ineffective or ambiguous. Article 29 declared an unopposed candidate elected, a bonus granted to local wheeling and dealing which, paradoxically, benefited the Liberals. The originality of Maura's local government reforms has been overestimated: his 1907 Bill was a complicated summary—it had 409 clauses—of previous Liberal and Conservative drafts; nor were its provisions for local autonomy exceptionally generous. Moreover, Liberals were correct in arguing that the introduction of a corporate franchise in municipal elections was 'unconstitutional' and undemocratic and would give over the municipalities of Spain to 'a social oligarchy' of local caciques. The Liberals rejected the whole premise of Maura's reform: the existence of an enslaved 'real Spain'. 'Local life', the Liberal democrat Canalejas argued, 'can't be a force for anything.' The electorate, he held, must be educated before it could be an effective force in politics. In 1907 40 per cent of the electorate was illiterate and in the backward provinces of the south the proportion rose to 70 per cent.

Maura's Conservative revolution from above assumed that the neutral masses he would liberate were natural Conservative voters. Maura professed to take public opinion as his political compass, yet what the Liberals regarded as public opinion he rejected as the creation of demagogues and a venal press—'the tinkle of a baby's rattle'. He never faced up to the problem of what would happen if the neutral mass voted—sincerely—for 'dissolvent' and 'anti-patriotic' Republicans and Socialists. His own election of April 1907, managed by his Minister of the

Interior La Cierva, was amongst the dirtiest in Spanish history. His contempt for hostile 'opinion' was that of a high Tory; to the end of his career he held, as firmly as the Duke of Wellington, that the duty of a government was to govern and that those who sought to prevent it governing by organizing public opinion against it must either be dismissed as slanderers or, if protest took to the streets, suppressed in the name of public order.

The originality of Maura's 1907 Bill was that it attempted to incorporate the Catalan demand for autonomy within a comprehensive local government reform. Here the stubborn opposition of Liberal doctrinaire centralists to the recognition of a 'region' helped to defeat any prospect of a settlement of the Catalan question through an agreement between Cambó and Maura (see p. 65). Such a settlement, Liberals believed, would turn Catalonia into a Conservative preserve. In any case the possibilities of a settlement were ruled out because Maura's desire to revitalize politics by dismantling 'Jacobin' centralization could not encompass Cambó's determination that Catalonia should be granted autonomy because it was already a 'live' region. Nor could Cambó himself prevent Solidaridad Catalana (see p. 65), on which his political leverage was based, from dissolution. The Catalan 'all-or-nothing' left regarded Cambó's approaches to Maura as illicit collaboration with a clerical Conservative. Catalan deputies' talk of the 'absurd Spanish state' encouraged Liberal centralists to argue that 'when you [the Catalans] talk of your region and recount its history you are not raising a regional problem, but a problem of independence', i.e. that they were separatists under the skin.

Maura's Bill, after 3,000 speeches and 1,387 amendments, never became law. To the Liberals he appeared increasingly as a parliamentary dictator out to destroy the 'liberal conquests'. During his first ministry (1903–4) they had joined with Republicans in a violent anti-clerical campaign, in the press and in street demonstrations, against his appointment of a monk to the See of Valencia, a Republican city.

It was Maura's reaction to terrorist outrages in Barcelona that united the left against him with the cry 'Maura No'. His Terrorist Law led to the formation, in November 1908, of the Bloc of the Left, in which dynastic Liberals and anti-dynastic Republicans united with the sole purpose of driving him from office. To Maura, this alliance of dynastic Liberals and the 'sewer' of street politics was little short of treason: if Liberals went 'outside the monarchical orbit' they must be denied power by the monarchy.

His supporters attributed—and still attribute—the defeat of Maura's attempt at regeneration from above to the blind party passions of his opponents. There was, however, a fundamental flaw in Conservative regenerationism. 'Revolution from above', conceived in purely political terms as a cleansing operation, was morally impeccable; but without a reform of the antiquated social structure that supported *caciquismo* it was doomed to failure. For all his criticisms of the 'shapelessness' of Spanish society, Maura was a social conservative; he believed that honest elections in a conservative society would ensure a permanent Conservative majority, ending the irruption into political life of a Liberal party sustained by electoral corruption and little else.

The same criticism applies to Cambó's programme of regenerating Spain from Catalonia (see pp. 64–5): the regeneration of Spain had to be achieved without imperilling the class structure of the Catalan base.

II

The final crisis which drove Maura from the leadership of a united Conservative party, denied him the possibility of office, and exposed the conservatism of the Lliga, came with the Tragic Week of 1909. Maura had been drawn into a minor colonial war to defend the Spanish mining concessions in Morocco against an attack by native *harkas*. An ill-managed call-up of reservists released a revolt reminiscent of the revolutionary *journées* of the mid-nineteenth century.

In Barcelona and other towns in Catalonia, the Tragic Week was a muddled, confused affair of street demonstrations, a strike, and an outburst of church-burning; a quasi-revolution, never mastered and directed by those elements whose policies had helped to unleash it. All involved were dominated by 'the everlasting obsession of attracting the working population'. The workers' protest against the call-up provided a groundswell of resentment that could be exploited. Maura had been warned that 'to go to Morocco is to go to the revolution'.

As we have seen (p. 49) the great achievement of Alejandro Lerroux was to organize the workers of Barcelona in his Radical Republican party. Particularly after 1903, when the workers' own organizations had been exhausted by strikes and broken by an employers' lock-out, anarchists drifted into Lerroux's party, radicalizing its revolutionary postures. However, in 1907 working-class leaders, influenced by both the success of Solidaridad Catalana and French syndicalism, formed an independent federation of unions—Solidaridad Obrera (SO), an apolitical *ouvrieriste* organization; bitter at the employers' savage response to recession, the leaders of Solidaridad saw in the unpopularity of the call-up a pretext for a general strike.

On Sunday, 25 July 1909, the Socialists, anarchists, and Solidaridad

Obrera, with the sympathy of left-wing nationalists, declared a general strike for the following Monday. It began at four o'clock in the morning with the organizers stopping workers in the streets and at the factory gates. The strike was successful in Barcelona and other Catalan towns; but it did not spread outside Catalonia.

Disarray and indecision above (once martial law was declared the Civil Governor, Ossorio y Gallardo—a follower of Maura and the only politician ready to infuse jargon with wit—packed his bags and retired to his house overlooking the city) was matched by lack of leadership from below. 'The sedition', wrote Ossorio, echoing de Tocqueville in 1848, 'had no unity of thought, nor homogeneity of action, nor a leader to personify it, no tribune to influence it and no war cry to solidify it.' A protest strike turned into an armed rebellion that fell into the hands of revolutionary *meneurs* deserted by the leaders—Iglesias, Lerroux's deputy, was alleged to have taken a laxative to incapacitate himself for the barricades.[1]

Thus the revolutionary strike degenerated into leaderless, purposeless barricades and church-burning. It was this incendiarism that made the Tragic Week a unique phenomenon: 21 churches and 40 convents were burnt, the work of radical enthusiasts and anarchists bred on the counter-culture of anti-clericalism.

The Tragic Week was not a social revolution. It was a *revuelta*, a revolt, and its consequences for both Catalonia and Spain were political. The conservative bourgeoisie, 'the honourable and peaceful citizens', did nothing to save their churches from burning; after it was all over they clamoured for vengeance and the Lliga supported La Cierva in his determination, as Minister of the Interior, to liquidate the 'revolutionary elements'. This stamped the Lliga as a Conservative concern, ending any hope of reviving the alliance with the left in another Solidaridad Catalana.

To the Catalan poet Joan Maragall, to whom Solidaridad had been a great emotional experience, a national revival, the Tragic Week and the vengeance of conservative reaction were profoundly dispiriting. In noble articles, mauled or rejected by the Lliga's press, he pleaded for understanding and mercy. The Catalan bourgeoisie were cowards twice over and their cowardice only served to inject life into moribund Lerrouxism. 'Catalonia', wrote Maragall, 'still does not exist.'[2]

If the Tragic Week discredited bourgeois Catalanism, its consequence

---

[1] J. Connelly Ullman, *The Tragic Week* (1968), 203.
[2] For his attitude see Josep Benet, *Maragall y la Semana Trágica* (1966).

in Spain was the end of Maura's 'revolution from above', wrecked on Maura's hubris and on the determination of the Liberals to drive him from office. He bore responsibility for the execution of Francisco Ferrer for his ambiguous role in the *journées* of 1909. The execution unleashed the concerted protest of the European left: there were mass demonstrations and storming of embassies from London to Budapest. Alfonso XIII was alarmed by the strength of this reaction in Spain and elsewhere. He 'sacked' Maura and called on the Liberal leader, Moret. Maura never forgave the King and staged a political strike: he refused to alternate with the Liberals, who were 'unfit' for office and who, as the allies of revolution from below, could only be treated with 'implacable hostility'. Conservatives who did not take Maura's catastrophist view grouped together under Eduardo Dato (1856-1921); to continue on strike not merely denied the party the chance of office but 'left the monarchy defenceless' with no alternative to the Liberals. The result of Maura's political pride was thus to divide the Conservative party and to weaken the whole political system.

By 1913 Maura had ceased to be a party leader and had become the chief of a movement, Maurism. It attracted conservative youth, especially students, and was devoted to the denigration of the 'traitor' Dato and his accomplices as 'oligarchs' who sacrificed conservative principle to power. Since it professed to abstain, like its leader, from politics (without a party organization it made little impression on the electorate), it degenerated into 'street Maurism'. Maurism was the first indication of a disturbing phenomenon: the emergence of quasi-violent youth movements. With its parades and monster meetings it focused on a parliamentary statesman the discontents of violent men and youth; applauded by such enthusiasts, Maura sensed at last his 'reawakening of citizenship'. He began to appeal to the true Catholic Spain beyond politics, the 'essential Spain' which *must* be accepted by *all* who wished to participate in public life—an appeal to be made later by the Patriotic Union of Primo de Rivera's dictatorship and by the Falange, both attempts to replace democratic political parties by an all-embracing movement or national 'communion'.

Maura was to disappoint his followers: having failed to accomplish his revolution from above within the constitutional monarchy, he jibbed at the final stage of his political metamorphosis; he would neither become an anti-parliamentary dictator himself nor allow that position to anyone else. Thus he did not become, as the Carlist Vázquez de Mella hoped, 'a Mussolini before Mussolini'. His fate was to be Prime Minister in 'national' governments at moments of crisis, when the orthodox parties he had helped to destroy were in impotent confusion.

III

Confusion was confounded by the disputes among Liberal leaders for the leadership of the party after the death of the 'old Shepherd' Sagasta in 1903. It was left to the King to sort out these squabbles by selecting a Prime Minister from among the faction leaders—a striking illustration of how the disruption of the 'artificial' two-party system exposed the monarchy.

The strong man of Liberalism who aimed to unite a moribund party behind a regenerationist programme was José Canalejas (Prime Minister March 1910 to November 1912). His project for the democratization and revitalizing of Liberalism was much wider than a mere exploitation of anti-clericalism—a posture into which he had been forced by the sheer violence of the clericalist reaction. More important, he hoped to win the confidence of a working class not yet irretrievably committed to socialism or anarchism, for a Liberal party weaned from *laissez-faire* and prepared to accept the state as an instrument for social justice. He therefore favoured state arbitration in wage settlements, legislation on labour conditions, workers' insurance, and compensation for accidents. He was the first politician to make an attack on the latifundia with the notion of expropriation on grounds of public utility.

Yet Canalejas failed to become the Lloyd George of Spanish Liberalism. Confronted with serious strikes his instincts as a man of order, which gained him the grudging sympathy of Maura, lost him any credit with the Socialists. While his lenience towards a naval mutiny and an outburst of primitive violence in the now smart resort of Cullera was criticized in the conservative press, to the Socialists he was a 'murderer'. He was assassinated while looking in a Madrid bookshop window in November 1912. He had not, as the King had hoped, absorbed the radical threat; he had given radicalism 'nothing but a few crumbs'.

The last two governments of the monarchy before the Great War were formed by remnants of the old parties of the *turno*: the Conde de Romanones (1863–1950) and his followers among the Liberals; Dato with the anti-Maura Conservatives. Both were targets of those attacks by journalists and intellectuals which did so much to discredit the parliamentary system. Romanones was dismissed as the archetypal party manager, an expert in the trivialities of political manœuvre: a man who saw the immoralities of the system but who 'instead of reforming them, exploited them'. Dato was dismissed as a rich company lawyer, a 'mellifluous doctor', with no policy except political survival.

These judgements are harsh if not unjust. Romanones not merely took a serious interest in education; like his rival for the leadership of the party, García Prieto, he kept the Liberals open to the notion of regenerationism from the left, preserving their role as 'lightning conductors'. It was this opening to the left that brought Santiago Alba into Romanones' government of 1912–13. Alba's vision of politics derived from Costa's version of regenerationism. Power, for Alba—though he was a slippery politician—was not an end in itself but an instrument for the modernization of Spain, a channel for the influence of 'producers' as opposed to the 'proletariat of lawyers' who manned the political apparatus. He wanted productive investment in agriculture (he represented the wheat interests of Castile) and industry. To finance this the army and the bureaucracy must be cut down to size and the tax system reformed. This was not an attractive proposition to the middle class which Alba hoped to woo. The fate of his war-profits tax (see p. 83 proved to him that the conservative middle classes were unwilling to win social peace 'at the price of a small sacrifice ... [they] as so many other times in Spanish history, did not know how to look beyond the end of their noses'.

Nevertheless Alba's 'programme of realizations' weaned the newly formed Reformist Republicans from the Republican–Socialist conjunction. The Reformist notables sought an interview with the King and became 'govermental Republicans'. If the monarchy accepted practical reform, then it would survive. This *grand trahison* signalled the temporary eclipse of historical Republicanism. Even Ortega was optimistic at the prospect of power for a party that was the new home of his fellow intellectuals. It would replace the parties of the *turno*, 'monstrous parties which are still on their feet, as they say elephants remain standing after their death'.

One of these standing elephants was Dato. As the 'man of vaseline' he appeared colourless beside the trumpet calls of Maura. Yet it was to Dato that Spain owed her first labour legislation, beginning with his Workers' Compensation Act in 1900 and culminating in Romanones' eight-hour day in 1918 and the creation of a Ministry of Labour in 1920.

The failure of the modest ambitions of politicians like Dato and Romanones was not solely due to their attachment to, and their imprisonment in, 'old politics'. Certainly, their precarious parliamentary position, the fact that both Dato and Romanones owed their power to the King rather than to the electorate, weakened any 'policy of realizations'. Yet the real obstacle was the poverty of the Spanish state: Romanones could not find the money to build schools and pay teachers; the labour legislation of Dato achieved meagre results because the state could pay so few inspectors. It was not the quality of Spanish politicians so much as an incapacity to reform the tax system and cut back bureaucratic expenditure that lamed all efforts at 'Europeanization'. The Spanish middle classes wanted modernization without paying for it. 'I am not one of those', declared Villaverde, 'who sees in taxation an instrument to correct social inequality. I believe that these inequalities should not be corrected. Social inequality is necessary and beneficial, like the inequalities in nature to which it owes its development.' Yet even Villaverde's modest tax reforms unleashed a middle-class taxpayers' strike.

6 The Crisis of the Parliamentary Monarchy 1917–1923

Politicians, their parties enfeebled and fragmented by the aftermath of 1909, were called upon to face the prolonged crisis that lasted from 1917 until the overthrow of the parliamentary monarchy by the Barcelona garrison in September 1923. Spain was not unique. In all countries of southern and eastern Europe the strains imposed by the Great War of 1914–18 proved too great for democratic and quasi-democratic regimes; apart from Czechoslovakia, all experienced some form of authoritarian take-over.

Between 1914 and 1923 the parliamentary system was sorely tested by a complex of challenges; indeed for long periods the Cortes was prorogued, the press censored, the constitutional guarantees suspended, and the country ruled by decree. A wartime boom and the Russian Revolution of 1917 increased the strength and militancy of organized labour. The Catalan question remained unsolved. A 'dirty' colonial war in Morocco brought a disgraceful defeat in 1921. The political system might have survived these strains had not the army resumed its intervention in politics and had not the King deserted the politicians. The coup of 1923 was but the last episode in a series of military incursions. In 1917, declared the Liberal politician Romanones, the armed forces became 'the masters of Spain'. Alfonso XIII, confronted with the incapacity of party politicians to provide him with a strong government (and only if they did so could the crown avoid becoming the football of parties) was forced to become a maker of ministries—an occupation for which he acquired a taste but which disillusioned him with the mechanics of the constitutional system of which he was the apex as the 'moderating power'. Increasingly he was tempted by some essay in strong government and in 1923 he placed his bets on the strong.

I

The most immediate effect of the war in Europe was to divide the political class: Conservatives, army officers, and the right in general supported Germany and 'authority' against 'decadence'; the left, particularly intellectuals, supported 'civilization' against German 'barbarism'. Both raised the political temperature by mass meetings. This division, bitter as it was, troubled the surface of politics; the economic and social effects of the war and its immediate aftermath were deep and lasting.

Spain's neutrality was the key to wartime prosperity. Once the immediate dislocations were overcome the belligerents' demands were insatiable, feeding an export-led boom in a country with a weak domestic market. This domestic market was now 'protected' by the war more effectively than by tariff walls; this led, in turn, to a 'mushroom' process of import substitution (e.g. in the chemical and electrical industries when German imports fell off). It was an era of effortless profits and soaring dividends in shipping, steel, and mining. All this immensely strengthened the domination of the Basque banks. Prosperity was not confined to the Basque Provinces. Catalan factories worked overtime to supply the French armies. Agricultural prices soared. The ostentation of a new race of war profiteers, the '*nouveaux riches*' with their 'strident luxury', was an affront to 'traditional middle-class mores and an insult to the workers'.[1]

To the average Spaniard the war meant high prices, as all the government attempts to control prices led to bottlenecks and black-marketeering. Inflation, as always, upset the existing social balance. While the 'suffering middle classes' and the non-unionized workers were hit by high prices, industrial workers saw the opportunity for successful strikes against employers with full order books. There is a sense in which the labour troubles of the war years—and this applies to the agricultural labourers of the south, enthused by rumours of the great revolution in Russia—were part of a revolution of rising expectations.

The exceptional advantages enjoyed by Spain as a neutral producer vanished with the peace. 'Normality' exposed the weaknesses of a prosperity based on the exploitation of under-utilized capacity. Now the gains of wartime withered away. Basque shipping collapsed, its yards idle. Mines which had survived in wartime scarcities closed down. The new steel mills went over to half-time; 140 Catalan textile factories closed down throwing an estimated 20,000 out of work. Landowners who had ploughed up marginal lands allowed them to revert to scrub pasture, lowered wages and dismissed hands. The agricultural unemployed could no longer migrate to find jobs in a depressed industry. The industrialists have been blamed for a short-sighted failure to invest wartime profits in modernization, the better to face the postwar slump. Rather, they were obsessed with a realization of the fragility of wartime profits and hampered by the incapacity to import capital goods from the belligerents.

[1] cf. A. Hurtado, *Quarenta anys d'advocat. Historia del meu temps* (1956), i, 266.

Catalan industrialists reacted both to the war boom and to the postwar slump in a way that labelled them, once more, as hard-faced individualists unwilling to sacrifice the traditional independence of small-time employers for the advantages of concentration and modernization. The sudden rush to form employers' associations represented less an attack on the evils of cut-throat competition than a response to labour militancy and as a means to resist the 'interference' of an incompetent government. In 1916 Alba, the Liberal Finance Minister, proposed a tax on excess war profits. This met with an orchestrated storm of protest from Catalan and Basque industrialists against 'a piece of tyrannical legislation', yet another attempt of agrarian Castile to 'punish' the productive classes.[2] The Catalan industrialists met the postwar depression with their usual reaction to hard times: protection and an offensive against organized labour. It looked as if Catalan employers preferred, as left-wing critics of Spanish capitalism now argue, the comforts of protection to the risks of modernization; that they cared less about regionalism *per se* than its use as a weapon to extort economic concessions.

II

The re-entry of the army was to dominate politics until 1923. Cánovas had successfully ended the era of the old-fashioned party *pronunciamiento*. Soldiers reappeared in the political arena, no longer as political mutineers led by a general, but as a pressure group of younger officers professedly acting as saviours of the nation.

As in other spheres, the Cuban disaster of 1898 lay at the root of discontent. Soldiers blamed defeat on the selfish neglect of the politicians—'pseudo fathers of the *patria*'. There was a new note of military messianism which claimed for the army a 'national dynamic function' as 'the only healthy force' in a corrupt society.

Structurally the army was a far from healthy element. It was a sedentary, bureaucratic monstrosity rather than a fighting machine; attempts to reform it in the 1880s had broken on vested interests. The officer corps was grossly inflated—one officer to every five enlisted men in 1915; 60 per cent of the army budget went on officers' pay. This officer corps was divided. The 'specialized' corps, the Artillery, Engineers, and the General Staff, enforced by officer committees (Juntas) strict promotion by seniority—the bureaucratic ideal; the infantry and cavalry were not so protected against 'political' or 'merit' promotions.

For this sedentary, bureaucratic middle-class army, pay and promo-

[2] S. Roldán et al., *La consolidación del capitalismo en España* (1973), i, 275.

tion prospects and the status of the officer in society were all-important. It was the poverty of the Spanish state that was at the root of the military problem. Only the higher officers enjoyed a decent standard of living and felt themselves part of the political establishment. Majors and captains often worked part-time in relatively humble occupations in the struggle to keep up appearances, to buy the uniform that was the symbol of status in a provincial garrison. A permanent sense of frustration, what the military press of the time called 'a lack of interior satisfaction', explains the morbid sensitivity of the officers that was exhibited in a defence of their 'honour'. All attempts at reform aimed at reducing the size of the inflated officer corps in order to create a smaller, better equipped, better paid army broke on the vested interests of serving officers. Only if the politicians left the army alone would the army let the politicians alone: that was the basis of the *modus vivendi* of officers and politicians in the Restoration.

Neither the vested interests of the army nor its honour could be attacked by civilians. Since it regarded itself as the ultimate protector of national unity, its opposition to Catalanism as a threat to that unity was violent and vocal. 'The remedy against the separatist *canaille*', declared *El Ejército Español* in 1905, 'lies in the army.' Catalanist activists replied in kind by caricaturing officers in a comic paper; the young officers of the Barcelona garrison broke up the offices of the paper and demanded a Law of Jurisdictions to remove all attacks on the army from civilian courts. To 'save the discipline of the army' the generals of the establishment gave in. This forced the resignation of the government and the choice, by the King, of a new government that gave the army its Law of Jurisdictions in 1906. As Melquíades Álvarez declared, the law was 'the bastard fruit of a bloodless revolution', the triumph of a pressure group over civilian politicians who could not face a showdown with soldiers.

In 1917 civilian politicians gave in once more; this time to what was a junior officers' strike for higher wages in a period of wartime inflation and for promotion by seniority—the bureaucratic ideal of a sedentary army—upset by merit promotions earned in the Moroccan war.

The Barcelona infantry garrison formed a Junta de Defensa in imitation of the specialized corps and, with the support of junior officers all over Spain, defied the government's attempt to dissolve it. Moreover, their demands that all decisions be taken by majority vote and the exclusion of generals from the Juntas meant that the whole hierarchical structure of the army was in peril. This time, in contrast to 1905–6, the generals did not—with a few exceptions—seek to 'save discipline' by siding with the junior officers.

From the beginning the *Junteros* presented their 'material demands' (i.e. better pay and secure promotions) and their plea for the recognition of their dignity as part of a general movement for 'morality and justice'. They thundered against '*caciquismo* and oligarchy'. Their leader, Colonel Márquez, was a political simpleton. What is, in retrospect, astonishing is the reaction of the civilian critics of the Restoration system in accepting these tetchy mutineers as national saviours, capable of renovating the political establishment. Ortega greeted the Junta movement as 'the most noble, healthy and original act which Spain has shown to Europe in the last hundred years'. Neither he, nor large sections of the middle class, saw that mutineers who proved powerful enough to bring down successive governments threatened a new era of praetorian politics.

III

Because the *Junteros*' trade union demands were cast in the language of regenerationist patriotism, their protest became the opening move in the generalized crisis of 1917, a crisis that the regime surmounted but which left its structure shaken. 'The military crisis which broke out in Spain on the first of June', wrote the *Statesman*, 'is the first sign that the political structure known as the Restoration is beginning to crumble on its own.' For a brief moment it seemed as if the conservative Catalanist Cambó might become the civilian *caudillo* of a middle-class revolution supported by a general strike.

As usual the renovating coalition was composed of incompatible elements. Cambó's Lliga campaigned for an autonomous Catalonia as the invigorating element within a 'Great Spain', coupled with 'selfish' economic demands: export subsidies and a free port. The bourgeois Reformist Republicans of Melquíades Álvarez and Lerroux's Radicals allied to secure 'the triumph of national sovereignty' in a constituent Cortes which should endow Spain with a democratic constitution and a government that would include the 'new left'. The UGT was to support this bourgeois revolution by a general strike, which would go beyond a demand for wage increases to combat wartime inflation, in order to secure 'a fundamental change in the system'.

This language of renovation which should liberate Spain from the governance of selfish factions was similar in tone to that of the *Junteros*: all through 1917 they were obsessed by the notion of an alliance between king, army, and people against the 'oligarchs'.[3] 'Remember, Your Majesty, that if a king opposes the oligarchs [i.e. his ministers] relying on the support of his army and his people, that king strengthens his crown,

---

[3] J.A. Lacomba, *La Crisis española de 1917* (1970), 158.

since the hour of monarchies has not passed.' Such pretensions earned for the deaf, eccentric Márquez the title of 'Benito I'; but Márquez and his fellow officers regarded the bourgeois revolution led by Cambó with suspicion. They refused to surrender their role as regenerators to Republicans and the Catalan '*canaille*'.

García Prieto, the Liberal Prime Minister, was forced out of office on 9 June when he refused to recognize the Juntas as a legally constituted military trade union. His successor, Dato, gave in to military mutiny, recognizing the Juntas, probably in order to keep the loyalty of the army in his coming confrontation with civilian sedition. Dato met the mounting crisis by the standard wartime procedure of suspending the sessions of the Cortes. This united the disparate strands of protest in the 'Assembly Movement'. With the constitutional road barred, the coalition of renovators decided to call a meeting to demand the opening of the Cortes. Boycotted by the orthodox parties and without the support of the great critic of the *turno* and enemy of Dato, Maura, the Assembly could be presented as a seditious convention of Republicans and 'separatists'. It met in Barcelona on 19 July. After a show of Roman dignity it was dissolved as seditious after agreeing on the constituent Cortes, a government including the renovators, and autonomy for Catalonia. It was to meet in Madrid on 20 October to force these demands on the government.

Before this could happen, against the advice of its leadership, the UGT staged its revolutionary general strike on 13 August. According to plan, the strike should have reinforced the demands of the Assembly. Coming when it did, it split the movement and forced the army to support the government. The *Junteros* put the preservation of order and loyalty to the King above all else; they were outraged when Marcelino Domingo, a left-wing Catalan Republican, exhorted conscripts not to obey their officers and talked of their commander-in-chief, the King, suffering the fate of the Tsar or Louis XVI. Given the firm attitude of the army, the general strike accomplished nothing; but that there were 170 casualties shows that the revolutionary strike of 1917 was a more serious affair than the pseudo-revolution of 1909.

For the Socialists, the lurch into revolution was a traumatic shock, reinforcing the conservatism of the organization men in the union and the party. To Cambó the strike revealed that he was playing with forces he could not control; a Girondin confronted by Jacobin *enragés*, he reverted to his natural conservatism as a 'man of government'. His business colleagues proposed donations for the soldiers who had saved society and turned a revolutionary strike into 'a comic week'.

When the Assembly met in Madrid on 30 October Cambó 'put his cards on the table' and deserted the Assembly Movement. Called to an interview in the Royal Palace, in return for two Catalan ministers he dropped the constituent Cortes and the idea of a government including the left. A 'government of concentration' of Liberals and Conservatives was the formula invented to cover the retreat. This weak, divided government under García Prieto could not 'renovate' Spain; the Assembly Movement, dissolving into its constituent elements, had turned out to be a damp squib.

When García Prieto's government fell on 22 March 1918 the confusion of parties was so acute that it seemed as if no government would be formed at all. The King threatened abdication to bring the politicians to their senses. Maura came out of political ostracism to head what was called a National Government. Greeted with mass demonstrations in Madrid, it was in fact a government of the old gang with the addition of Alba, who represented the 'modern' wing of Liberalism, and Cambó, ready to implement his 'blind faith in Spain'. Cambó, the great capitalist, had deserted *laissez-faire* for an ambitious programme of state investment which was to 'harmonize public and private enterprise': a state take-over of a railway system starved of capital; agricultural credit; hydro-electric schemes; mining laws that would end foreign 'colonial' control of natural resources.

Once again the government fell apart over the old contradictions that had bedevilled regenerationism since 1898. For Cambó, regeneration should come from the right and pay special attention to Catalan claims. To Alba the monarchy as a 'Republic with a crown on it' must absorb the left or perish. As a centralist he rejected as covert separatism Cambó's 'Great Spain' in which the regions, led by Catalonia, were to find a place. Alba had suffered from Catalan 'selfishness' in 1916 and resented the Catalanist programme as a recipe for regeneration. Maura, who had lost his old faith in his capacities to save Spain, resigned. It was the end of an illusion.

From November 1918 to September 1923 Spain had a series of short-lived governments. Ten in all, not one lasted a year. These feeble governments faced two acute problems: the war in Morocco and the labour war in Barcelona. Both involved the army which, in these years, at times reduced civilian government to a fiction.

In August 1917 the army appeared to have saved the political establishment; the politicians, unsupported by a wavering king, were unwilling to face a show-down with an officer corps that might still be needed, in Cánovas' phrase, as the last resort against a proletarian revolution. Strike-breaking was not a task all officers relished and if they were to be expected to 'save capitalism' they demanded complete independence from civilian control. Márquez accused the politicians of letting a crisis develop and then calling in the army; if they acted thus then the army would be compelled to force on them 'procedures of morality, justice and foresight'. In 1918 La Cierva (concerned by the spread of Juntas to the post office telephones and the Ministry of Finance) as War Minister hoped to split the Superior Junta by satisfying the 'material interests' of the army and isolating political mavericks like Márquez. With sovereign contempt for parliamentary processes he granted by decree a pay rise and promotion by strict seniority. The Juntas refused to disappear but their influence waned.

This was less the result of a resolute return to civilian rule than the consequence of a split in the army itself. Officers in the privileged corps had never shared the political ambitions of the infantry. Above all, the African Army fighting in Morocco wanted promotion by merit, i.e. earned on the battlefield. Mola, an *Africanista* who was to organize the military rising of July 1936, castigated 'that cursed officers' trades union . . . an affair of unemployed bureaucrats—a military union legalized by the weakness of public power'.[4] Increasingly public opinion (including the King, more and more committed to the African Army) turned against the *Junteros*. In November 1922 the Conservative Sánchez Guerra finally dissolved the Juntas.

With the Juntas gone, it was the Moroccan war (see p. 93) that kept the army, now more or less united, in politics. As in the colonial war against Cuban separatists in the 1890s, the military press was to complain that politicians were expecting soldiers to do their dirty work for them without supplying them with the arms and the men to fight, because politicians would not risk their political careers by defying a public opinion indifferent to the war and unwilling to make any sacrifices to win it.

IV

Between 1918 and 1923 Spain was to be the scene of one of the more savage social conflicts of postwar Europe. The dramatic surge in militancy and membership came not to the Socialists, but to the CNT. In 1914, after three years of clandestinity, the CNT membership was 14,000; by 1919 with 700,000 members it was over three times as large as the UGT (200,000 members). The revolutionary epicentres of anarcho-syndicalism were Andalusia and Barcelona.

To understand the history of anarcho-syndicalism we must remember that its peculiar nature derived from the fact that unions organized for

[4] E. Mola, *Obras Completas* (1940), 990, 997, 998.

'direct action' against the employers were superimposed on a pre-existing tradition of libertarian anarchism and terrorism. There always remained a residuum of idealists, a moral élite including the 'saint' of Andalusian anarchism, Salvochea. But the anarchist tradition was also represented by the small 'action-groups', *grupos de afinidad*, firm in their belief that the revolution could be triggered off by acts of violence which became ends in themselves. At the other extreme were the 'pure' syndicalists who believed that the first step must be the organization of a strong union which must avoid wasting its strength in futile revolutionary gymnastics and must produce results in the form of wage settlements and better working conditions. The 'moderate' union leaders, Salvador Seguí, known as 'Sugar Boy', and Angel Pestaña, were typical anarchists in background and character. Seguí was an indifferent house-painter and enthusiastic reader of Nietzsche; but he was an organizer who could control crowds by his oratory. Pestaña had tried his hand as railway worker, bricklayer, watchmaker, glass-worker, stage manager, and minor actor before he found his *métier* as a journalist. Union strength, they argued, must be built up by *successful* strikes and harboured for the day when a general strike could destroy capitalism and usher in a society based on the great unions. They were fully aware that the CNT was infiltrated by terrorists whom they could not disown and whom they even had to pay. The heroes of the action groups appealed to an immigrant lumpenproletariat, a 'special class of men who live on the indefinite frontier between labour and common crime' (Pestaña).

The moderates, led by Seguí, fought a constant battle against the revolutionary energumens of the movement. It was the attitude of the Catalan employers in alliance with the Barcelona garrison, combined with the vacillating policy of the government, that brought their efforts to nought, the eclipse of the CNT as an organization, and its decline into impotent terrorism.

The Catalan employers organized in the Employers' Federation were determined, as they put it, 'to give battle to syndicalism' and destroy it. Madrid governments wavered between attempts to come to an understanding with the moderate CNT leaders, which were consistently sabotaged by the employers, and a reversion to repression. Repression, by the simple expedient of imprisoning the moderate leaders, left the CNT at the mercy of the activists. It was the employers' intransigence, backed by an army the government could not control, that turned the Canadiense strike of 1919—the most famous strike in Spanish labour history—from a dispute over pay into a general strike that plunged Barcelona into darkness, closing its cafés and theatres and threatening food supplies.

Seguí courageously resisted extremist demands and accepted the government's efforts at conciliation: he failed when, after agreement had been reached on the pay dispute, the Captain General refused to release arrested militants. A revolutionary general strike was declared 'against our will'. It was broken by massive arrests. Two Civil Governors came to the conclusion that 'a sincere respect for the right of association' was the best way to restore social peace and keep the CNT out of the hands of violent men; such efforts were finally sabotaged when the employers declared a lock-out that flung 20,000 men out of work and completely destroyed the influence of the moderates. 'Stubborn men of retrograde opinions' had played into the hands of the terrorists. The government surrendered to the employers and in November 1920 gave them as Civil Governor General Martínez Anido. For two years he ruled Barcelona as an independent fief on behalf of the Employers' Federation. 'Let them [the Madrid government] get rid of me if they can' was his customary reply to inquisitive journalists.

Martínez Anido now had to deal with terrorism: in January 1921 there were twenty-one assassinations in thirty-six hours. He did not use only police repression. He relied on the counter-terror of the Free Syndicates (Sindicatos Libres), organized by his own police chief. The Free Syndicates were in origin a Catholic right-wing union recruiting its members from workers 'sick ... of the tyranny of our so-called redeemers ... the union bullies and rowdies' of the CNT activist groups who extorted union dues at pistol point. They became *pistoleros* at the service of the employers, engaging in an urban guerrilla war with the CNT gunmen. There can be no doubt that the CNT extremists, for whom terrorism was 'the moral equivalent of the revolution they wanted but did not know how to make', began the war. And there can be no doubt that Martínez Anido's illegal methods, in the narrowest sense, were successful; today we know that the suppression of organized terrorism by legal means is a difficult task. In 1920 terrorism claimed fifty-seven deaths; in 1922, twenty-four. The number rose sharply again when the government at last dismissed Martínez Anido as Civil Governor. One of the victims of this last wave was Seguí himself, shot down in March 1923.

To conservative Spain the revolutionary wave that swept over Andalusia in the 'Bolshevik years' 1918-20 was as alarming as the labour war in Barcelona. It was neither solely a *jacquerie* of landless labourers (it included, as had the invasion of Jerez in 1892, small proprietors) nor a revolt of desperation; rather, it was a revolution of rising expectations. Vague rumours of a revolution in Russia—one anarchist organizer changed his name from Cordón to Cordoniev—set off new waves of strikes in Andalusia, where there had been a period of intense propaganda effort since 1910; militants had built up local agricultural unions with a paper, *The Voice of the Peasant*, and a central congress. These strikes were therefore semi-organized as no previous agrarian protest had been: they were strikes for the concrete demands put forward at the Congress of Agricultural Workers held at Castro in October 1918. These demands were the abolition of piece-work, negotiated wages, and recognition of the workers' syndicates or centres.

At first the strikes were remarkably successful, and employers— terrified by a revolutionary solidarity which included cooks, maids, and wet-nurses—negotiated wage settlements. Strike committees took over municipal government; the landowners lost their nerve and retired to the security of the provincial capitals. In the spring of 1919 the government sent troops to suppress the strike, and the rural anarchism of the south was left, once more, in the keeping of the 'men with ideas'. Yet this was one of the most active periods of anarchist propaganda, when over fifty *pueblos* had their papers and when the anarchists of the south were formally joined to the workers of Catalonia in the CNT. Above all, the anarchists had penetrated the 'hard' regions of Valencia and Levante.

In their Madrid Congress of La Comedia in 1919, the CNT militants could believe that 'their' revolution was a distinct possibility; in the pride of strength they rejected any alliance with the UGT because they believed they would absorb 'anaemic socialism'. This was the zenith of the postwar revolutionary mood; by 1923 the CNT had been broken by a depression which strengthened the employers' bargaining position, futile strikes, and the employers' offensive. The two great unions fell to fighting each other and among themselves.

To compound and embitter divisions came the question of whether to join the Third International established in Moscow. To all revolutionaries the Bolshevik revolution was 'a beacon of hope . . . the revolution we had dreamed of'. In the CNT Nin and Maurín, later to found the revolutionary workers' party the POUM (see p. 139), sympathized with Leninism but failed to win over their union. In the Socialist party the bureaucrats, the old men of the party counselled by Pablo Iglesias from his deathbed, fought a successful rear-guard action against the pro-Bolshevik *enragés* of Madrid Socialist Youth. In 1921 these latter broke away to form the minute Spanish Communist party, consisting largely of intellectuals under the age of thirty. The Communists were close to the activists of the CNT: a revolutionary *coup* would release a counter-revolution and open up new opportunities. At least one part of the equation was valid. The Communists organized a mutiny in Malaga and it was the government's pardon of a corporal that hardened army opinion in favour of Primo de Rivera's *pronunciamiento*.

With the CNT broken and torn by dissension it was the UGT and the Socialists who survived as the organized representatives of the working class; with six members in the Cortes of 1918, the Socialists were replacing the Republican party as the vehicle of moral protest against the 'system'. Socialists confessed scorn for a movement whose leaders were dragged along by *pistoleros*; as an instinctive reply to police repression, the infantile revolutionism of the CNT lacked any understanding of the 'processes of historical evolution' so dear to Marxists. It was futile to reject day-to-day gains if a union was to help its masses. The party could not, however, keep lip service to the revolution out of its rhetoric. 'Evolution and revolution are the same thing; revolution is no more than the acceleration of evolution.' Socialists like professors Julián Besteiro (1870–1939) and Fernando de los Ríos (1879–1949) were unlikely combatants on the barricades; both believed that a long period of education must fit the workers for power. Largo Caballero (1869–1946), a self-educated plasterer and the rising figure in the UGT, was much concerned with municipal politics and the organization of burial societies. A trade union official above all, he despised the secret meetings and pistol-toting of the CNT.

The consequence of the labour war, accompanied as it was by assassinations and violence—a Prime Minister, Dato, and an archbishop had been shot by CNT gunmen in the war of reprisals—was that it scared the propertied classes, in particular the bourgeoisie of Barcelona and the landowners of the south. Since 1914 the employers had seen in the creation of associations the weapon to 'break the pacts, contracts and conditions of work with workers' unions ... restoring to the employer the liberty of action that his dignity demands in order to hire and fire without restraint'.[5] In the Barcelona Federation and in the clubs of the Andalusian capitals the employers felt that, not merely their living, but their lives were at stake. Successive governments refused to take this dramatic view: Conservatives like Dato and Sánchez de Toca, and Liberals like Romanones were prepared to use the Institute of Social Reform as an instrument for the settlement of strikes. The conservative classes dismissed governmental conciliation as weakness and bitterly attacked ministers who would not 'string up anarchists on lamp-posts' and grant every request of the employers for armed force.

This lack of faith in civilian government accounts, in part, for the ready acceptance of a military dictatorship in 1923. The Barcelona employers had already appealed to the military when civilian governments refused to protect their interests. The dictatorship of Primo de

[5] *El Trabajo Nacional*, 1 January 1914.

Rivera may be seen as the transposition of this local condominium of autocratic soldiers and frightened businessmen into a national regime.

V

In July 1921, the news of the most terrible disaster in Spanish military annals fell on the Cabinet 'like a bomb'. The Spanish army in the eastern zone of the Moroccan Protectorate had been driven in a panic retreat from its position around Annual. Spaniards could only guess from the censored newspaper accounts that thousands of conscripts had been massacred by Moorish tribesmen.

The Spanish government had accepted the protectorate in 1912 not in any fit of colonialist enthusiasm, but simply to keep France from occupying the coastline opposite Spain. Spanish Morocco was a poor, roadless region divided into two military zones, unconnected except by sea, inhabited by restless tribes which had never been brought under control by their nominal sovereign, the Sultan of Morocco. A twentieth the size of French Morocco, unmapped and unexplored by Europeans— those who sought to penetrate the mountainous interior were castrated or murdered—Spanish Morocco presented every conceivable military difficulty.

Military disaster was the result, as Alcalá Zamora, the future President of the Second Republic, was to argue, of fighting a colonial war with an ill-trained conscript army.[6] The consequence was an unworkable compromise between the civilian politicians' determination to avoid trouble at home by conducting a difficult and unpopular colonial war on the cheap in terms of conscript casualties ('relative war'), and the military view that there was no alternative to the methodical conquest by trained and reliable troops ('absolute war'). The result was an embittered officer corps in Africa; Goded, Franco, Mola, Sanjurjo—the military conspirators of 1936—had all experienced frustration. It was to overcome the difficulties of waging a dirty war with unwilling conscripts and the carping of the despised *Junteros* (*Africanistas* resigned from the Juntas *en masse*) that the *Africanistas* created, in imitation of the French, a long-term volunteer force, the Legion or Tercio. Major Franco designed its uniform, joined it, and wrote its history. Subject to iron discipline, inspired by the mystique of comradeship in arms, and encouraged by higher pay, the Tercio became a legendary unit, the finest fighting force in the Spanish army.

During the war of 1914–18 Morocco had been quiet. Operations were

[6] Niceto Alcalá Zamora, *Discursos* (1979), 158.

resumed in 1919. The High Commissioner was General Damaso Beren-guer, a cultivated soldier who had studied French 'scientific warfare' in Morroco. In the eastern zone Berenguer conducted a successful, meth-odical campaign against an aristocratic cattle thief, El Raisuli, whose cruelty and guile gave him ascendancy over the tribes of Jibala. When news of Annual reached him he was within six kilometres of El Raisuli's capital and in sight of the definitive subjection of the eastern zone. Once this was accomplished, he would turn to the west.

The commander in the western zone was the ambitious, 'virile' General Silvestre, a friend of Alfonso XIII and of Berenguer. He committed himself to a perilous advance against the tribes which had been organized and armed by Abd el Krim. Abd el Krim had served the Spanish administration and had been decorated for his loyalty. Impris-oned for his contacts with the Germans during the war, he became fiercely anti-Spanish. Educated and ambitious, he was to become a hero of Arab nationalists and of Catalan separatists alike.

Berenguer's responsibility for the disaster was that, knowing its dangers, he did not firmly countermand Silvestre's proposed advance; Silvestre's that, until disaster was upon him, he did not make clear the danger of his exposed position without a secure line of retreat. Silvestre's conscripts broke when Abd el Krim attacked Annual, and fled in uncontrollable panic; in a few days 5,000 square kilometres were lost and the remnants of a demoralized army cooped up in Melilla.

VI

In 1917 the slogan around which opposition had crystallized was 'renovation'. Between 1921 and 1923 politics were dominated by the cry 'responsibilities': who and what were to blame for Annual?

The Conservatives, as the party in power at the time of Annual, were anxious to restrict the quest for responsibilities to military questions; they set up a commission of enquiry under General Picasso limited to this purpose. The Liberals were prepared to use 'responsibilities' to unseat the Conservatives and gain office. The opposition—particularly the Socialists—sought to use responsibilities not merely to discredit the army by accusations of incompetence and corruption, but to attack the whole political system—above all to involve the King, supposed to have encouraged Silvestre on the road to disaster. The accusations against Alfonso XIII became a nail which the Socialists were determined to hammer into the coffin of the monarchy. In the municipal elections of April 1931 which became a plebiscite on the future of the monarchy, *El Socialista* ran a cartoon 'Monarchy No!' with a skeleton in a soldier's cap beside the caption 'The candidature of the soldier of Annual'.

It was the 'gesture' of the Conservative Sánchez Guerra, Prime Minister, from March to December 1922, that politicized the issue. After a year's delay he submitted the Picasso report to a committee of the Cortes. The left could now use 'responsibilities' as a platform to mobilize middle-class support behind a demand to democratize the system. Sánchez Guerra had hoped to modernize the Conservative party and, by making his own party responsive to public opinion, to dish the Liberals, anxious for power after two years in the wilderness; but by opening responsibilities to political debate he killed his own ministry.

His successor was García Prieto (December 1922). This was the last government of the monarchy, the final attempt of the dynastic Liberals to act as 'lightning conductors', as architects of an opening to the left. The new cabinet included a representative of Melquíades Álvarez's Reformists and Alba, the Liberal financial reformer and the *bête noire* of the army and the Catalan bourgeoisie. Its programme included a revision of the religious settlement, a reform of the Senate, a modern budget, the pursuit of responsibilities and civilian control of Morocco, even agrarian reform. It had no chance to implement this programme: Morocco dominated politics.

Alba forced through the old compromise of war on the cheap in Morocco, the appointment of a civilian High Commissioner and the ransom of Abd el Krim's prisoners. All this was an 'insult' to the 'honour of the army' which made its discontents known to Alfonso XIII.

The parliamentary system had been consistently attacked by the anti-dynastic parties and their intellectual allies as corrupt and ineffective, an artificial construction that served the interests of politicians who manned it, men incapable of a national vision. There was a mood that some sort of dictatorship was a necessary prelude to a renewal of political life. Alfonso XIII suffered from indiscreet anti-parliamentary outbursts, alarming his ministers—whom he regarded as political cowards unwilling to defend him from the slanders of the left—by appeals for support for a royal reform 'with or without the constitution'. He argued that a temporary dictatorship was permissible in 'moments of extreme gravity' in order to clear the way for governments 'that respected the popular will'. He was dissuaded by Maura from attempting to create a 'King's' government under a soldier: if soldiers wanted to govern, Maura told the King, they must govern by themselves.

Ortega, the bitterest critic of the 'old politics', detected in the desire for a dictatorship that he observed in many circles a symptom of the old 'belief in miracles . . . in the prize in the political lottery'. The problem was that there was no dictator in sight. The candidate finally appeared in the general García Prieto had appointed as Captain General of Catalonia: Miguel Primo de Rivera.

During the night of 13 September Primo summoned Barcelona journalists and presented them with a manifesto to the Spanish army and people to be printed without comment. He would 'liberate Spain from professional politicians' like the 'depraved and cynical' Alba who had dishonoured the *patria*. He struck out against separatists and Communists and appealed to all men of good will to join a national Somaten (the self-defence force of the Catalan bourgeoisie) to restore social order. He clearly expected that his appeal would meet with general assent. He was a hero to the Catalan bourgeoisie, to whom Alba's proposal to lower tariffs was the monstrous scheme of a sworn enemy of Catalonia's prosperity.

If the King had resolutely backed his government, the *coup* would probably have failed. Primo de Rivera, with the declared support of only one garrison outside Barcelona, had taken an extraordinary gamble—he was a gambler by nature—on the general disenchantment of public opinion and the attitude of the King. Once Alfonso's attitude was apparent, the government resigned and Primo's gamble came off. Fully aware of the constitutional consequences of his action, Alfonso appointed Primo as President of a Directory of unknown generals. By thus giving legitimacy to a bloodless military revolt, Alfonso sealed the fate of the constitutional monarchy. The degree of his foreknowledge of or complicity in the *coup* was irrelevant.

The Socialist deputy Prieto had talked of the army 'imposing its mandate by a dictatorship from the shadows'. The army had come out of the shadows to the approval of the intellectuals, the indifference of the Socialists, and possibly even to the relief of the politicians. García Prieto professed to offer prayers to Saint Miguel Primo de Rivera who had relieved him of the 'impossible task of governing Spain'.

The central question must be: did Primo de Rivera, as his supporters claimed, kill off a diseased body or was he strangling a new birth?

The record of the 'corpse' was not encouraging: fifteen governments since 1917; repeated suspensions of the Cortes; intermittent censorship of the press. In the elections of April 1923 half the electorate had not voted. It can only be a personal opinion that the 'responsibilities' issue had been used successfully by the left to alter the political balance; that new forces were entering political life—the left emerged stronger than ever in the 1918 elections.

Nor was it only on the left that there were stirrings of vitality: a group of enthusiasts had begun to organize a Catholic Christian Democrat party, the PSP. The party, split internally, never got off the ground before the *coup*. Its programme nevertheless represented a more convincing attack on the *turno pacífico* than the utterances of jaundiced intellectuals. It was to be a *mass* party, not a party of notables manipulated from above. It saw that first-past-the-post elections in single-member constituencies were a gift to the caciques of the dynastic parties. To destroy them Spain must have proportional representation and multi-member constituencies which could not be managed by electoral manipulation of the neutral mass. But the 'corrupt' Cortes would never pass the necessary legislation. The era of mass politics was to be ushered in by a royal decree.[7]

It was these signs of life rather than the death agonies of parliamentarianism or any fear of a *specific* attack on the responsibilities issue in the Cortes that alarmed the King and the army: Primo de Rivera caught parliamentary rule in a painful transition from oligarchy to democracy; the old political machine was showing evident signs of wear even though it could still turn out a comfortable government majority. But the prospects of transformation envisaged by advanced liberals had not conquered the indifference of the electorate—in the last election of the monarchy 146 deputies owed their seats to uncontested elections under Article 29 (see p. 73).

The destruction of the parliamentary monarchy created by Cánovas, whatever its shortcomings, was the decisive break in modern Spanish history. It opened what constitutional lawyers called 'a constituent period', the search for a stable form of government, a process that might be considered a waste of historical time. In 1977, after two dictatorships and a Republic, Spain returned to the form of government the soldiers had overthrown in 1923: a parliamentary monarchy based on universal suffrage.

[7] O. Alzaga, *La primera democracia cristiana en España* (1973), Part IV.

7 The Dictatorship of Primo de Rivera and the Fall of the Monarchy 1923–1931

I

'Our aim', ran Primo de Rivera's first proclamation to the country, 'is to open a brief parenthesis in the constitutional life of Spain and to re-establish it as soon as the country offers us men uncontaminated with the vices of political organization. We will then hasten to present these men to Your Majesty so that normality can be established as soon as possible.'

Primo de Rivera's political thinking was primitive, personal, and naïve. Unpatriotic professional politicians had destroyed Spain; a patriotic amateur would restore her. A political caste had, through the farce of elections, isolated government from the people; he himself would enter once more into direct and personal touch with the people, restoring to government its democratic spirit. As ruler of Spain he 'talked' with the people, explaining his decrees and frankly confessing his errors, creating a picture of the benevolent despot under Divine Guidance doing his best but not always succeeding, scribbling pencil notes to his subjects in the small hours of the morning after a hard day's work at his desk.

The dictator's 'intuitions' were raised by his propagandists to the status of a political doctrine. Hatred of the old gang of party politicians was rationalized into an anti-parliamentary political theory which professed to be more truly democratic than parliamentary liberalism; it attacked individualism and individual rights: men were born in society and must respect what, in that society, was 'real'. Doctrines of individual rights were 'the arabesques of unemployed intellectuals'. The dictatorship would be pragmatic: it would respect the great existing social creations: the Nation, Church, and King *in that order*.

The dictator and his party were not enthusiastic monarchists; they accepted the monarchy because the vast majority of Spaniards did. As to the Church, the dictator, as repentant rakes so often are, was a devout Catholic, who thought all other Spaniards were too, or ought to be. Materialism was for oxen who had no history. All this meant that the dictatorship was a less tolerant society than 'decadent' parliamentarianism. In 1926 a woman was imprisoned for maintaining that the Virgin Mary bore other children after Jesus; Protestant sects saw administrative hindrances multiplying about them. Even so, the regime's relations with the Church, particularly in Catalonia, became uneasy. As it lost prestige and popularity, so the Church sought to separate its destinies from those of the dictator.

Primo de Riverism was not fascism. Its theory of sovereignty as the amalgamation of autonomous social entities, anterior to political society, was nearer to Aristotelian scholasticism than to totalitarianism. Mussolini was much admired and fascist trappings and linguistic usages were imported; but as a cursory examination of the writings of the regime's apologists reveals, Catholic reactionaries and native regenerationists supplied the ideology of the dictatorship. Costa was the dictator's John the Baptist, prophesying the coming of an 'iron surgeon'. Ortega had pleaded for an élite, rejecting the 'false assumption of the real equality of men'; his attacks on the old political system became biblical texts, bandied about by the supporters of Miguel Primo de Rivera and of his son, José Antonio. Above all others loomed the great liberal heretic, Antonio Maura. The dictator claimed that he was putting into effect Maura's revolution from above, which had been thwarted by parliamentary liberalism. If Maura himself regarded the dictator as a political trick-cyclist, doomed to fall once his initial momentum weakened, many Mauristas found in Primo the leader they had sought in vain on the benches of the Cortes. Other critics of the *turno pacífico*—the right-wingers of the young PSP for instance (see pp. 96–7)—welcomed the dictatorship as dealing a death blow to 'the decaying and corrupt organization of the official state' which represented 'private interest, the greed of caciques and the ambitions of plutocrats'.

II

There was nothing novel about the content of Primo de Rivera's policies. It was as if he set out to show that he could accomplish what 'decadent' parliamentarianism had failed to accomplish. By royal decrees he would put into effect the reform projects that had been sabotaged in the Cortes by the intrigues of factious party politicians. Thus the Municipal Statute of 1924 was based on twenty-two bills, all of which had failed, over forty years, to get through the Cortes. Other projects came out of Costa's bible for regenerators: the plans for the hydraulic confederations were the work of a disciple of Costa. The dictator paid tribute to Maura and incorporated in the Municipal Statute his corporate suffrage; but, as with so many constructive ideas of the dictatorship, the Municipal Statute was stillborn because the dictator dared not risk the elections which would have given it life.

Like many authoritarian politicians Primo was an eclectic when it came to specific policies. Moreover, apart from clearing out the old politicians like his *bête noire*, Alba, he had no fixed idea as to the regime with which he should endow Spain. His first *ad hoc* solution was military rule, with elderly generals as pseudo-ministers; lesser officers took over as provincial governors and mayors—'pocket regenerators' with instructions to clean up local politics by booting out the old gang and to encourage patriotism and gymnastics. The virtue of military government, the dictator proudly claimed, was that it saved salaries.

In 1926 rule by military amateurs was replaced by the Civil Directory, a mixture of young, bright technocrats and older generals like Martínez Anido. Since parties in the orthodox sense were mere emanations of a parliamentary system condemned by history, popular support was to be mobilized by a *movement*—the Unión Patriótica (UP). The UP was conceived as a form of moral regeneration, as a league of citizens open to all true patriots, as the dynamic élite of a state purified of the politics of place and power.

The language of the dictator reflected a profound political ignorance. He refused to see that the UP was a party in the ordinary sense of the word; that is, a group of men who shared a common conviction that a given political solution—the dictatorship—was in their interest. It was to this communion of patriots with clean hands that Primo proposed to hand over the task of ruling Spain. 'We are going to prepare Spain for government by those who have never governed.' Yet in spite of these prospects, the party refused to grow: great rallies, rousing speeches, and almost complete control of governmental patronage failed to bring in the men of goodwill. The dictator had fallen victim to the regenerationist myth of a 'real', popular Spain buried under an artificial political class. There was no such reserve. When Primo suspected his error it was too late to rectify it and win back the outraged and rejected politicians.

III

Primo shared the common conviction that society was sound and that all that was amiss in Spain was the superstructure of politics. Once it became apparent that the simplest operation of iron surgery—the elimination of 'old politics' and politicians—did not of itself regenerate the *patria*, then he must take upon himself the task of regeneration. For Primo this was to be achieved by economic advance, particularly industrial growth.

To the technocrats and planners of the regime Spain was a poor economy because private capital and enterprise had never been able to overcome the backwardness that had obsessed Spaniards since 1898. The state must grant weak or 'missing' industries monopoly conditions and invest heavily in basic public works.

The public works programme of the dictatorship, intended to provide the stimulus and infrastructure for the take-off, was criticized as the economic exhibitionism of an upstart regime. Primo boasted that he had turned cattle tracks into European-style roads; his opponents that he had at great expense given 'gentlemen [*señoritos*] roads to roar along in their cars'. His railway legislation was based on Cambó's plans. The state was prepared to undertake capital expenditure which the feeble financial structure of the companies could not support; in return, the state had a right to supervise the management of those companies in the national interest. The proudest and most durable creations of the dictatorship were the Hydraulic Confederations which grouped together various interests in an attempt to rationalize the great river systems as a source of electrical power, and for irrigation and a programme of reafforestation. The effort to organize the Confederations as a local version of a corporate 'democracy' failed; but they were the successful origin of the modern electrification of Spain.

The problem for the regime was to find the money to finance these ambitious undertakings. This exposed the central weakness of the dictatorship. Primo had come to power to save society, not to reform it. But when he refused to become a mere instrument of the upper classes, when he professed to listen to 'the clamour of the people' and indulged in mild social radicalism, he met the entrenched opposition of the economic establishment. Thus he could not finance his public works by reforming a tax system which his Finance Minister, the former Maurista Calvo Sotelo (1893–1936) recognized as unjust in its reliance on indirect taxation and in its tolerance of widespread tax evasion by the rich. In 1926 Calvo Sotelo proposed to base the budget on an effective, progressive income tax. This he defended as modern, efficient, and socially just. 'True democracy is recognized today by the distribution of public taxation, not by a formal political constitution.' The government, nevertheless, dared not rally the masses against the classes; it gave in to a bitter press campaign led by the aristocracy of the banking world. However great his utility as the restorer of social peace, the conservatives had no time for the dictator's financial 'amateurism': the campaign against the income tax became a campaign against the government itself.

Once tax reform had failed there was no alternative to borrowing. The loans for public works appeared in an Extraordinary Budget and were the most criticized aspect of the dictatorship. Critics pointed to the inflationary effects of the Extraordinary Budget (which the regime denied by pointing to the stable level of domestic prices) and to the almost total lack of financial control. The result of the regime's efforts to keep domestic prices down was a pressure on the peseta; its fall, partly due to an overvaluation that had attracted capital which then began to leave the country in 1928, allowed the opposition in financial circles to mount a campaign against Calvo Sotelo's attempts to save exchange rates, a campaign which forced his resignation.

At the same time the government was determined to regulate every aspect of the economy that was stimulated by this public expenditure. Haunted by fears of overproduction and 'wasteful' competition and by dreams of autarky—Primo was pained by the upper-class predilection for French wines and the doctors' preference for imported scalpels—the Council of National Economy embarked on a programme of wholesale intervention. Every article that could be produced in Spain must be produced, regardless of production costs: hence 'intervention' to save domestic coal production, lead, and resin; hence the raising of tariff barriers by a third; hence the attempts to create a national car industry, to finance home-grown cotton by a levy on imported cotton, to intensify 'cerealist' policies; hence the nationalization of the distribution of petrol, partly to produce revenue, partly to save Spain from 'Cubanization' by the oil companies. The Spanish economy fell into the hands of committees regulating everything from hydro-electric power to the rabbit-skin industry. Intervention and control were criticized by those groups that suffered, or those that were not rewarded, as laming an economy still dependent on private enterprise.

But in spite of fierce criticism the regime could point to a steady if modest increase in production. The dictatorship had an air of optimism and expansion, though the continued prosperity was to a large extent the result of favourable outside circumstances for which the regime could take no credit. Spain's import prices fell as its export prices rose. As the dictator saw, his hopes of autarky rested on the continued growth of Spain's agricultural exports which alone could finance industrial growth and heal the deficit in the balance of payments. The tourism which the regime did all it could to encourage by building roads and state hotels in historic buildings was luxury tourism; it could not, as did the mass tourism of the 1960s, underwrite an industrial take-off.

IV

The regime professed to be devoted to greater social justice. There were much-publicized schemes for cheap workers' housing; the social services were improved—particularly maternity benefits, for Primo avowed great concern for women's rights. It was the fundamental conservatism of the regime, its sensitivity to criticism from the financial and landowning establishment that inhibited any serious attack on inequality and injustice. Primo's successes lay in uncontroversial fields like primary education, with 8,000 new schools. Land reform is the test case. The dictatorship fell back on the anodyne solution of colonization on land sold voluntarily by the owners: a mere 4,000 peasants were resettled. Agricultural labourers remained outside the social security system. Nor did the conditions of the industrial worker improve; real wages probably fell slightly overall and the poor provinces, as always, came off badly: real wages rose dramatically in industrial Vizcaya, falling sharply in Jaén; and it was only the favoured regions that benefited from the compensation of increased social security benefits.

Why, then, it may be asked, was the working class so docile? The answer lies partly in the efficacy of repression, partly in the attitude of the Socialist party. Primo de Rivera's political reputation, like that of Napoleon III, was based on a liquidation of the red spectre combined with sympathy for virtuous labour. Abolition of the jury, censorship of the press, and the revival of the Somaten, as a militia or special armed police reserve, helped to break the already shaken cadres of the CNT. Martínez Anido, as Minister of the Interior, was the government expert on the suppression of anarchism. Repression, as always, split the movement. Pestaña argued that the CNT should accept the government's labour arbitration machinery, saving the organization at the expense of the principles of revolutionary syndicalism; at the other extreme, anarchist purists revived the 'revolutionary and moral genius of Bakunin' by founding, in 1927, the FAI (the Iberian Anarchist Federation), a pure revolutionary organization of small groups of activists. Although there was a clandestine organization of the CNT and occasional conferences took place, with its militants scattered by jail and exile 'the movement', wrote its historian Buenacasa, 'ceased to exist for seven years'.

There was more to the dictator's labour policy than mere repression. Why should workers' leaders lament the destruction of the bourgeois state of the 'old politicians' when they were offered a satisfactory machinery of wage arbitration by the new government? Primo hoped to integrate the UGT into the new state.

In 1924 this looked by no means an impossible ambition. The concern of labour leaders like Largo Caballero, favourite of Pablo Iglesias, was to preserve the UGT, outdistance its rivals, and maintain and enlarge the legislation that protected labour. This did not entail *political* collaboration but merely an acceptance of the existing situation—an opportunism encouraged by the formation of Ramsay MacDonald's Labour Government in Britain, which seems to have induced a passing hope that socialism might attain power in a capitalist monarchy. All Spanish Socialists had to do for the moment was to accept posts in the various government agencies concerned with labour issues, *without* committing themselves to overt support of the regime—Largo Caballero as Councillor of State for Labour refused an invitation to a palace ball. In 1926, in imitation of Spanish precedents and in line with social Catholicism and current fascist models, Aunós as Minister of Labour set up a corporate Labour Organization as the social centrepiece of a new state. His mixed committees with equal representation of labour and capital were accepted by the UGT whose officials became, in effect, state-paid bureaucrats.[1]

The co-operation with the dictator by the UGT, dominated by a reformist leadership, was opposed by Prieto and the left of the Socialist party and earned the party the obloquy of the CNT. Largo Caballero continued to defend co-operation as preserving the UGT from the fate of the CNT and giving Socialism a monopoly of the labour movement— immediate advantages which would vanish if Socialists showed signs of co-operation with bourgeois politicians against the dictatorship. In 1929 the Socialists abandoned the dictator by rejecting the invitation to elect members to Primo's National Assembly. This was a body blow for the dictator's attempt to legitimize his rule. The Socialist movement, preserved by collaboration from destruction, was now prepared for its 'historic mission' as the party of the future.

If Primo de Rivera failed to 'integrate' the Socialist movement and win over the UGT for a programme of 'national production', his failure with the Catalans was even more resounding. Though he expressed mild sympathy for Catalan aspirations in 1923 in order to secure support in Barcelona, he shared the Castilian view that regionalism that went beyond folklore and home crafts was a cover for 'blind and perverse separatists'. He thought that Catalanism was the work of a small minority of university professors and intellectuals; its manifestations—the use of Catalan in church, the Catalan flag and the national dance—were suppressed. The one regional institution granted by corrupt parliamentarianism, the Mancomunidad, was dissolved as a financial and political disaster. This was too much even for conservative Catalans, who had opposed the political pretensions of the nationalist left and who had greeted Primo de Rivera as a saviour of society.

In exile Primo seems to have believed that he had come to power to destroy Catalanism; he could believe Catalanism was dead because, in a regime of silence, he could take his desires as accomplished facts.

[1] J. Andrés Gallego, *El socialismo durante la dictadura 1923–36* (1977), 49–191.

Repression strengthened Catalanism: Cambó argued that the dramatic expansion of Catalan literature, the boom in Catalan books, proved that repression accomplished a conversion in depth where his own autonomy campaign had failed. Cambó still hoped for his moderate solution 'within the monarchy'. This solution was already outdated. Just as repression had strengthened the extremists in the CNT, so it gained sympathy for Maciá's Republican separatism. The *grande bourgeoisie* had lost control. Catalanism was now the affair of middle-class radicals and convinced Republicans.

V

It was in Morocco, where the politicians had come to grief, that the dictator would score his greatest triumph. By 1924 Abd el Krim's ruthless leadership and primitive Berber nationalism had given the Rif tribes the appearances of a state. He began to attract the sympathies of the left, in a campaign against the 'colonial oppression' of Spain. Primo's first intuition was to risk the possibility of a mutiny in the African Army by acceding to the politicians' desire for an inexpensive 'relative' war and withdrawing to the 'Primo de Rivera line'—Franco was one of the dedicated Africanist officers who openly opposed 'abandonism'.

Just as he had been favoured by the terms of trade, so a change in French policy gave Primo his opportunity in Morocco. In 1925 Abd el Krim attacked the French advance posts; before we condemn the Spanish for the débâcle of Annual in 1921, it is well to remember the French defeats in this year which shook the fabric of the protectorate. French willingness to co-operate with the Spanish army allowed the crowning victory of Alhucemas.

The wheel had come full circle with the triumph of the army's maximalist policy of conquest and military occupation. This was not because Primo de Rivera had been weak and subject to military bullying but because events, above all the possibility of military co-operation with France, had made possible a policy he had rightly considered dangerous and beyond Spain's capacity in 1923. In 1924 he had been courageous enough to force his views on the African command. In 1925 he assumed direct responsibility for the risky combined operation of Alhucemas. By 1927 the protectorate was pacified. Primo de Rivera deserved the rewards of courage.

VI

By 1929 Primo's Moroccan laurels had faded and the prosperity that had supported the regime seemed under threat; the public works programme was cut back. As in most countries, a fall in the exchange rate was regarded as a national calamity. It was not, however, the symptoms of an economic crisis that undermined the regime. Its failure was a political failure. It could not solve the problem that haunts all authoritarian regimes: the establishment of a political system with an appearance of legitimacy that could succeed the dictatorship.

There can be no doubt that Primo de Rivera originally regarded his dictatorship in the classical sense as a short, sharp interlude. Through a variety of metaphors, ranging from surgery to pyrotechnics, the dictator declared his intention of returning to 'normality'. Difficulties arose in his differing judgements as to the moment at which it would be prudent to withdraw and as to the nature of the regime that would constitute normality. Hence his repeated rectifications in his attempts to re-cross the Rubicon.

From his original idea of the constitution of 1876 run by new men, Primo accepted the idea of a new constitution to be drawn up by a National Assembly that might attract some of the old men; to the committed members of the Unión Patriótica this was a way to institution-alize the 'movement' and secure their political survival—much as the Francoist political élite were later to pin their hopes on the slogan 'After Franco, the institutions'. The Assembly was intended to represent the great interests of the nation. In fact it became a forum for competing pressure groups. The constitution which it drafted expressed the current right-wing hostility to the practices of liberal, responsible parliamentary government: in the name of efficiency—'getting things done' was Primo's favourite motto—speeches were limited. Corporative representatives sat beside elected deputies. The main departures from classical parliamen-tarianism were the absence of any ministerial responsibility and the suppression of the royal prerogative of appointing and dismissing ministries, a power now shared with a body which was an imitation of the Fascist Grand Council. This constitution did not please the King—though Primo, under the influence of Mussolini, believed the royal prerogatives were too extensive—and the Assembly had been boycotted from the outset by the old politicians and later by the Socialists. The new constitution had to be abandoned as a political flop.

The public debate on the constitution in 1929 revealed the extent of the opposition to a regime which could not be made acceptable to the forces that still counted in Spanish society. The opposition of the maligned politicians is understandable; they were the insulted and injured. Legally minded, they could not accept Primo's 'constant plebiscite of public opinion', sensed in homages at railway stations, as a substitute for a constitution. Sánchez Guerra, leader of the Conservative party, advised the King to dismiss the dictator. In 1928, with the help of discontented officers and the declared enemies of the monarchy, Sánchez Guerra staged in Valencia a feeble imitation of a nineteenth-century *pronunciamiento*, in what was declared to be an attempt to save the King from the dictator. That the revolt was a fiasco (the wife of the compromised general in Valencia, fearing the social consequences of failure, persuaded her husband to arrest Sánchez Guerra) was less important than that the conspirators became national heroes.

The most surprising feature of the opposition of the politicians to the dictatorship was that it secured the support of the intellectuals. It is important to realize that Spanish culture was entering on what has been called a second Golden Age. At no time, until the declining years of Francoism, was the potential influence of intellectuals as great and their prestige so little impaired. Unamuno, the Christian existentialist of Salamanca, had become a national and international figure; Ortega was at the height of his reputation as a journalist-philosopher in the *Revista de Occidente* and with his articles in the liberal daily *El Sol*; there was a new generation of poets like García Lorca. The universities, especially Madrid, were more 'European' than at any previous time.[2]

Almost the totality of this intellectual establishment came out in bitter opposition to the dictatorship and by implication to the monarchy that supported it. Given that writers like Azorin had been equally bitter critics of the 'old politics' and that Ortega had given Primo's *coup* a qualified welcome as giving them the final push, their *renversement des alliances* is, to say the least, somewhat inconsistent. Politicians, many of whom were lawyers, and intellectuals alike were outraged by what they termed the dictator's 'lack of juridical sense'. Primo had an endearing sense of Wild West justice and it was a particular scandalous interference with the due course of law that brought the intellectuals into declared and permanent opposition. Unamuno was dismissed from his chair, and went into exile; from Paris, he savagely attacked the dictator in language that did him little credit as a stylist and with scant regard for truth, as he himself later confessed. Blasco Ibáñez, the popular novelist and Republican agitator whose fame had been secured when Valentino starred in the film version of *Four Horsemen of the Apocalypse*, slandered the dictator and the King with false accusations of immorality. Apart from Maeztu— he joined the UP and became an ambassador and was sent to Coventry by his peers—and D'Ors, not a single intellectual of standing supported the

[2] For the universities see Schlomo Ben-Ami, 'Los Estudiantes contra el Rey', in *Historia 16* no.6 (October 1976), 37–47.

regime. The Ateneo, the literary club that symbolized the worst and the best in Spanish intellectual life, was closed down.

The opposition of the intellectuals merged with the opposition of the university students—their numbers had doubled since 1923. Unamuno became a father figure to student rebels, addressing them letters in which he called the dictator a felon, a miserable robber, and a coward. Student opposition originated in the defence of student interests by the non-Catholic Students' Union, the FUE, against the attempt to allow Catholic private universities to confer degrees which represented essential certificates for government jobs. This first overt opposition Primo de Rivera struck down with contempt. 'Spain', he observed, 'does not need universities.'

Thus, throughout its decline his government was subjected to a series of minor assaults which discredited it. Special squads of bicycle police were employed to remove seditious graffiti; the students' committee circulated clandestine leaflets; laudatory poems of which the initial letters of each line spelled 'Primo is a Drunk', appeared in the press. Primo de Rivera came to hate the students—he was particularly outraged by the presence of women in student demonstrations which he connected with the rise of pornography. To the King the student protest was particularly distressing. He had spent a great deal of energy on the new University City in order to conciliate the youth of Spain; his reward was the destruction of his bust by students, a clear indication of the dangers of continued support of the dictatorship. When Primo de Rivera fell it looked as if he had been defeated by a students' rag.

The grumblings of the old politicians and the sedition of the intellectuals he could have resisted; what he could not afford to lose was the loyalty of the army and the support of the King.

The discontents of the army originated in the dictator's 'lack of respect' for those conventions which had protected the military career from interfering civilians. Primo politicized promotions. General Queipo de Llano was placed on reserve for a joke in poor taste—UP, he observed, signified public urinal as well as Patriotic Union. Such actions threatened the autonomy of the army and revived the old *Juntero* spirit. 'If soldiers can do this, how on earth shall we defend ourselves against civilians?'

It was Primo de Rivera's onslaught on the artillery corps which, in Berenguer's words, 'broke the harmony of the military family' and made his fall inevitable. Unable to push through the drastic reduction of officers which might have created a modern army, the dictator's reforming zeal concentrated on one glaring anomaly—the 'closed scale' by which artillery officers declined promotion which broke strict seniority.

So serious was the resistance of the artillery corps to this attack on its privileges that the government suspended the whole artillery officer corps. The struggle had seriously weakened Primo de Rivera. The artillery officers were bitter against the dictator and lost faith in a king who did not defend their interests. The King himself disliked the way in which the dictator had dissolved the proudest corps in the army without consulting its commander-in-chief.

VII

Nineteen twenty-nine was, in his son's phrase, the year of the dictator's agony. He had failed in his attempt at an *entente* with the Socialists. In August they published a manifesto declaring themselves supporters of 'a Republican state of freedom and democracy'. His interventionism had alienated all but those who had benefitted from it: his attempts to gain Socialist support and his labour tribunals irritated the employers. The bankers had successfully resisted his modest proposal for cheap agrarian credit; the railway interests resented the control of his Railway Council. Capitalists, who had been saved in 1923—strikes had fallen from 465 in 1923 to around 100 in the following years—and who had flourished under his rule (if the soaring profits of the big banks were any indication), turned against Primo. He was, declared the Minister of Labour, 'overwhelmed in an avalanche of gold'. Calvo Sotelo, who believed that only social reform would stave off social revolution, found all his projects as Finance Minister sabotaged by what he called the 'obstinate passivity of the conservative classes'. The great landowners treated his attempts to rationalize the land tax and to limit tax evasion as 'Bolshevism'. Landowners and bankers were 'men of narrow vision'.

Once the peseta began to fall—largely for causes outside the government's control—the decline was attributed by the financial establishment *solely* to the inflationary effects of lavish and uncontrolled public spending. The monetary debate weakened confidence in a regime that appeared to be floundering in problems beyond its competence when the dictator himself, in one of his characteristic notes, confessed that he was 'too tired' to remember the arguments of his Finance Minister. Cambó, the most influential figure in the financial and business world, declared that capital would never flow into Spain 'while the present regime has not prepared its normal substitution'—that is, until the dictator announced his resignation.

All these discontents reached the aristocratic court, which considered the dictator a vulgar amateur. The King knew that the ministry was deeply divided over the problem of the return to 'normality'; that the regime was supported only by 'interests' and the men of the UP who had no other political home. Determined to escape the consequences of Primo's growing unpopularity, which were involving the monarchy—a pamphlet on 'Alfonso XIII as a dancing partner' had appeared—the King hoped that, by dismissing the dictator, he might not merely recover the prerogatives sequestered by the dictator, but appear as a liberator and thus wash himself clean of the responsibilities of 1923.

The opportunity for which the King and court had been seeking was created by the last of the dictator's erratic intuitions. On 26 January 1929, after a sleepless night and *without consulting the King*, he circularized the Captains General. The army had made him, did it still support him? If not, he would resign 'in five minutes'. This was the most extraordinary offer ever made by a modern dictator; it infuriated the King as commander-in-chief of an army whose loyalty to the crown had been under a severe strain. It was not merely the unenthusiastic replies of his fellow generals, but the realization that the King could dismiss him, that forced Primo de Rivera's resignation. He retired to Paris and died a broken man within a few months.

The dictatorship is often dismissed as an irrelevant interlude in Spanish history, the temporary intrusion into politics of an eccentric, well-meaning soldier. This it was not. The *pronunciamiento* opened up a search that lasted half a century for a legitimate government to replace that destroyed in 1923. Even more important, the dictatorship was both a model and a warning to General Franco. Many of his economic notions were lifted straight from the policies of the dictatorship. The idea of a movement, of a communion of all patriots and men of good will as opposed to an orthodox party, came to life once more under Francoism as the instrument to rally support for the regime, only to become in the end the agglutinate of a political élite. The Nationalist slogan 'Spain one and great' was an invention of the UP. General Franco saw that authoritarian rule implies a degree of repression that Primo was unwilling, or unable, to impose. Catalanism in all its manifestations must be ruthlessly suppressed; organized labour destroyed. Above all, the loyalty of the army must not be sacrificed to inclinations to reform its antiquated structure; 'the harmony of the military family' was a precondition for the survival of a dictatorship. For both Primo's rise to power and his fall proved that, in the last resort, the army was the final arbiter.

VIII

With the dictator gone, the task of returning to 'normality' was entrusted, first to General Berenguer, an honest, cultured, but ailing soldier confined much of the time to a wheelchair, and then to Admiral Aznar, a political innocent given to reading novels in moments of crisis. They failed. On 14 April 1931, King Alfonso left for exile and Spain became a republic.

Regimes fall as much as a consequence of the ineptitude of their defenders as a result of the strength of the opposition. Monarchists perceived the necessity for the creation of a strong, modern mass party to replace the dynastic parties in ruins after the hiatus of the dictatorship; but they could not sink their congenital feuds or abandon the mores of the 'old politics'. Romanones and Alba failed to form a united Liberal party; Romanones helped to sabotage Berenguer's plans for a return, via clean elections, to the constitution of 1876 simply because he regarded Berenguer as a Conservative competitor for office who could not be trusted to 'make' an election.

The hesitations of Berenguer—if he had called elections immediately it is conceivable that the monarchists might have scraped home—allowed the extent of the disenchantment and disarray of the politicians to emerge in public. They could not forgive the King for the treason of 1923; he must wash away his sins by submitting his conduct and the monarchy as such to the judgement of a constituent Cortes. Others went further. Miguel Maura, son of the great Antonio, led the monarchist defections to the Republican camp. A flood of press statements and speeches to enthusiastic audiences made the politics of 1930 a suspense story.

Given the historic weakness of the Republican movement outside the great cities, the revival and reorganization of the Republican parties was the political phenomenon of 1930, in sharp contrast to the declining prestige of the monarchist parties. It is an indication of the relative mildness of the dictatorship that the Republicans had been organizing in public since 1926. The Republican Alliance of that year included 'old' Republicans like Lerroux, whose progress towards his new role of middle-class messiah made him suspect to 'new' Republicans like Azaña, the intellectual driving force of the Republican revival, and to the Radical Socialists who were making a bid for working-class support. Conservatives were alarmed that Republicanism represented, not merely the desire for political renovation, but a social revolution, the moral prodrome of which was revealed in a press that discussed abortion and the evils of clericalism. Azaña's concern was precisely the opposite: that the Republican revival represented only 'a negative Republicanism born out of the corruptions of the old regime', a feeling directed against the person of Alfonso XIII as symbol of that corruption. The Republican revival was more than this. It did represent a desire for renovation, for citizenship in a modern, European state; but the moral isolation of Alfonso achieved by the Republicans' propaganda campaign and such publications as Blasco Ibáñez's *Alfonso XIII Unmasked* was a crucial factor in the overthrow of the monarchy. Once the King had vanished, there were few issues on which the Republicans could unite.

It was the alliance of the intellectual establishment (intellectuals were the lions of fashionable salons and flattered and courted by the press) that facilitated this task of moral isolation. In February the leading writers formed 'The Group at the Service of the Republic'. In November came Ortega's famous article 'Delenda est Monarchia'. This growth in the influence of the intellectuals escaped the blind world of the court. The King, after a brief essay at a *rapprochement* early in his reign, had neglected them. They now took their revenge. 'Our campaign', confessed Unamuno, 'was less anti-monarchist than anti-Alfonsist.'

But how were the Republicans to overthrow the monarchy? The revolutionary tactics of 1930 are incomprehensible unless we assume that the anti-monarchical coalition doubted whether the personal unpopularity of the King was great enough to drown residual monarchical conservatism in a general election. To hide this lack of faith in the general will Republicans could point to Berenguer's disastrous hesitations, and revive the historic accusation that elections run by monarchical politicians would be 'insincere'. Hence a republic could legitimately be imposed by a *coup*. But for a Republican rising to be successful it must be supported by the army in a *pronunciamiento*, by the workers in a general strike, and by rebellion in Catalonia.

In Catalonia the dictatorship had damaged the monarchy beyond repair and discredited the Lliga: Cambó was a Conservative and a monarchist—at the last moment he proposed the creation of a national Conservative centre party. Catalanism was now a concern of the middle-class Republicans, divided between non-revolutionary intellectual groups and Maciá's Estat Catalá. Maciá, who had 'invaded' Spain in 1926 with a small force of enthusiasts, was a separatist and a revolutionary. In July 1930 Republican Catalanists of all shades agreed to co-operate with Spanish Republicans in overthrowing the monarchy once the Spanish Republicans, in their turn, could present a united front; their price for co-operation was complete autonomy for Catalonia as the first claim on a victorious republic.

As for the workers, Berenguer failed to gain the Socialists as a 'government force'. Those who had opposed collaboration with the dictatorship, above all Prieto whose contacts with Republicans were long-standing, swung into an alliance with the Republican conspirators. The CNT had been legalized in April and rapidly recovered its strength. Unlike the Socialists in their belief that the next stage in the march of history was a bourgeois revolution, the CNT was committed doctrinally to a *workers'* revolution and outright rejection of co-operation in a bourgeois, Republican conspiracy; but the leadership, smothering their principles in a distinction between illicit pacts with bourgeois parties and licit intelligence, signed an agreement with the Republicans in May 1930—a step for which they were to be bitterly criticized by the purists.

The conspirators knew that without the sympathy, or at least the neutrality, of the army their projected *coup* must fail. Thirty years of royal flattery had turned sour in the latter years of the dictatorship. Berenguer had failed to restore the 'harmony of the military family'. Senior officers, personally loyal to Alfonso, would not denounce their juniors engaged in plots. Once more two theories of military obedience were in conflict. Mola, head of the security forces, maintained that it was the duty of soldiers to obey a legal government; to potential conspirators like the unruly Queipo de Llano it was the duty of soldiers to examine the legality of the government before obeying it. Mechanical discipline was subject to the higher discipline of loyalty to the *patria*: a perjured king, who had broken his contract with the nation in 1923, could no longer command obedience.

A separate revolutionary committee controlled the military side of the rising. This military rising was never properly put to the test and it may be doubted whether the army would have risen against the King. What mattered was that in the crisis of April 1931 officers would not risk a civil war as they did in 1936; they were responsible for what has been called a 'negative *pronunciamiento*', since their abstention left the monarchy defenceless. Rather than to monarchical institutions as such, their true loyalty lay to a conception of national order, which they saw imperilled in 1936. Then it was the turn of Mola to use the arguments he rejected as treason in 1930.

In August of that year all the conspirators met in a San Sebastian hotel and signed a pact which committed the united Spanish Republican groups and the Catalan left to joint action. The Republican bloc accepted the terms of the Catalan left. The presence of Prieto, in a personal capacity, implied the co-operation of the Socialists. It was a figure from the past, Alcalá Zamora, a Republican convert of a year's standing, who became the central figure of the conspiracy, because his promise of a conservative Catholic republic would reassure the bourgeoisie on the right: it was symbolic that he was arrested for conspiracy coming home from mass. Thus a cacique from Andalusia, a Liberal politician remembered for his emotional anti-Catalanism, became the chairman of the Revolutionary Committee set up at San Sebastian to overthrow the monarch he had served as a minister; this committee was to become the

Provisional Government of the Second Republic.

The rebellion was planned for 15 December, but at the last moment changes of plan confused the conspirators; on the 12th one of them, Captain Galán, rose at Jaca, an Aragonese garrison town. He was to become the martyr of Republicanism; his action was that of a megalomaniac who dreamed of becoming the Robespierre of the Republic. He would liberate women, impose birth control, and set up a world council of the Republic of Humanity. His rising was ineptly directed and the rebels, without food or transport, were easily defeated by loyal troops.[3] The Madrid conspirators, taken by surprise, were compelled to follow his action by issuing a mimeographed manifesto, signed by members of the Revolutionary Committee, who were promptly arrested by the government. The leaders of the UGT and the PSOE were divided and inept; they were unable to call a general strike in the capital. A few bar pianos playing the 'Marseillaise', a few groups of undecided workmen, had been the only overt signs of rebellion. Neither the army nor the workers, controlled by the reformist leadership of the UGT, had moved and the only serious support was given by a series of peaceful general strikes in provincial capitals.

To outside observers the government had mastered an unsupported rebellion and a mood of pessimism overwhelmed Republicans. Yet the failure of the December plot was the greatest blessing for the future Republic; had it succeeded, the Republic would have come, observed a Republican, as a result of yet another *militarada*. Its failure and the martyrdom of Galán and his fellow conspirator Hernández, whose execution was exploited as an example of Alfonso's personal cruelty, accelerated a conversion of opinion to a Republican solution. Throughout the Republic portraits of Galán and Hernández were to be found pinned on working-class walls.

It was Berenguer's long-postponed summons for a Cortes to meet in March 1931 which exposed the attrition that was working havoc in the monarchical forces. In February, to his surprise, his offer of an election was met by a wave of abstentions; party leaders refused to accept his election as sincere while the old government-appointed municipalities were still in being. The bottom had dropped out of Berenguer's planned return to normality; he therefore resigned.

The King now did what he might have done with success a year before: he called on Sánchez Guerra to form a ministry, accepting his terms of a constituent Cortes and the temporary suspension of the royal prerogatives. Sánchez Guerra visited the imprisoned Revolutionary Committee which rejected his offers. The consultations achieved nothing except to

[3] M. Tuñon de Lara, 'La sublevación de Jaca', in *Historia 16* no.1 (May 1976), 57–64.

reveal that the monarchy was 'already in the antechambers of the revolution' and that the imprisoned Revolutionary Committee was more powerful than the King himself. This strangely old-fashioned crisis was resolved by the appointment of Admiral Aznar as Prime Minister, with a Cabinet of old-fashioned monarchist politicians—both La Cierva and Romanones were ministers. The concession of municipal elections was the ministry's bid for popularity and acceptance by opinion.

The Aznar government rapidly lost what prestige surrounded its inception: from the outset it was divided between those like La Cierva, who believed the monarchy could and should resist to the point of armed conflict, and those like Romanones who put their faith in concession. From the cells of the Model Prison the Revolutionary Committee saw its influence grow. The trial of the Committee was turned into a Republican demonstration: the defendants were allowed to come from prison in private cars and were treated by the public as the future governors of Spain. On top of all came the worst of the student riots. Students barricaded themselves in the Medical Faculty and fired on Civil Guards; the Minister of the Interior came to terms with the Dean and withdrew his forces. Afraid of creating martyrs by strong measures, the government trusted to a victory in the forthcoming elections as the only hope.

On the eve of Sunday, 12 April, the returns from the municipal elections in the provincial capitals came in; to the stupefaction of the ministry the Republican–Socialist bloc had triumphed in the large towns. Though there was a majority of monarchist municipal councillors elected in Spain as a whole, Republicans could argue that 'numbers' (i.e. the larger constituencies) and 'intellect' (i.e. the 'enlightened' urban voter) had rejected, in what they treated as a plebiscite, a monarchy acceptable only to rural caciques.

The events from Sunday to Tuesday have been raked over by historians to establish responsibilities for the final débâcle and the rejection of La Cierva's passionate pleas to the King that he should soldier on.

From the monarchist point of view there were three men who abandoned hope. Berenguer, as Minister of War, in the small hours of Monday morning sent a telegram to all Captains General which seemed to imply that the army should accept the verdict of 'the national will'. Sanjurjo, as commander of the Civil Guard, let the government—and perhaps the Revolutionary Committee—think that he would not commit his forces to a last-ditch defence of the monarchy in the streets. The reasons for the two men's actions are clear: they did not wish to destroy the harmony of a military family already divided in its loyalties, or to make the army the predestined sacrificial victim of a victorious Republic.

The final surrender was negotiated by Romanones, independently of his divided Cabinet colleagues. On the morning of 14 April he proposed to the Revolutionary Committee that they should wait till the full results came in and for the general election. Alcalá Zamora refused all concessions and demanded that the King leave the country by that evening; he made it clear that the Committee knew of Sanjurjo's 'negative *pronunciamiento*'. 'I said no more,' Romanones confessed; 'the battle was irretrievably lost.' To his critics he had gone to the committee 'with a white flag', already convinced 'that the monarchy of Alfonso XIII had passed into history'.[4]

The King's intentions during Sunday and Monday are unclear. His only course would have been to remain *in situ* until a general election which might have inflicted an even more decisive defeat on the monarchy. But if the street agitation that began on the afternoon of 14 April became serious this would risk a bloody repression against cities like Barcelona and Seville which had already declared for the Republic. Alfonso decided to leave Spain at 6.30 in the evening. The Revolutionary Committee could scarcely believe their luck; Miguel Maura called a taxi and, pushing through the crowds, installed the Provisional Government in the Ministry of the Interior.

There are such things as purely political events, and one such was the fall of the Bourbon monarchy. It was all very sudden. 'The fall of the monarchy', wrote Alfonso's polo tutor, 'gave me a greater shock than any fall from a pony.' There was no economic crisis. The sharp reversal of the public spending of the dictator had had, as yet, no serious consequences. A rash of strikes and student riots did not portend a social revolution; but unrest was enough to make 'the interests' desert the monarchy for a Conservative Republic as a better safeguard for the social order. 'We are out of fashion,' Alfonso complained.

There can be no doubt that the 'negative *pronunciamiento*' of the army and the morale of the security forces dealt the final blow. All government services were subject to a creeping paralysis, a loss of confidence; the government, wrote Miguel Maura, was possessed by 'the suicide complex that gripped the governing class of the monarchy', by the psychology of 'abandonism'. General Mola describes how he found his office invaded by journalists, his security forces riddled by jealousies, inefficient, corrupt, and ill-equipped—the Madrid police had to use taxis which were scarce in times of crisis. Officers and men alike sensed that a republic was coming and acted accordingly by failing to arrest their future masters. Tired out by student riots and strikes, the police voted Republican, it was said, in order to get a good night's sleep.

[4] J. Pabón, *Días de ayer* (1963), 367–433.

8 The Second Republic 1931–1936

On the day after the declaration of the Republic Ortega wrote: 'Whether we like it or not, after 14 April we shall all be something other than we were.' Not merely people would be somehow or other transformed; the Republic would be a 'new dawn'—the phrase was current in April—in Spanish politics. Yet it has become popular to describe the Republic as 'the monarchy disguised'. Political mores did not change overnight. There were eighteen governments in just over five years with the President of the Republic manipulating a series of political crises in the manner of Alfonso XIII; the iconography of the regime, in posed photographs of new ministries, reflected this continuity. Civil Governors were, according to Miguel Maura who appointed them, second-rate party hacks; enchufismo—the 'plugging oneself in'—was a Republican version of the political patronage of the ancien régime; Lerroux's followers were finally discredited in 1936 by a sordid financial scandal in the old style.

Yet this is to emphasize appearances at the expense of reality. The parties of the Republic became what the parties of the monarchy were only beginning to become in 1923: mass parties with programmes appealing to the electorate. Politics penetrated the countryside instead of 'passing through it like an express train', upsetting the old social balances.

We can best understand this phenomenon at local level. A study of a small Arâgonese town has shown how violent, sudden and apparently thorough was this process of mass politicization. The town had been a relatively stable society of smallish proprietors and labourers, historically dominated by the pudientes (the 'powerful ones') who possessed enough land to enable them to set the tone of town life. Suddenly, after April 1931, the tensions between rich and less rich were dramatized and publicized; and they corresponded with the division between Catholic and anti-Catholic. Party organizers came from the city; there were mass meetings. The municipal council became the focal point for the new political rivalries. Personal relations, in the old style, became impossible. Catholics turned religious fiestas into political demonstrations; the left soaped the church steps so that the devout would slip up. Socialist control of labour exchanges destroyed old relationships in agriculture. Even women, excluded from public life in traditional Spain, began to take part in politics.[1]

Why then did the Republic fail to establish itself, falling victim to an army *coup* in July 1936? Apart from the inadequacies of the party system (see p. 122) and the complications of regional politics, it was because, by rhetoric and half measures, the 'Jacobin' governments of 1932–3 and of February 1936 to July 1936 raised expectations among the under-privileged which were not satisfied, while the mere existence of these expectations and of parties to promote them was regarded by the privileged as the prelude to social revolution. Ortega in *The Rebellion of the Masses* had deplored the intrusion of the barbarian mass on to the stage that should be occupied by the élite. Now the barbarians were on stage. It was this process that had brought the masses into politics that the Nationalists' Civil War was fought to reverse: Franco destroyed the mass politics of 'inorganic democracy'.

II

All the members of the 1931 Provisional Government believed that it was the task of the new regime to bring Spanish society up to date, to close the gap between Europe and Spain, however different their recipes for modernization might be. To transform traditional society by democratic parliamentary processes is, at the very least, a difficult task; it is an impossible undertaking on a tight budget. Every reforming enterprise of the Republic was lamed for lack of money: Azaña's military reforms; agrarian reform; Prieto's programme for agricultural regeneration through irrigation; the ambitious projects of a generation of intellectuals in the tradition of the Institute of Free Education (see p. 43) determined to create a 'neutral', lay, educational system.

While it is true that the relatively insulated economy of Spain suffered far less than other European economies from the Great Depression of the '30s, the Republic was unlucky that its advent corresponded with the era of budget slashing and deflation. By 1934 exports had fallen by 75 per cent, industrial production was stagnant, and there were close on a million unemployed, 70 per cent of them in the countryside.[2]

With all the difficulties created by world economic circumstance the Republic's failure to finance reform by altering the distribution of income exposed its dilemma. In its early years it was a bourgeois concern supported by reformist Socialists who shared the budgetary orthodoxy of

[1] Cf. C. Lisón Tolosana, *Belmonte de los caballeros* (1966).
[2] See A. Balcells, *Crisis económica y agitación social en Cataluña 1930–1936* (1971), 30–142.

the British Labour Government when confronted with a recession, and who feared the political and social consequences of dismantling capitalism by a stout blow. There was no point, Prieto argued, in socializing misery and promoting a fascist reaction. No Republican government could bump up revenue by forcing through a tax reform that would shift the burden of taxation away from regressive indirect taxes, which hit rich and poor alike, to a progressive tax on income.

The result was doubly unfortunate. Reform perished through lack of funds and the very prospect of reform threw into opposition a conservative class whose economic and social power remained much as it was in 1931. The agrarian reform was intended to dismantle a 'feudal establishment'. It was a threat rather than a resolute attack and the economic establishment was left *in situ*.

That left-wing Republicans between 1931 and 1936 and their Socialist allies failed as social revolutionaries became the standard accusation of Marxists. Since all the governmental parties *in 1931* were democrats concerned with making a parliamentary democracy acceptable, they can scarcely be blamed for refusing to institute a revolutionary dictatorship as the instrument to destroy conservative interests by decree. They paid a high price for their respect for the democratic processes, for settling for 'humanist socialism', as the compromise between the Republican left and the Socialists was termed. The conservative interests they failed to render innocuous consistently blocked even modest social reform (and thus disabused Socialists with the bourgeois Republic), finally combining with military rebels in 1936 to destroy democracy for forty years. In Sender's novel, when militiamen enter the house of an aristocrat on the outbreak of the Civil War they marvel that 'having all this the Duke wanted more and rebelled to get it'.

III

The political history of the Second Republic can be divided into four phases. First, the constituent period from April to December 1931 which ended with the promulgation of the Republican constitution of 1932 and the collapse of the Provisional Government; second, the swing to the left with the Republican–Socialist coalition under Azaña which lasted until its defeat in the elections of November 1933; third, the phase dominated by the right which, in turn, suffered electoral defeat in the Popular Front elections of February 1936; finally, the descent into the Civil War unleashed by the military *coup* of 18 July 1936.

Like the provisional government of the French Republic of 1848, which Marx described as 'a compromise between the different classes which together had overturned the throne but whose interests were mutually antagonistic', the government presided over by Alcalá Zamora was, in terms of political conviction and party history, such a mixed bunch that it could agree on little but principles of good intent. The Prime Minister, whose main attributes were an astonishing memory and a talent for the florid political oratory of the *ancien régime*, and his Minister of the Interior Miguel Maura, strong-willed and emotional, represented the Catholic conservative wing of the government. Their ambition was to found a Conservative centre party. The now 'tamed lion' of the Radical Republican party, Lerroux, though still committed to a secular society, was emerging as the leader of the middle classes alarmed by the radicalism of his Socialist ministerial colleagues.[3] Like Alcalá Zamora, Lerroux believed in a Republic open to all Spaniards, regardless of their political past or their social class, provided they accepted the Republic as the legal government; what this meant was a conservative Republic of order—in Lerroux's phrase, 'revolutionary against conservative reaction: conservative against the revolution'.

The notion of an open Republic managed by some centre coalition was unacceptable to the left wing of the government. For them the Republic must be for Republicans; it must have a Republican content which entailed loyalty to a specific programme beyond mere loyalty to a particular form of government. To open the Republic to the right would destroy its 'content'. The strong man of the left was Manuel Azaña, Secretary of the Ateneo—all the members of the Cabinet except for Largo Caballero were *Atenistas*, a striking proof of the influence of intellectuals and pseudo-intellectuals in what was called the Republic of Professors. The Radical Socialists were the Jacobins of the ministry. Their social radicalism was overshadowed by their violent anti-clericalism. The Socialists were represented by the rivals for the leadership of the movement: Prieto the journalist and friend of the bourgeois Republicans; Largo Caballero, the ex-plasterer who had left school at seven.

However much the legalism of the Provisional Government persuaded it to postpone fundamental reforms till the meeting of the constituent Cortes, urgent problems demanded action. The Socialists were concerned with the pool of agrarian unemployment, the plight of the small tenant farmer, and the achievement of a machinery for wage settlements that would strengthen their union. Azaña was committed to a democratic reform of the army. The Catalan question demanded an immediate solution.

[3] O. Ruiz Manjón, op.cit., 205 ff.

Socialist concern with the fate of the landless labourers was prompted by the mushroom growth of their own landworkers' union, the Federación Nacional de Trabajadores de la Tierra (FNTT), from 36,000 members in December 1931 to roughly 400,000 a year later—37 per cent of the total membership of the UGT. Largo Caballero, as Minister of Labour, issued decrees which forbade landowners to employ labour from outside the municipality as they had done to lower wages and break strikes; leases were frozen in order to favour the tenant farmer; agricultural labourers were granted access to the Mixed Committees to settle labour disputes. These decrees, which were the first modest attempt of any government to do something to alleviate the lot of the most depressed class in Spain, were resisted—and sabotaged—by conservatives as indefensible attacks on private property and economically counter-productive.

A spate of decrees applied to all workers: an eight-hour day, sickness benefits, holidays with pay. Most important was the remodelling of the Mixed Committees inherited from the dictatorship which gave increased powers to the workers' representatives. The Committees became the fief of a new Socialist bureaucracy. With the only effective means of improving wages and conditions in its own hands, the UGT was in a strong position against the CNT with its lack of 'socialist sensibility'. But once the Socialists' defence of the economic stability of a bourgeois Republic led them to resist 'excessive' wage demands, the bureaucrats were in danger of coming under attack by an unsatisfied, increasingly militant base. As we shall see, the political defeat of the Socialists in the elections of November 1933, which deprived Largo Caballero of his patronage as Minister of Labour, combined with his concern over the radicalization of the masses were to turn him from the enthusiastic collaborator with the left Republicans into the proponent of a Socialist take-over. The bourgeois Republic proved incapable of taking the first step on the Marxist road to socialism: the destruction of 'feudalism'.

Azaña's military reforms were intended to produce an efficient modern army to replace an army overloaded with officers. Nearly half the generals and 40 per cent of the officers accepted his offer of retirement on full pensions. Even so, the army remained lopsided and the anti-militarist vigour with which the remaining aspects of the reforms were imposed alienated army opinion when, according to Mola, the vast majority of officers had accepted the Republic. Azaña's 'Black Cabinet' of military advisers fell into the error of politicizing promotions and thus disrupting 'the harmony of the military family'. In August 1932 Sanjurjo, sacked as chief of the Civil Guard, hoped, vainly, that these discontents would provide recruits for a successful *pronunciamiento* (see p. 125).

IV

The task of modernizing Spain began in earnest with the constituent Cortes elected in June 1931. The constitution was drawn up under the chairmanship of a Socialist professor and its single chamber was intended as an instrument for radical reform.

If this was the intention of its authors it was thwarted in practice by the mechanisms of parliamentarianism as they developed in the Second Republic. It was characteristic of the sudden arrival of democracy that parties were numerous (twenty-six in the constituent Cortes of 1931), ill-disciplined, and divided from each other and within themselves; moreover, the whole party system was complicated by the existence of regional parties—a left and a right in Catalonia distinct from their Spanish equivalents with whom they had to make deals. Given this multiplicity of parties and factions, no single party achieved more than 115 seats in a Cortes of 470. All governments were perforce coalition governments. Policies had first to be agreed between the competing political families in the Cabinet and then forced on the various supporting groupings in the Cortes. To make the task of turning reformist intentions into legislation even more difficult, the opportunities for filibustering by a wrecking opposition were extensive, and even on vital issues governments were reluctant to use the guillotine. The debates on the Catalan Statute dragged on for four months, prolonged by the 'dead weight' of interventions from prestigious non-party intellectuals like Ortega and Unamuno.[4]

This governmental impotence in the Cortes was particularly evident over three crucial issues: Catalan autonomy; the religious settlement; agrarian reform. Azaña had great difficulties in bringing his Socialist colleagues, conscious of the weakness of their own party in Catalonia, to support a generous autonomy statute for the province; by giving in to the Socialist demand that labour and social legislation remain with the central government, Azaña ensured that a clash came in 1934 when a conservative government in Madrid was confronted by a left-wing reformist government in Catalonia. In the religious settlement the doctrinaire anti-clericalism which gave the Radical Socialists their political identity caused endless parliamentary difficulties. The component parties of successive governments were divided over agrarian reform and these divisions were exploited in the Cortes debates. Agrarian reform began to get government muscle only after February 1936.

All the coalition governments of the Republic—with the exception of

4 Ventura Gassol, Generalidad Counsellor for Culture, in reply to Unamuno. Quoted S. Varela, *Partidos y parlamento en la Segunda República* (1978), 161.

the 'constructive' phase of the Azaña coalition and the governments of the Popular Front between February and July 1936—were liable to destruction by the withdrawal of a faction or a revolt within a precarious parliamentary majority. All but two of the eighteen ministries of the Republic fell as the result of an internal crisis, much in the style of the crises of the parliamentary monarchy. Much of the failure of the Republic to 'solve' the social problems of the '30s must be attributed to this insecure political superstructure.

V

It was not the democratic radicalism or the social content of the constitution but its religious settlement that enraged conservatives, split the Cabinet, and created the opportunity for a rally on the right to defend a persecuted Church.

The attack on the privileged position of the Catholic Church was understandable, given the enormous emotional significance of the Church as a pillar of the *ancien régime*; but it was a godsend to conservatives searching for a decent stick with which to beat the Republic. Anti-clericalism was part of the Spanish progressive tradition or, as Prieto put it more crudely, 'its only intellectual baggage'. The creation of a lay state and secular education was the historic mission of Republicanism; in the words of *El Socialista*, the PSOE daily, it was 'an elementary aspiration of democracy'. With the benefits of hindsight we can see (especially since the Vatican would have gone a long way to come to terms with the new government) that the attack on the Church was a mistaken priority. Article 26 of the new constitution and the subsequent legislation separated Church and State, expelled the Jesuits, and clipped the Regular Orders' control over education. It must be admitted that, however conciliatory the Vatican may have been, Catholic influence over education was the one thing it would not surrender and this was, at the same time, the one thing that the left Republicans were determined to destroy.

In May 1931 the Provisional Government did nothing to stop a savage outburst of what Ortega called 'Mediterranean fetishism'—the church-burning which had been a standard performance of Spanish extreme radicalism. It started in Madrid as a protest against a monarchist meeting. Only Miguel Maura, Minister of the Interior, demanded that the Civil Guard should be used; the rest of the government, fearful of its popularity should there be casualties, did nothing. For this act of political cowardice Azaña must take the blame.

The defence of a 'persecuted Church' provided the rallying cry of the right. Gil Robles (see p. 127 ff.), who was to make his political career as the leader of this Catholic reaction, called the Republican legislation not merely an injustice but an error. 'The religious problem from that moment [the passing of Article 26] was converted into a battle-cry, sharpening to the point of paroxysm the combat between the two Spains.'

It is characteristic of the Second Republic that the right both gained the propaganda value of 'persecution' and yet avoided its consequences; the legislation against the schools of Regular Orders was evaded by subterfuge—the formation of limited companies which ran schools staffed by monks and nuns in civilian clothing while the rachitic finances of the state could not provide alternatives. But with the legalization of divorce, the creation of secular cemeteries, and the removal of the crucifix from schools, it seemed to traditionalists that Spain was to be given over to the excesses of materialism and free love. It was not that the faithful were driven into the catacombs. They suffered, rather, a host of minor persecutions at the hands of some of the new Republican municipalities: fines for ringing of church bells, prohibition of religious processions; the removal of religious sculptures on the façades of churches; the civil burial of those who had not, in their wills, specified a religious burial.

Alcalá Zamora and Miguel Maura had long been uneasy at what they regarded as a drift towards a sectarian, 'exclusive' Republic dominated by a majority formed by Azaña's left Republicans and the Socialists. Article 26 they could not swallow, nor tolerate the 'glacial hostility' and vindictive rancour of its supporters. They resigned on 14 October 1931. Alcalá Zamora became the Republic's first President under the new constitution; Azaña succeeded him as Prime Minister with a government which included the Socialists. The Socialists paid a high price for power and for their initial conviction that the Republicans would carry through a bourgeois revolution, in restraining their own militants from pressing 'unacceptable demands' (Prieto, for instance, broke a strike of the multinational Telephone Company); their alliance with bourgeois Republicans in government would last only as long as the minimum demands of the party could be satisfied. Yet even the most modest reforms were resisted by conservatives (the Basques and the Agrarians in the Cortes) as the prolegomena to a Socialist take-over. 'What is all this talk of handing over the Republic to the Socialists?' Azaña declared. 'When will this fantasy end?' But the fantasy worked. Lerroux, as the *caudillo* of conservative resistance to creeping socialism, was, after the June elections, the leader of the single largest party in the constituent Cortes. Azaña regarded Lerroux and his Radicals as morally discredited and intellectually old-hat; to the Socialists they constituted the main impediment to the introduction of socialist measures in a bourgeois democracy. The Radicals had been excluded from Azaña's government. To conservatives, the Republic had fallen into the sectarian hands of Masons and Marxists.

The government's reformist programme—the autonomy statute for Catalonia and agrarian reform—was being mauled in the Cortes when Azaña's position was strengthened by a forlorn attempt to revive nineteenth-century procedures: the *pronunciamiento* of General Sanjurjo in Seville (10 August 1932). It aimed to install a right-wing Republican government in place of a government that had ceased to represent 'the nation', whose unity it threatened to destroy by giving in to Catalan 'separatists'. The *coup* was a fiasco and in Madrid Azaña watched its collapse with cold satisfaction; he could point the lesson that talk of a Republic open to the right had ended in a military rising by making 'idiot generals believe that the country would support them'. But no significant portion of the country was then prepared to support a discontented general. By 1936 the equation had changed.

Thus strengthened, Azaña could push through the Catalan Statute and the Law of Agrarian Reform.

The Catalan Statute appeared as the one substantial success of the new regime. In the euphoria of April 1931 it seemed for a moment as if Catalonia would put in jeopardy the whole future of the Republic as a Spanish government. The dominant force was now the Catalan Republican left, the Esquerra. A mushroom growth, it was a party of petty bourgeois and intellectuals with the support of the *rabassaires* whose threatened tenancies (see p. 19) it defended. It was also the party of the national hero Maciá and his lieutenant, Companys. Maciá declared on 14 April for an independent Catalan state in an Iberian federal republic. He was persuaded to withdraw and accept that Catalonia be granted a provisional government—the Generalidad—which would draft an autonomy statute and submit it to a plebiscite and ratification by the constituent Cortes. Maciá made clear that the sacrifice of independence was only relative: 'a privation, for a brief interlude, of a part of the sovereignty to which we have a right'.

The Generalidad's draft of the Catalan Autonomy Statute was overwhelmingly endorsed in the plebiscite. 'At last we are free,' Maciá told enthusiastic crowds. 'No human power will be able to thwart the will of the Catalan people. . . . Catalonia will become great among the civilized nations.' In the Cortes the Statute revived the old accusations by conservatives of covert separatism. Azaña's speech in support of the Statute was his finest and the Statute, as modified by the Cortes, satisfied the minimum demands of the Esquerra. It set about the task of

Catalanization, from the reform of the university to the changing of street names and the labelling of museum exhibits. That there would be serious conflicts when powers were transferred to the Generalidad and when the governments of Madrid and Barcelona were of opposing political persuasions, was not apparent in the atmosphere of mutual congratulation.

If the Catalan Statute appeared as a triumph over the past, the Law of Agrarian Reform was a crucial failure.

Agrarian reform in a democratic society which respects existing property rights and has not the financial resources to compensate for the expropriation of large landowners is a contradiction in terms. In Spain, the legal and technical complexities of reform were exploited by a ruthless opposition in marathon debates. The Republicans, many of whom came from the urban petty bourgeoisie, had no gut-feeling for the plight of the agrarian dispossessed—Azaña made no speech on the agrarian issue. The Agrarian Law of 1932 gave the Republic the legal instrument to tackle the agrarian question; but it did not provide the cash or the determination. Starved of money—its budget was less than half the expenditure on the Civil Guard—the Institute of Agrarian Reform handed over to peasant settlers an area the size of one huge estate. The Agrarian Law was typical of the Republic's reforms in that it was mild in practice but threatening in principle. 'It seriously threatened the strongest economic class in Spain ... and awakened the hopes of the impoverished peasantry.'[5] Moreover, though the Law was intended to break up the great absentee-owned estates, it threatened some 70,000 modest proprietors—an aspect insistently criticized by the right, which aimed to create an alliance of poor farmers and rich landowners—and created a general atmosphere of uncertainty in the countryside. This helped to turn the peasants of Castile against a Republic that had made the mistake of allowing imports of wheat in a year of a bumper harvest.

The failure of agrarian reform was central to the fate of the Republic. The Socialist Federation of Agricultural Workers (FNTT) had so grown in strength that the Socialist leaders could not be indifferent to demand for redistribution of land. The failure of the Republic to deal with the agrarian problem therefore disabused leaders like Largo Caballero of the possibilities of socialist progress within a bourgeois democracy.

VI

By the summer of 1933 the prestige of the Azaña government was, in the Spanish phrase, 'exhausted'. It had long lost the enthusiastic support of

---

[5] The verdict of Edward Malefakis, whose *Agrarian Reform and Peasant Revolution in Spain* (1970) is central to understanding the history of the Second Republic.

the older generation of intellectuals who had greeted April 1931 as a new dawn. Ortega declared, 'This [the Republic] is not it'; Unamuno's attacks were consistently bitter. Under fire from both left and right, its glamour was clouded by sterile debates and the repression of outbreaks of rural violence which culminated in the 'massacre of Casas Viejas'. Moreover its political base, the working alliance of left Republicans and Socialists, was in peril. Besteiro, the Marxist professor, opposed a collaboration which had brought no rewards. By the summer of 1933 Largo Caballero, the apostle of collaborationism, declared his conviction that 'to accomplish socialist aims in a bourgeois democracy is impossible'.

The revolutionary left of the CNT had never accepted the Republic and scorned Socialist reformism as treason. Prieto broke CNT strikes mounted by the 'brutally ignorant leadership' of a 'labour organization based on pistols'. The CNT fell into the hands of extremists. Pestaña and the moderate syndicalists were expelled. The CNT was now in the grip of the 'representatives of revolutionary romanticism'—the Federación Anarquista Ibérica (FAI), determined to keep the movement true to anarchist purity: to the FAI, which had been moulded in the political morality of clandestinity during the dictatorship of Primo, parliamentary democracy was a farce and the Cortes 'a brothel'. 'Our revolution is made, not on the benches of Parliament but in the streets.' In January 1932 and 1933 they dragged the movement into abortive attempts at social revolution.

The conservative Catholic right had no popular party to represent it in the constituent Cortes except for the Basque-Navarese bloc and a handful of Agrarians: *faute de mieux* the conservative-minded had voted for Lerroux. In the November elections of 1933 this was no longer the case; the Catholic right had built up a modern mass party—the CEDA, a confederation of Catholic parties.

The new party sprang from the group of political Catholics whose mentor, Angel Herrera, was the former editor of the daily *El Debate*; its leader was José María Gil Robles (b.1898), whose pear-shaped figure hid a powerful debater and formidable mass orator.

The immediate aim of the CEDA was the defence of the persecuted Church against the onslaught of the secularizing left. Its ultimate aim was the implanting in Spain of a Catholic corporate state. The problem arose over means. It professed the doctrine of 'accidentalism' (i.e. that forms of government were immaterial provided Catholic interests were respected) and the old Catholic tactic of accepting and exploiting the 'lesser evil'. Thus without openly acknowledging the Republic it could operate as a legal political party within it.

The nature and fate of the CEDA is one of the keys to the fall of the

Second Republic. What was it? Was Gil Robles a 'fascist' out to destroy democracy, or was he ready to accept its processes provided he was allowed to use them? As the election speeches of November 1933 prove, Gil Robles' 'accidentalism was not far removed from the position of those Socialists who argued that democracy was acceptable provided it was a socialist democracy. To his opponents 'accidentalism' was a sham and, as long as his party was financed by rich monarchists, he kept it together by studied ambiguities and by outbursts against decadent democracies. 'We must impose our will with all the force of our rightness, and with other forces if this is insufficient. The cowardice of the Right has allowed those who come from the cesspools of iniquity to take control of the destinies of the fatherland.'

At the time and since, it has been argued that these outbursts made clear Robles' hidden intention to destroy the Republic by *violent* means. He resisted the pressures of the monarchists in the party: after Sanjurjo's military *coup* the activists were expelled. 'The right', Gil Robles later confessed, 'had no other means of gaining power than by using the established regime [i.e. the Republic], introducing themselves into it and *making it their own.*' Was this not, his enemies argued, to use Trojan horse tactics to modify democracy out of existence and substitute for it the institutions of the corporate state? 'Deep down,' the Socialist Prieto argued, 'Gil Robles wanted a dictatorship.' His verbal concessions to the right of his party—and it can be argued that the duty of a party leader is to keep his party together at all costs—merely confirmed this suspicion.

Just as the Socialists were divided, so was the CEDA. Even after the monarchist activists had been expelled it embraced monarchist conservatives and genuine Christian Democrats like Jiménez Fernández, who, as CEDA Minister of Agriculture in 1934–5, tried to implement his ideal of a property-owning peasantry and the social policies of Leo XIII and Pius XI. But the social programme of the CEDA remained a dead letter in a party weighed down by the conservatives on its right. It became more and more a party of the frightened upper and middle classes and in the end Gil Robles gave party funds to the conspirators of July 1936.

To the right of the CEDA were those who could not accept the ambiguities of Gil Robles' 'accidentalism'; counter-revolutionaries, they were committed to the violent overthrow of the Marxist Republic. They found a theological justification for violence in sixteenth-century theological treatises on 'resistance to tyranny'. The Carlists were openly arming in Navarre and though the plans for a dynastic fusion with the Alfonsine monarchists collapsed on the intransigence of the Integrists, the Carlists were co-operating with militant Alfonsine aristocrats who had become disciples of the French counter-revolutionary right. They were not a serious electoral threat; but they believed that the Republic must be overthrown and were ready to conspire actively against it.

In September 1933 Azaña finally resigned and elections were called for November.

These elections revealed the consequences of the electoral laws of the Republic. In order to end the *caciquismo* that flourished in the manipulable single-member constituencies of the monarchy, the new voting system was by lists in large constituencies. This was to favour the widest electoral coalitions and eliminate those parties that fought alone. In 1933 the system favoured the right, because it formed such a coalition while the Socialists and left Republicans fought separately. The Socialists lost half their seats and the left Republicans were almost wiped out.

The election was characterized by oratorical violence: 'The triumph of reaction [i.e. the victory of the right at the polls] must be avoided', declared Largo Caballero, 'first in the ballot box, then in the streets.' Gil Robles was making similar threatening noises. The tragedy of the Republic was that, in the end, those who used inflammatory language had to live out their rhetoric. Since Gil Robles won an electoral victory that allowed him to ease first his party and finally himself into power, his threats did not materialize. Largo Caballero and his party, fighting the elections without the Republican left, lost. Their threats became, in October 1934, a reality.

VII

The left came to regard the 'Two Black Years' (December 1933–February 1936) as a period of quasi-fascist government. Rather than governments of resolute reaction, the unstable coalitions of Lerroux and Gil Robles represented what Gil Robles was later to call 'the suicidal egoism of the rich'; it was a 'sterile period' devoted to the reversal of the work of the Azaña coalition, from the restoration of priests' salaries to the sacking of ministry cleaners. The CEDA was revealed as a coalition of rigid conservatives which rejected the schemes for agrarian reform, proposed by the handful of social Catholics within the party, as 'Bolshevik' if not a heretical interference with private property rights. Perhaps the most revealing symptom of a period when governments let landowners have it their own way was the sharp drop in rural wages and the spate of evictions.

While the left—as we shall call the components of the Azaña coalition—could scarcely reject a Lerroux ministry as a threat to the survival of democracy, it regarded as inadmissible the claim of Gil Robles, now leader of the largest single party in the Cortes, to enter the government. To the left, above all to the Socialists, his 'accidentalism' was the tactic of a *führer* of the right, hiding an intention to establish an authoritarian corporate state from within democracy. The issue was confused by accusations of lack of loyalty to the *form* of a republic. This was not the point. Gil Robles would have been content with a conservative, clerical republic. The Socialists were equally prepared to legislate a socialist society into existence. They were as guilty of the sin of accidentalism as Gil Robles. It was clear, too, that Republicans to the left of Lerroux would boycott a ministry that included *Cedistas* as threatening to modify the 'content' of the Republic as bequeathed by Azaña.

Gil Robles declared himself to be anti-Marxist. To Socialists 'an anti-Marxist Front is a Fascist Front'. With the fate of European Socialists at the hands of Dollfuss and Hitler in mind, in February 1934 the party prepared for armed revolution should the CEDA enter the government. Its instrument would be the Workers' Alliance, to include all proletarian parties and unions. In October three CEDA ministers— scarcely a fascist take-over—entered the government. Ill-prepared (the Workers' Alliance was a reality only in Asturias where it included the CNT, the Socialists, and the Communists), the Socialist party lurched into a revolution. The leadership was propelled by its own youth movements (on right and left youth movements were becoming more powerful), and by a conviction that failure to revolt against a Spanish Dollfuss would be 'the death certificate of the party'.

The October 1934 revolution was a heroic proletarian epic only in Asturias: the workers set up a Socialist Republic defended by a 'red army' militia. In Catalonia the revolution was a fiasco. When the Generalidad passed a law favouring the tenant *rabassaires*, a constitutional conflict developed between the Generalidad controlled by the Catalan left—the Esquerra—and the conservative Radical government in Madrid. The Esquerra's rural strength was based on the *rabassaires*; the Madrid government supported the Catalan landlords who regarded the law as an outrageous and unconstitutional attack on property rights. Compromise failed and Companys was driven to 'revolution' by a handful of fascistoid nationalists. As Maciá had done in April 1931, he declared for a Catalan state in a federal republic. The CNT stood aside, denied arms by the nationalists. and the *rabassaires* could not march on Barcelona. Companys capitulated and was arrested.

The revolution of October was an irresponsible act. If the Socialists intended a revolution, with the Workers' Alliance in a poor way they lacked the means. If Largo Caballero (smarting at his electoral defeat in 1933 which had deprived him and his party of the immense patronage of the Ministry of Labour) intended by the threat of a revolution merely to force Alcalá Zamora to re-install the Azaña coalition, then he and the more militant Socialists who had ousted the moderates in February badly overplayed their hand. Though the left Republicans did not participate in the revolution and had intended by threats and by disowning the government merely to force the President's hand, they would have taken power if it had been handed to them 'by the streets'. Madariaga's verdict must stand—even if it was later assiduously circulated by General Franco's apologists. By revolting against an elected government in October 1934, the forces of the left denied themselves the legal if not the moral possibility of denouncing the rising of July 1936.

VIII

It was the repression of the October revolution that created the political will and emotional solidarity for the re-creation of the Azaña coalition of Socialists and left Republicans (with the addition of the Communists, who claimed a heroic role in the Asturias revolution) in order to fight the February elections as the Popular Front. It won the elections by a narrow majority. The conservative forces in Spanish society still represented roughly half the nation. By 1936 the process of polarization (induced, as has been said, by the necessity of large electoral coalitions at the mercy of their more extreme components), already evident in the 1933 elections, was intensified. But whereas in 1933 the left had been caught in the disarray of disunity, in 1936 it was the right that found the patching up of electoral pacts difficult.

The Socialists did not join the government which was committed to the programme of 'humanist socialism'. The split which went back to the days of Primo de Rivera now came to the surface in what often appeared to be a bitter personal quarrel between Prieto and Largo Caballero for control of the Socialist movement.[6] Prieto was in favour of co-operation with the bourgeois Republic and would have been willing in May to re-form the Azaña coalition in government. Largo Caballero, the apostle of collaboration with the left Republicans when it gave him the powers and patronage to build up the UGT as the best defence for the workers, now considered the Popular Front as 'an alliance with no future'. Alarmed by the possibility of losses on his left to the more resolute revolutionaries of the CNT, he was talking of a workers' take-over to be engineered by constant extra-parliamentary pressure on the government. In his Marxist outbursts it appeared to moderates like Besteiro that the

[6] For the Socialists' internal divisions see Paul Preston, *The Coming of the Spanish Civil War* (1978), 131 ff.

cold bureaucrat of reformism was now 'playing the part of a mad fanatic'. Yet Largo was no Spanish Lenin. Far from edging towards revolution, the moderates in the party were gaining influence and Largo himself cooling down.

The military conspirators justified their rebellion on the grounds that they were thwarting an organized Communist plot. This was a propaganda invention based on a great deal of talk about revolution which convinced the 'respectable classes', fearful of some general societal collapse of which pornography and the Republican divorce laws were a symptom, that they were on the edge of some Spanish 1917. 'All the militants,' wrote a sympathetic observer in May, 'both anarchists and socialists, believe that only an armed insurrection can give decisive victory to the workers.' But in so far as there was any plan beyond rhetoric, it was based on the prospect of a revolutionary counter-*coup* to defeat a right-wing rising. This is precisely what happened.

The hard right had long seen no alternative to the counter-revolution of violence based on an army rising. The National Bloc of their leader, Calvo Sotelo, was to the conspirators 'a cover-up, a stimulus to the military *coup*'.[7] Gil Robles' 'milk and water' legalism and famous 'tactic' had failed. Once the Basque Provinces of Guipúzcoa and Vizcaya accepted the godless Republic of 'Jews, Masons, and Communists' in return for the promise of autonomy, Carlist Navarre became the bastion of a militant Catholicism committed to a defence of national unity against the 'dissolvent' Basques. It was to be the only region where there was mass support for the rising; the Navarese Requetés, already armed and training in secret, were to prove Franco's best troops.

The Falangist militia were likewise ready for battle. Founded in October 1933, the Falange was a collection of authoritarian nationalist groupings formed around the vivid personality of José Antonio Primo de Rivera, son of the dictator. His aim was to win over the working classes to the *patria* and a dream of Empire, weaning them from Marxism and 'foreign' liberalism. A mixture of rhetorical poetry and gang warfare, a party of students with a sprinkling of enthusiasts from the middle class 'crushed' by the *laissez-faire* capitalism the movement denounced, bankrupt, its organization torn by local feuds and without a single deputy in the Cortes, the Falange scarcely constituted a serious threat; its relations with the rich monarchists who had once seen it as an instrument to overthrow the Republic, were strained; its contacts with the army fragile. Because of its sudden expansion after July and its prominence in the early days, the role of the Falange in the rising has been exaggerated;

[7] See J.A. Ansaldo, ¿*Para Qúe*? (1951), for the conspiratorial right.

its most important contribution was to heighten the atmosphere of violence. The core of the counter-revolution was not this collection of fanatics and dreamers, but the hard conservative right.

All the conspirators realized that without the army the counter-revolution must fail: 'without your force it will be titanically difficult for us to conquer,' José Antonio wrote to Mola. The military conspiracy appeared a ramshackle affair; Mola, since March its organizer, twice contemplated suicide. The hesitations of Franco, who feared for the 'moral unity of the army', drove the active conspirators to despair.

The rising of 17/18 July 1936 was called the 'generals' rising' by the world press. This was a misnomer. The driving forces of the conspiracy were the younger officers; senior officers were, on the whole, loyal to the Republic. Why, given the threat to the 'moral unity' of the army, did the conspirators rise in Morocco and why did sedate family men risk their careers in a hazardous enterprise?

They were true to their middle-class origins and professional interests. 'Officers', wrote Colonel Casado, destined to lead the last *pronunciamiento* of Spanish history, 'lived outside the social and political problems of the world and Spain. They only wanted to better their conditions and receive from people the consideration they believed they deserved.' They had not got better conditions from Republican anti-militarists and, like many middle-class Spaniards, they were not getting the consideration they deserved from the Popular Front. They were also conditioned by a political theory which made them servants of the *nation* and not of any particular government. 'Discipline', wrote General Mola, 'must not be confused with lack of dignity. Indiscipline [i.e. military revolt] is justified when the abuses of power [i.e. the acts of a legal government] constitute opprobrium or lead the nation to ruin. Meek obedience, in the first case, is infamy; in the second, treason.' To General Kindelán, who was to become chief of the Nationalist Air Force, the army was the 'guardian of the values and historical constants of the nation, defending them against whoever seeks to attack them, whether foreign enemies or even the *state itself*'. It was up to the officers' clubs to interpret the general will when betrayed by a government; above all when 'government was in the gutter'. This, to military malcontents, seemed to be the condition of Spain in the summer of 1936. It was the collapse of public order—the extent of this collapse and the degree to which it was exaggerated by the propaganda of the right is open to question—symbolic of some greater social collapse, that brought the army back to its nineteenth-century role as the final arbiter of Spanish political life.

It may seem otiose to labour the point that without the intervention of the army there would have been neither a Civil War nor forty years of

Francoism. Italy has experienced a collapse of social discipline and political stability comparable to that which occurred in Spain in the 'Tragic Summer' of 1936; but there has been no authoritarian *coup* because there is no army to back it. There is a deeper reason: by 1960 Italy was an industrial society. Spain in 1936 was still an agrarian society in the process of industrialization. Such societies are fragile and can be mastered by a resolute minority ready to rally conservative interests against the emergence of mass politics.

9 The Civil War 1936–1939

I

If the conspirators had planned a painless military take-over by sympathetic garrisons in the provincial capitals, followed by a triumphant march on Madrid, they failed. If the government, blinded by optimistic reports, regarded the rising as what the Prime Minister called 'an absurd conspiracy', they were deluded. Where the security forces and the overwhelming majority of the population supported the government or where the military were divided or hesitant, the rising failed: this was true of Madrid, Barcelona, and Valencia. Where junior officers were resolute and leaders enterprising, cities with large working-class populations—Seville and Valladolid, for instance—fell to the rebels. In spite of the role of loyal security forces, the victory of the Popular Front was everywhere presented as a proletarian epic: the siege by the crowd of the Montana Barracks in Madrid; the barricades manned by the CNT in Barcelona. This half-truth gave the unions a moral claim to power as the saviours of the Republic, betrayed by a feeble government of bourgeois Republicans which had refused to arm the workers and sought to come to terms with factious generals.

The patchy success of the rebellion and the subsequent fortunes of war divided Spain into two zones that did not always correspond to social structure or previous political allegiance. The Civil War is incomprehensible without the concept of 'geographical loyalty': those caught in a hostile zone had either to conform, escape, or risk imprisonment or shooting. Loyalty was often a matter of locality.

For the Nationalists (whose cause is more easily defined in negatives—what they were against) the war was a class war against Marxists, a religious war against Masons and free-thinkers, and a war against separatists. The lines of class allegiance were crossed by religious conviction or regional loyalties. Thus the Catholic Basques fought for an 'atheist' Republic which had granted them the self-government the Nationalists were committed to destroying. Respectable Catalan bourgeois, horrified by the assassinations by the 'uncontrollables' of the CNT, for the same reason, supported a government dominated by working-class parties. Nevertheless, where they were free to choose, the working classes chose the Republic and the upper classes were, with few exceptions, fanatic Nationalists. It was the loyalty of the middle class that was in doubt. Many followed in the footsteps of the older generation of intellectuals, disenchanted with the 'proletarian' style of the latter days of the Republic. Communist propagandists set out to capture the loyalty of the 'little man' by presenting the war as the defence of his interests in a bourgeois democracy.

The Civil War separated and split families. There was a generational divide. Falangist students hid their pistols from their parents in hol-lowed-out books; the street dust-ups of the Socialist Youth alarmed the older party members; the Carlist youth found the abrasive oratory of Fal Conde more to their taste than the speeches of the accommodating, aristocratic Rodezno. The military rising itself was an affair of captains and majors; only three generals in command of divisions 'declared' on 18 July. 'In the military, as in the civil sphere,' wrote the Catalan Falangist José María Fontana, 'the bulk of the movement was *cosa de gente joven*—a young people's affair.' If these young enthusiasts imagined they were making a world safe for the under-forties, they were to be sadly disillusioned.

Two factors need emphasis. Firstly, 'the army' as an institution did not revolt. It was divided, and without the loyalty of senior officers the Republic could never have organized an army.[1] If all officers had joined the rising it might have been over in a matter of days: in Madrid the divisions of the garrison doomed the conspirators to be thrown, like rag dolls, from the windows of the Montaña Barracks. The fact that the Nationalist 'army' and the columns of civilian volunteers in metropolitan Spain were, in the early days, a relatively weak fighting force made the African Army under General Franco the decisive element. Without these disciplined units the rising might have turned out to be a disastrous gamble. Once Franco had ferried his troops from Morocco to the mainland his military and, ultimately, his political pre-eminence were assured.

The second decisive factor was the distribution of resources between the two zones. On any calculation, the material resources of the government—from maps to gold reserves—outweighed those of the rebels. In the early days the Republic held the industrial resources of Spain, and the Nationalists more of the rural heartland of Castile together with Andalusia and Galicia. This balance seemed to favour the Republic; but industry demanded imported raw materials and the great cities needed food. Republican exports never covered raw material imports—

[1] For the divisions in the army see R. Salas Larrazabal, *Historia del ejército popular* (1973), especially chs. 1, 2, and 3.

especially after the loss of the mines of the north—and industry was starved; so was the civilian population, struggling by 1938 on a diet of Dr. Negrín's Resistance Pills—lentils—and at the mercy of a new race of black marketeers, listening in secret (this was the first war in which radio was an important weapon) to Nationalist propaganda which promised 'the white bread of Franco'.

II

The Madrid government's first reaction to the military rising that spread from Morocco to the mainland on 18 July was to resign. The response of the proletarian parties was to demand arms for the workers. 'A government that refuses to arm the workers is a Fascist government,' thundered Largo Caballero. This the new government of Martínez Barrio, formed on 19 July, refused to do. By seeking, at the last moment, to negotiate with Mola, it has been accused of failing 'to rise to its historic task' out of fear of a workers' take-over. When Giral's government—again a Cabinet of left Republicans—did arm the workers' militias such a take-over occurred. In every town and village that remained loyal to the Republic the normal machinery of government was replaced by local committees of party militants whose orders were enforced by armleted patrols of militiamen; this was the era of confiscated cars, huge posters, and lorry-loads of enthusiasts with clenched fists.

'The whole state apparatus was destroyed' wrote Dolores Ibarruri, the Communist orator famous as La Pasionaria, 'and power lay in the streets.' It was picked up by the great proletarian organizations: the UGT, the PSOE, and the CNT. The officers' counter-revolution had unleashed the most profound European working-class revolution since 1917. The immediate manifestation of the bohemian stage of this revolution was an outburst of terror and indiscriminate killing which the government could not control: 6,832 priests were slaughtered and churches were burnt. This mindless version of the September massacres of the French Revolution was of great importance. It confirmed the hostility of the upper middle classes and provided Nationalist propagandists with atrocity stories. The pornography of war, they were the emotional cement of 'the Cause'. Barcelona became a city where it was injudicious to wear a tie. In Madrid the rich crowded into embassies, waiting for an opportunity to slip over to the Nationalist zone where waiters and hotel porters existed: 'Now we are gentlemen again,' wrote one of Franco's future ministers on arriving in San Sebastian. The systematic execution of working-class leaders in the Nationalist zone put a river of blood between the working class and the gentlemen.

The constructive side of the summer revolution was contained in the concept of collectivization: the take-over of factories and estates by committees of workers or the unions. Collectivization was most intense where the CNT was dominant; with its epicentre in Catalonia, it must be emphasized that it left whole areas untouched—Madrid, for example, was more 'normal' than Barcelona. Collectivization sometimes institutionalized the *religiosité prolétarienne* of the 'men of ideas'. In industry the 'egoism of centuries' ended, according to the CNT press; on agrarian collectives the brutal force of landowners was replaced by 'social love' in self-governing communities where the local café was closed, money replaced by work chits, and prostitution, alcohol, and visits to the cinema frowned on.

The collectives have been defended as an inspiring social experiment and criticized as 'absurd' in a war economy that cried out for the rational distribution of scarce resources. Certainly the collectives tended to fragment the economy by a process known as 'syndical selfishness', in which each union and collective scrambled for raw materials and preferred higher wages to higher output 'as if in a capitalist system'. The CNT leadership and the Generalidad were fully aware of these shortcomings; but attempts to co-ordinate production via an Economic Council did not produce the CNT utopia of 'a planned economy without state intervention'.

Utopia could not be realized with wartime shortages and with the CNT collectives starved of credit and raw materials by their political enemies. These enemies pointed to the decline in industrial production, to the resentments created by the forced collectivization of artisans, butchers, bakers, and peasant proprietors. 'We succeeded in rousing the villages from their slumber. All the villages which *we control with an iron will* follow the norms of the CNT.'[2] This 'iron will' was exercised at the expense of the small-scale orange producers of the Levante—after 1937 the only export earners of the Republic.

The safeguard of the social revolution was the militia, which was formed by the workers' parties on an *ad hoc* basis, often round the personality of a leader who could bully army officers into giving him weapons or who had commandeered lorries. Units varied in size from a few dozen to the Communist party's Fifth Regiment. In the militia columns military discipline was replaced by revolutionary discipline: elected officers could only enforce orders after a wearying process of consultation; for CNT militiamen to salute an officer was 'a symbol of slavery'. To deploy such units, apt as they were to return home without

[2] See the reports in the Valencian CNT newspaper *Fragua Social* for July 1936.

orders, with any regard to logistics was a nightmare for the regular officers of the general staff.

III

Victory in war is the result of the successful organization of enthusiasm. In André Malraux's words the task of the Republican government at war was 'to organize the Apocalypse'. To prevent the collapse of loyalty in large sectors of the population the excesses of the spontaneous revolution had to be curbed. To conduct a regular war, the control of the central government over improvised committees had to be restored. This dilemma divided the politicians of the Republic: there were those to whom the sacrifice of the conquests of the revolution meant the betrayal of the working class which had saved the Republic in the July days, and those who believed the war against fascism could only be won by a strong centralized government which could mount an efficient war effort—and that meant dismantling the revolutionary conquests and the reversal of the revolution in order to retain a Popular Front embracing the bourgeois parties.

The primacy of revolution was defended by the CNT and the POUM. The latter, a revolutionary workers' party of Trotskyite ideas, but not affiliated with the Fourth Trotskyist International, was led by two able Marxist intellectuals: Joaquín Maurín and Andrés Nin. In the eyes of the POUM, sympathetic to the CNT and, as a small party, dependent on the CNT masses for any effective action, the great fault of anarcho-syndicalism was the large syndicates' dogmatic refusal to seize *political* power, a step they could have taken on 18–19 July and for which an opportunity would never recur.

The proponents of social normality and an orthodox war effort controlled by the central government were the Republican party, the right wing of the Socialist party which followed Prieto, and the Communists.

The Spanish Communists' transformation into social conservatives was partly in response to the policies of Stalin searching for support from Popular Fronts in respectable democracies. The war, therefore, was presented in Communist propaganda as a war to defend a bourgeois democracy 'with a profound social content'. But the Communist defence of ordered government was based on its lack of working-class support in Spain. 'Objective historical conditions do not permit a proletarian revolution.' Recruits must come from the middle classes, scared by the upheavals of July and seeking some stronger protector than the left Republicans who, as Largo Caballero told Stalin, were 'doing very little to assert their own political personality'. This protection the professional classes found in a disciplined party with impeccable proletarian credentials and an immensely efficient propaganda machine, a party that could halt the spontaneous revolution without being accused of betraying the working class.

The rapid growth of the party's strength and influence is explained by its control of the all-important Soviet arms supplies, a leverage denied to Republicans and Socialists who looked in vain for help from their allies in the West. But the Communists would have remained powerless without the support of the left Republicans and Prieto's Socialists. These allies were not Communist dupes; they were conventional politicians appalled by revolutionary chaos, the dissolution of government control—Azaña's diaries reflect his horror at the excesses of July—and the military failures of the militia system. They saw in the Communist party the necessary ally.

IV

How, given the strength of the unions and the mystique of a proletarian revolution, were governmental concentration and a purposeful articulation of the anti-Fascist forces to be achieved? Clearly the task was beyond Giral's pure Republican ministry, which Largo Caballero dismissed as a reactionary farce. The government, as Azaña put it, must either adopt the revolution or repress it. Since it lacked the means, or the resolution, to risk a civil war within the Civil War, there was no alternative but to adopt the revolution in the hope of controlling it.

The task was entrusted to Largo Caballero, who became Prime Minister on 4 September 1936. Obstinate and secretive, avoiding awkward interviews by retiring to bed at nine o'clock, he was to Prieto 'an imbecile'; but he alone possessed the prestige, if not the will, to bring the workers' organizations into a co-operative mood. On 4 November, with Franco's armies outside Madrid, the CNT joined his government. For the first time in European history Communist and anarchist ministers sat with bourgeois colleagues in the same cabinet.

The decision of the CNT leaders to join the government was the most momentous decision in the history of Spanish anarcho-syndicalism. It was to split the movement and to open a rift between the leadership and the militant masses. It meant the rejection of the whole tradition of the movement. Federica Montseny, one of the new ministers, was the daughter of anarchists 'to whom the words *government* and *authority* signified the negation of every possibility of freedom for man'.

The revolution 'we all wanted but none of us expected' was threatened by the Communists and their allies who wished to turn the militia, the safeguard of that revolution, into a disciplined army, dismantle the parallel government of the revolutionary committees, and halt collectivization. For the CNT, joining the government was a defensive move, a last resort to save the revolution, 'to prevent trickery and impose radicalism'. With its power ebbing away, the CNT must shed its principles 'so that we should not be without influence in Spanish public life'. The only alternative would have been to force its principles on Spain by a revolutionary dictatorship; but such a dictatorship, possible only in Catalonia in July, would not merely have outraged libertarian principles; it would have failed, and thus weakened the war effort against fascism, which if it triumphed would destroy bourgeois democracy and the CNT alike. The CNT could not be 'in the streets and in government'; after a painful examination of her conscience Federica Montseny opted for government 'with tears in her eyes'. But from the outset the militants did not share this pessimistic collaborationism, which in the end brought no rewards. When the Republican ministers fled from Madrid to Valencia, they narrowly escaped being shot up *en route* by a CNT column.

The new government proceeded in an attempt to stabilize the revolution. Militia committees were dissolved; collectivization was slowed down and regulated; peasant proprietors were reassured by the Communist Minister of Agriculture; the police were cut off from the political parties; the process of turning the militia into a regular army began. But Largo Caballero was not the man to dismantle the revolutionary conquests. As President Azaña insisted, the dilemma of July persisted: the revolution had not been absorbed.

It was not only the competing claims of parties and unions that weakened the central government. It is important to realize that central government control was never established throughout the whole Republican zone.

This was particularly the case in Catalonia and the Basque Provinces. Both had Statutes of Autonomy (the Basque Provinces, christened Euzkadi, had been granted theirs in July 1936) and both sought to push autonomy to its limits. Companys declared that the generals' rebellion had turned Spain into a federal state and that the position of Catalonia, as a separate unit in that state, was an 'irreversible reality'; more resolute nationalists argued that the Spanish state was 'a historical souvenir' destroyed by its own collapse in July.

To the politicians of Madrid this was a selfish exploitation of 'the crisis of the democratic state'. Catalonia seized the assets of the Bank of Spain, issued its own banknotes, and 'robbed' the central government of all the powers it could lay its hands on. Companys was accused of military inactivity, and of failure to take a stand against the collectivizations of the CNT in return for the implicit support of anarcho-syndicalists for Catalan independence. That this tacit alliance existed after 19 July cannot be denied; Companys gave effective power to the Anti-Fascist Militia Committee, dominated by the CNT, perhaps in the hope of domesticating the 'blind destructive revolution' of the CNT. When the central government recovered its control of Barcelona in May 1937 it destroyed both the CNT and Catalan autonomy alike.

What Azaña called 'frivolous provincialism' was not confined to Catalonia and Euzkadi, where President Aguirre resisted all attempts by the central government to control military operations. Until it was destroyed by Communist troops, the fief carved out in Aragon in the early days of the war by the anarchist hero Durutti was controlled by the CNT Council of Aragon as an enclave of libertarian communism. To the historians of the CNT it was a utopia of agrarian collectives, 'the marvel of the revolution', where 'speculation and usury' vanished; to the Communists it was a tyranny of brutal energumens. Asturias had its own UGT–CNT Council; Santander even its own diplomatic representative in London.

There can be little doubt that the competing power centres that emerged in the summer of 1936 put great difficulties in the way of a unified economy and an efficient war effort. 'Revolutionary cantonalism' in the economic sphere was reflected in the multiplicity of local paper currency. Even more serious was the failure to achieve a united military command, a single general staff—the *mando único* of the Communist slogan—immune and insulated from the pressures of political parties. This failure led General Rojo (who had to bear the military consequences of political fragmentation) to a verdict that must stand: 'In the political field, General Franco triumphed.'

V

In the spring of 1937 both the Nationalists and the Republicans experienced the most severe political crisis of the war. The resolution of these crises revealed the relative ease with which political divisions could be surmounted and a wartime concentration of power achieved in a military-authoritarian regime, and the difficulties confronting such a concentration in a democracy. If the formal apparatus of democracy had been dismantled (a disciple of Ortega passed the war crossing out clauses of the constitution of 1932 which had been abrogated *de facto*), the rivalries of parties survived the demise of true parliamentary life.

In the Republic the May crisis represented the final conflict between the defenders of the spontaneous revolution and the apostles of ordered government and social conservatism. The predominant role of the Communists is explained by their advocacy of a 'concentration of government', a regular army, and the organization of the economy with one end in view: victory in the war. 'Either the government takes the necessary steps to win the war,' the party Secretary warned, 'or it ceases to be the government.'

The propitiatory victim was Largo Caballero, who resisted the advance of the Communists in his own party, in the administration, and in the army where they sought to monopolize the Corps of Commissars. In what Largo called their reptilian intrigues the Communists found allies in Prieto and the left Republicans who shared their own conviction that Largo Caballero was 'burnt out' as a war leader and not the man to reverse the revolutionary conquests of July.

The catalyst of the May crisis, which gave Largo Caballero's enemies the chance to move in for the kill, was the troubles in Barcelona, which cost perhaps five hundred lives and left an enduring legacy of political bitterness.

In Barcelona the revolutionary spontaneity of the previous summer—the months when George Orwell found the 'working class in the saddle' in a city with no tipping and no ties—had turned to sectarian bitterness and 'ugly little rows' between the Communist party of Catalonia (the PSUC), the CNT, and the POUM. The PSUC chose to regard the POUM as Trotskyites (this was the era of the great purges in Moscow) to be eliminated as 'wild beasts' and fascist spies. *La Batalla*, the POUM daily, replied in kind. The PSUC was also attacking the revolutionary conquests and the militia. The entry of the CNT into the government was not saving the movement from its enemies. The CNT militants who rejected the leadership's 'collaborationism' entered into an informal common front with the POUM.

When the government police attacked the Telephone Exchange manned by the CNT, these discontents erupted in inconclusive street fighting, the 'dust-up' so brilliantly described by Orwell. The POUM leaders had long been pressing on the CNT the necessity of a *political* take-over by the workers. The moment of truth had come. They had no alternative but to fling in their lot with the CNT militants who had, according to the Secretary General, 'lapsed into the old mentality where everything can be solved by bombs and rifles'. The POUM leaders were committed to a revolution which they knew was bound to fail.[3] The CNT

[3] Victor Alba, *El marxismo en España* (1973), i, 287 ff.

leaders in Valencia were appalled and sought to mediate. To Prieto the May Days provided the chance to destroy the revolution in Barcelona and establish the control of the central government in Catalonia. On the evening of 7 May government Assault Guards entered Barcelona as a conquered city.

The Communists used Largo Caballero's reluctance to punish the POUM as fascist traitors as an excuse to get rid of 'the old man'. The vengeance of the Communist party—Nin, the bespectacled POUM leader, was murdered, others arraigned as traitors—remains a stain on the party's history. It was not that Communist overall strategies were mistaken; their plea for strong government, the maintenance of a Popular Front that included the bourgeois Republicans and concentration on the war effort was, in their own jargon, 'objectively correct'. The policies of the POUM, the consequences of a naïve Marxist–Leninist dogmatism, would have been a disaster, dissolving the Popular Front, cutting the Republic off from Soviet supplies in the vain hope of winning the war by a working-class revolution. It was Communist *methods* which stank: the night-time rap at the door by the secret police, the mysterious disappearance of once-valued comrades and the 'horrible atmosphere of suspicion and hatred' (Orwell), the ruthless promotion of party members and the destruction of enemies by vilification. This last was the fate of Largo Caballero and of his rival Prieto once the latter became convinced that the Communist policy of resistance was mistaken.

Largo Caballero's successor as Prime Minister was a physiologist, Dr. Juan Negrín. A man of colossal energy and enormous appetites, he was presented, in the postwar recriminations of the exile world, as a Communist dupe and a dictator. This he was not. He realized both the necessity to avoid offending the Soviet Union, which alone supplied the Republic with arms, and the need for the 'concentration of government' advocated alike by the Communists and the right-wing Socialists of Prieto. Concentration he achieved; but at the price of excluding those forces—Largo Caballero's followers and the CNT—which claimed victory over the generals' rising, and of creating enduring political feuds.

The concentration of power that the Republic struggled to achieve came naturally to the Nationalists; hierarchy and discipline were the dominant values of an anti-democratic movement. The prevailing style was military: whereas a uniform was the insignia of reaction in Madrid, it was a passport to privilege in the Nationalist capitals of Burgos and Salamanca. Ordered government was a psychological necessity for the Nationalists.

From the outset Nationalist Spain was a military state where power lay with the generals, conscious of the need for a single command. They elected Franco as Commander-in-Chief, and when he insisted on supreme political power granted it to him, on 29 September 1936, as 'Head of Government of the Spanish State ... who will assume all the powers of the New State'. The generals believed that they were creating a wartime dictatorship which, after victory, would restore the monarchy. In fact they had created a Hobbesian sovereign endowed with greater powers than Napoleon, a sovereign who was to shed few of those powers over forty years and whose model was Philip II, the solitary, all-powerful bureaucrat of the Escorial.

The achievement of political unity in the Nationalist camp provides a sharp contrast to the Republican political feuding. To Franco the determination of the Carlist leader, Fal Conde, and the Falangist Hedilla to maintain the independence of their respective movements threatened a return to the sterile party conflict of 'inorganic' democracy. On 18 April Franco announced from the balcony of his office in Salamanca the creation of a single movement that would unify *all* the political forces of Nationalist Spain. Unification was imposed from above. Franco declared on the radio that he embodied in himself 'the national will to unity'. The two main constituents, from which the new movement took its clumsy initials (FET de las JONS), were the Carlists and the Falange.

The Falange had grown prodigiously. Since the Carlist creed 'lacked a certain modernity', Falangism *faute de mieux* was the only available ideological clothing if a military revolt, barren of political ideas other than a commitment to order, was to attract 'the neutral mass'. The 'new shirts' who flocked to buy Falangist uniforms had little sympathy with the social radicalism of José Antonio, in prison in Alicante where he was executed on 20 November 1936, to become the 'Absent One' of party ceremonial. The provisional leader of the radical quasi-fascist wing, the austere Manuel Hedilla, feared for the future of the movement in the military, conservative atmosphere of Burgos and Salamanca. 'I prefer repentant Marxists to rightists corrupted by politics and *caciquismo*.' In his struggle to keep the movement pure and independent he was opposed by his rivals in the Falangist clans. On 16 April 1937, 'the blackest day in the history of the Falange', these ugly feuds erupted in gang warfare. The victor was neither Hedilla nor his rivals, but the Generalisimo.

Rumours of a conspiracy of Hedilla to prevent the virtual dissolution of the old Falange led to his arrest. He had refused the post of Secretary General of the new party. His fate was a warning to others; he became the forgotten man of the right. Falangists in the radical tradition might consider the Decree of Unification as a sell-out to clericalism; but with their jobs secure as long as they kept their mouths shut, most of them remained silent.

The militant Carlists were the greater losers in this process of unification from above; they had, an embittered Fal Conde remarked, 'lost the lot'. The programme of the new party was basically that of the Falange, and there was no promise to restore the true dynasty.

Franco now, as chief of the single party as well as Generalisimo and chief of state, controlled directly all important appointments in the government, the party, and the army. Apart from Franco, the victors were the old rightists who had slipped into the administration (as the Falange historian bitterly remarked, while the Falangists were fighting at the front) and the army. 'In the last resort,' wrote Serrano Suñer, Franco's brother-in-law and architect of the unification, 'the centre of gravity of the regime, its true support, was and continues to be, the army.'

VI

On 30 January 1938, after a ceremony 'fervent and devout, like a knight's vigil', Franco's first ministry took its oath of allegiance. Its composition revealed the simple secret of his statecraft: a cabinet appointed by himself that balanced the forces within the regime—three generals, one Carlist and two Falangists, and two technocrats. Two ministers came from conservative monarchist Renovación Española, an indication of the essentially conservative nature of a regime that had already turned its back on the Falangist 'national revolution'. What Hitler called 'the clerical monarchical scum' was floating to the top.

In this conservative state the Falangists were offered a consolation prize that was to give them a vast field of patronage and a continuing role: the control of the labour movement. It was the Falangist ideal of a radically transformed Spain in which liberal *laissez-faire* capitalism would be replaced by the co-operation of capitalist and worker in 'vertical syndicates' under the paternal direction of the state, 'without upsetting the respective situation of the different classes', that provided the ideological basis of the Labour Charter issued in March 1938.

One of Franco's biographers has praised the Charter as 'a law worthy of any enlightened British Labour leader'. On paper, yes. Few of the promises went into action in the war. Nationalist Spain emphasized war austerity (there was a 'one-course meal' campaign); while hours of work were reduced in Republican Spain they were raised in Nationalist Spain. The vertical syndicates were to prove a not altogether ineffective instrument for the protection of labour in postwar Spain. Nevertheless, the autonomy of the labour movement had been completely destroyed. 'The Vertical Syndicate is an instrument at the service of the state through which it realizes its economic policy'; it was an 'ordered hierarchy under the direction of the state'. Security of employment was, in these conditions, the minimum concession to labour denied the right to organize or to strike for better conditions.

Within this rigid authoritarian framework the war economy of the Nationalist zone was tolerably organized: wages were fixed, inflation was controlled. It was an economy based on confidence in victory: banks in the Nationalist zone gave loans on properties in territory still held by the Popular Front. Nor was this confidence confined to Spain: foreign exchange rates held well above those of the Republic.

In outward appearance and political language Franco's new state seemed a re-creation of the reign of the Catholic kings with Italian Fascist trimmings. The repellent early rhetoric of the regime was diffuse, indeed incomprehensible to the rational mind, in its attempts by 'renovating' tradition to reconcile the sixteenth century with the modern authoritarian reaction against 'the inorganic democracy of parties'.

Serrano Suñer was an admirer of Mussolini; yet he felt a mystical affinity with the Spain of the Catholic kings. The return of the Jesuits, the reappearance of the crucifix in schools, half-holidays for Aquinas, were symbols of this return to the past. The real conquest of the Church was its total recapture of the educational system. Republican teachers were purged, those who remained subjected to intensive retooling courses in Catholic thought. Though it was the Falange that was given control of the Students' Union, religious conformity was the test for students and professors alike.

From Navarre, the focal point of mass religious commitment, there radiated the brand of fierce orthodoxy and Catholic puritanism that was to mark the tone of life in Nationalist Spain. It was Navarre that first legislated against shirt sleeves in cafés and 'immodest' dress: there were to be no advertisements for bathing-dresses 'with women inside'; Nationalist puritanism even extended to an assault on modernisms in linguistic usage: '*ragoût*' on menus was criticized as a decadent word. Newspaper articles must be written 'in the language of Don Quixote'; libraries cleared of 'pornographic, Marxist, or corrupting works'.

Plastered over with this propaganda, Nationalist Spain had thus an old-world flavour. The Generalisimo's wartime headquarters were a reflection of the court of the monarchy. Refugees from the Republican zone arriving in Nationalist Spain were immensely relieved to find waiters ready to take orders. A few miles from the front, the hotels of Saragossa had hot baths and there were restaurants 'with bright lights and *animación*'. The Duke of Lerma, fighter pilot, found Valladolid replete with 'mountains of pretty girls'. San Sebastian was '*muy animado*';

he and a brother officer collected all the shoes put outside the doors of rooms in the best hotel, took them to another floor, and filled them with soda water. Such goings-on are difficult to imagine in Barcelona or Madrid, where the furnishings of upper-class life had been either consciously destroyed—palaces converted into offices or barracks—or had fallen into decay with war shortages. Nothing appalled the Nationalists more than this seemingly deliberate run-down of 'civilized' life. 'The stench was awful,' wrote Captain Bolín, head of Censorship and Tourism, on entering Barcelona, 'part of the accumulated filth the reds bequeathed to every town ... the dust at the Ritz was inches thick.'

So was the dust on Spanish intellectual life. While to liberals modern Spain had recovered, by her achievements in the realm of arts and sciences, an international repute unknown since the sixteenth century, to the average Nationalist the 'true' Spain of history had been betrayed by cosmopolitan professors. The rantings of one of the founding fathers of Falangism, Giménez Caballero, who had seen Mussolini as the saviour of 'Catholicity' and Cervantes as an anti-Spaniard betraying the true values embodied in Don Juan and the bullfight, were characteristic, not merely of an atmosphere that classed intellectuals as pessimists, 'eunuchs unworthy of a place in virile Spain', but of a relapse into verbal barbarism. The linguistic excesses of the Falange and of 'the ethical missionary state' were to debase political and literary language for a generation. Their counterpart in 'red' Spain was the slogan-soaked world of Marxist propaganda.

In spite of Falangist rhetoric which infected the public pronouncements of the government, the fundamental values of the new state were military order and Catholic orthodoxy, the values of Castile, creator of Spanish unity, hammer of heretics. Catalan refugees, apt to lapse into their 'spiritually inelegant' native tongue, were enjoined to speak the 'language of Empire'.

This return to the identification of Spain with intransigent Catholicism represented an interpretation of Spanish history profoundly different from that of the best minds of the Republic. The two interpretations started from a common premise: what the Spanish historian Américo Castro has called 'the state of progressive despair' at the disappointing performance of Spain, once the greatest imperial power in Europe, in a modern, technical, pragmatic world. The Republicans sought to raise Spain—for they were patriots too—by imitating the 'progressive' nations. For the more vocal Nationalist ideologists of 1936 only a return to the vision of a universal empire and the inward-looking values of Philip II could save Spain from the continuing ravages of a decadent materialism.

It was these institutions and these ideologies which were offered to 'liberated' Spain. The war was to Nationalists a war of liberation. Republican Spain was in slavery to a regime, absolutely evil in itself and dependent on a foreign power—the Soviet Union. The purpose of the war was to end this bondage: liberated Spain would be *independent*. The implications of this concept, central to Franco's whole thought, were never understood by his allies.

Germans and Italians were always advocating *Schrecklichkeit* or a *Blitzkrieg*. They could not understand why Franco did not bomb and shell enemy cities out of existence. His 'slowness' became an obsession with German staff officers and drove Ciano and Mussolini to fury. 'Are there no men in Spain?' 'Give me aeroplanes, artillery, tanks, and ammunition, give me diplomatic support and I shall be grateful,' Franco told the Italian Ambassador in April 1937, 'but above all *don't make me hurry*, do not force me to win at top speed, for this would mean killing more Spaniards, destroying a greater part of the wealth of the country.' Strategically this committed Franco to a war of attrition, of *desgaste* or 'wearing out'.

Liberated, Spain must be 'great'; and to be great she must be independent. Franco quickly saw that the most immediate threat to the independence of his new state lay in the economic demands and political pressures of his allies, Germany and Italy. Yet he desperately needed arms. To balance his necessities and his allies' importunities against the defence of his own freedom of action was a difficult exercise in brinkmanship. By 1939 Franco had proved himself the most successfully obstinate statesman ever produced by a secondary power.

The contest with Germany concerned the mineral resources of Spain. 'Germany', Hitler admitted, 'needs iron ore. That is why we want a Nationalist government—to be able to buy Spanish ore.' Franco was determined to keep his economic options open against German pressures to corner all Spain's minerals for the Reich—an operation called the 'Montana' scheme. 'The damned fellow', complained the German Ambassador, 'habitually does exactly the opposite of what we suggest, just to demonstrate his independence.' Every demand of the Germans was fought every inch of the way; but Franco's need for German military aid was so compelling that Nationalist Spain was on the way to becoming an economic colony of the Reich. The Nationalist government had to allow part of the huge debt to Germany to be paid off by the purchase of Spanish mines. The Montana scheme was, at last, home and dry.

VII

Military organization reflected political structure. The Nationalists created a conventional regular army round the core of the African Army.

The Republicans never fully overcame the defects of the voluntarism of the militia system. The Popular Army of the Republic was a remarkable creation given its unpromising *point de départ*. There were able commanders and planners, some with little military experience like the Communist Lister or Cipriano Mera of the CNT, some regular officers like General Rojo, the strategical brain of the Republican command; but the middle echelons were weak. The Nationalists started with a superior number of loyal junior officers; they trained the Provisional Lieutenants, later to become the staunchest supports of Franco's rule. Its notable achievements notwithstanding, the Popular Army, as a military machine that could be deployed by a unified command, was inferior to the Nationalist army.

These factors explain the main feature of the war: the Republicans could plan a series of surprise attacks that broke through the long front; but ambitious offensives bogged down after a few kilometres, and turned into a dogged defence of small gains. Franco, unimaginative as a strategist, was a methodical battle commander. His dictum was that no attack should be mounted unless its momentum could be maintained. 'To follow through' was all-important and it was precisely the incapacity to follow through that was the abiding weakness of the Popular Army.

Neither side got all the modern equipment it needed and both often fought with job lots of outdated and outworn weapons. It was a 'paupers' war' in which the only tactical innovation was dive-bombing. The supply of arms from the Soviet Union to the Republicans and from Germany and Italy to the Nationalists changed the balance of the war. Thus in November 1936 the Republic was well supplied and had command of the air; by the end of the war the Nationalist armies were better equipped and the supplies to the Republic erratic and irregular. By the last battles, as Azaña put it, 'you could break our front with bicycles'.

In the early months of the war, as we have seen, the critical factor was Franco's African Army, ferried by ship and air-lift (the only strategical novelty of the war) from Morocco to Andalusia. Trained troops, they advanced on Madrid through Extremadura, cutting through the militia 'like a knife through butter'. With Mola's columns held in the mountains to the north-east of Madrid, Franco's small and battle-weary army was held in the western suburbs by Rojo's newly organized army, to be strengthened morally and materially by the arrival of the first units of the International Brigades.

Madrid was Franco's 'obsession' and its successful defence was a decisive victory that determined the whole course of the war; had Madrid fallen in November Republican opposition would have collapsed in the winter of 1936. Franco's efforts to break through and surround the capital on the south were thwarted in the bloody battle of the Jarama (February 1937) in which the best units of the International Brigades suffered heavy casualties; a month later the Italian drive from the north, a badly planned motorized offensive along a single road in appalling winter conditions, was held in the battle of Guadalajara.

The defence of Madrid was more than a proof of the worth in defence of the Popular Army. It was turned by the propaganda of the left into an epic victory of Spanish democracy over the fascism triumphant in Europe. 'Madrid the tomb of fascism', ran the slogan; Madrid 'the universal frontier that separates liberty and slavery ... It is fighting for humanity ... with the mantle of its blood it shelters all human beings.' For the correspondent of the *New York Times* Guadalajara changed 'the stream of [world] history'. This euphoria concealed a failure in the north to retake Oviedo—its defence together with that of Toledo were the epics that corresponded to Madrid in Nationalist propaganda—and the total failure of the malformed militia system to prevent the fall of Malaga (7 February) to the Italians.

By the spring of 1937 Franco's military advisers had persuaded him to abandon his costly 'obsession' with Madrid and to concentrate his available forces on the conquest of the north. Once more the northern campaign exposed the military consequences of political fragmentation. There was no unified command. Aguirre, President of Euzkadi, wanted planes and tanks from Madrid, not an interfering general. 'Request Your Excellency', the general appointed by Madrid cabled the Minister of War, 'whether the army I had the honour to be appointed to command exists or not.'

On Monday 26 April came the most notorious event of the whole war: the complete destruction with high explosive and incendiary bombs of the small Basque town of Guernica. The bombardment was the work of the Condor Legion, the German squadrons serving with the Nationalist forces. Regarded by the German command as a legitimate operation of war, the destruction of Guernica was presented to Europe as an act of unparalleled barbarism. Fascists were not only barbarians but liars; the Nationalist press agencies maintained that the town had been burnt by 'red incendiaries', a palpable lie that was a gift to Republican propagandists. Dramatized in Picasso's *Guernica*, Guernica was exploited as a warning to Europe of the horrors of a war against fascism; it became a symbolic event, with a resonance out of all proportion to its military significance, resurrected in the 1970s to condemn U.S. bombings in Vietnam. So important are the myths of propaganda in war—especially in civil wars—that the Nationalists maintained their version against all evidence in order to fling the charge of barbarism back against their enemies.

Bilbao, blockaded and starved, fell on 19 June; the Catholic Basques, fighting to defend their autonomy rather than a lay Republic, lost heart. Santander was captured by a model manœuvre on 26 August; in Asturias, the Socialist stronghold, an initially tough resistance suddenly collapsed 'like a meringue dipped in water'.

The northern victories were decisive. The iron ore and industry of the north were in Nationalist hands; the retreating Basques had refused to blow up the foundations of the economic strength of their *patria*, the iron foundries and metal works around Bilbao. Franco now controlled 62 per cent of Spanish territory and over half the population; 25 per cent of the Republican armed forces had vanished in defeat.

The offensives mounted by the Republic to relieve the pressure on the north (Brunete in July, Belchite in August) revealed the strength and weaknesses of the Popular Army. Ambitious conceptions of General Rojo, they collapsed into muddles on the ground turning into costly defensive battles. The mastery of the air had passed to the Nationalists: Brunete saw the first appearance of the Messerschmidt 109.

VIII

Negrín inherited a disastrous military situation. The Republican offensive against Teruel (15 December 1937), fought in terrible winter conditions, failed. Franco had turned his forces through Aragon to cut the Republic in two by reaching the Mediterranean. The Aragon battles saw some of the worst collapses of morale and the most vicious politico-military infighting of the war. It is to Negrín's credit that he pulled together the Republic to fight its greatest battle. When Franco turned from Aragon to Valencia—a mistaken decision that committed his armies to a difficult campaign—the Republican army crossed the Ebro to fall on his rear. It was the classic story of the defence until November of a small territorial gain made in the first days of July. Franco used the battle to destroy the Republican army; when he attacked in Catalonia resistance disintegrated. On the first day a collapse opened a whole front. 'It was a rout,' wrote Rojo, 'one of the many which it has been my lot to witness.'

It was an astonishing propaganda achievement to maintain Republican enthusiasm in the face of a process of continual defeat interspersed by occasional triumphs. But by 1938 internecine feuds and mutual recrimination eroded morale. Shortages of food and consumer goods turned the Republican zone into a barter economy and life into a grim, grey struggle for existence. As final defeat drew close, the necessity of making oneself and one's family acceptable to the victors, their supporters waiting in the shadows of every town and village to take over power, triumphed.

Loyalty withered, sacrificed to survival. Confronted with massive desertions, the attempts to enforce loyalty by the government and its security forces—dominated by the Communists—resembled a generalized tyranny.

The tragic irony of the Civil War was that it ended as it had begun, with a *pronunciamiento* against a government which a section of the army maintained had ceased to represent the national will. Colonel Casado resented the growing power of the Communists in the army and believed that Negrín's policy of resistance after the collapse of Catalonia was suicidal. Supported by the old enemies of the Communists—the CNT and the moderate Socialist leader Besteiro—he formed a National Council, denouncing Negrín's government as a 'putrefying corpse' dominated by the Communists. When the Communist units in Madrid revolted and were suppressed by Casado's troops—both sides were wearing the same Republican uniform—perhaps 250 lives were sacrificed in a pointless eruption of irrelevant feuds.[4] Casado hoped that Franco would recognize a fellow soldier in his anti-Communist crusade and grant terms that would protect respectable Republicans. Franco insisted on the unconditional surrender of 'absolute evil'. With the naval base of Cartagena in chaos, with Republican troops deserting *en masse*, the Caudillo knew there was nothing to fight. On the evening of 31 March, down with influenza, General Franco was informed that his troops had occupied their objectives; the Civil War had ended.

IX

Both sides, for propaganda purposes and to win foreign support, presented the war as a battle for the ideologies that divided Europe. The generals presented themselves as Crusaders defending European civilization against a Communist plot rather than as defenders of Spanish conservative interests. For the left, the war was part of the wider struggle of democracy against fascism. What was in its origins a domestic tragedy thus became the great divide in the politics and intellectual discourse of Europe and Latin America.

The wrangles of the Non-Intervention Committee, sitting in London, not merely conveniently covered the reluctance of the Western democracies to aid the Republic; they exposed and crystallized the alignments of the great powers and gave the Fascist powers a sense of the weakness of the 'degenerate democracies' where the Spanish issue embittered domestic politics and divided political parties. In England and France it not

---

[4] See J.M. Martínez Bande, *Los cien últimos días de la República* (1973).

merely heightened the conflicts between right and left; both right and left emerged in 1939 riven by their attitudes to the war.

The war left a mark on a whole generation of intellectuals. Almost every European writer of significance supported the Republic: in America Hemingway wrote his longest novel on the war; James Baldwin his first short story. The Communist party orchestrated the writers' protest and the International Brigades, their hard core composed of party militants, later ruthlessly purged as 'cosmopolitan' agents of the American intelligence network.

The defeat of the Republic and the exposure of the role of the Communist party—for instance its attack on André Gide at the Writers' Conference of 1937 and its campaign against the POUM revealed by George Orwell—produced a sense of disenchantment. 'After Spain ... there was little left of the Thirties' movement but a feeling of resignation and a sense of guilt.' Liberals and socialists felt they had been taken in and used in Communist propaganda campaigns of 'screaming lies and hatred' (Orwell).

The war raised in its most acute form the problem of the political commitment of intellectuals and the sacrifices of artistic integrity commitment entails. There was no place for tender consciences in what the English poet, Cecil Day Lewis, described as 'a battle between light and darkness'. The effects of political polarization on Spain itself were unfortunate. The literary output of the Nationalists was repulsive (typical of the early outpourings was José María Pemán's 'Poem of the Beast and the Angel', 1939, with its crude anti-Semitic outbursts). On the Republican side a fine poet like Rafael Alberti became a Communist and abandoned poetry for political rhetoric; the only major party writer who could turn an ode on the Kharkov tractor factory into poetry was Miguel Hernández. The strains of war produced a distrust of the imagination which persisted in a generation of poets labouring under and against Francoism.

10 Francoism 1939–1975

General Franco, victor of the Civil War, was to rule Spain as Caudillo by the Grace of God until his death in 1975. If the political structure of his regime experienced only cosmetic changes, the society he governed was to change dramatically. Spain became an industrial society, every day more like the societies of western Europe. Hence the authoritarianism inherited from the victory of 1939 became increasingly anachronistic and out of place, not merely in Europe, where it was generally considered, with Portugal, as the last surviving 'fascist' regime in the West, but also unsuited to the 'modern' Spanish society of the 1970s. Economic change had produced conflicts and expectations that the political system absorbed only with increasing difficulty. The crucial break in the social and economic infrastructure came with the 'economic miracle' in the '60s: the political consequences in the early '70s.

I

In the immediately postwar years the problem was one of sheer physical survival, of feeding and finding jobs for a nation whose economy had been run down by its own Civil War and which was isolated from the economies of the West, first by the Second World War and then by the diplomatic and economic boycott imposed by the victorious democracies on a 'fascist' state which had, until 1943, openly supported the Axis powers. 'In 1940' wrote París Eguilaz, one of the foremost economists of the new regime, 'the national income, at constant prices, had fallen back to that of 1914, but since the population had increased the per capita income fell to nineteenth-century levels. That is, the Civil War had provoked an unprecedented economic recession.'

The instruments with which the regime sought recovery had been forged in the war itself with the help of Italian Fascist models: the regulation by the state of a 'capitalist' economy cut off, as far as possible, from the world market; an autarky that would embark on a massive programme of import substitution, producing everything at home regardless of economic cost. State *dirigisme* and protection were old traditions, but they were no longer justified on economic grounds, as protecting a weak economy. Rather, they were presented as political ideals: the recipe for a stable economy and a suitable policy for an 'imperial military state'. No nation, with the shortages of postwar Europe, could risk the perils of an uncontrolled market economy. The unique feature of Spain in the '40s—apart from the clumsiness of the apparatus that enforced regulation—was that autarky was presented as a permanent ideal.

It was not merely that intervention spawned regulations which created bottlenecks and supported a flourishing black market. There was a deeper contradiction. In spite of an enthusiasm for the peasant farmer as the 'core of the race', insulated from the subversive doctrines that had infected the urban workers after 1931, the regime early saw that industrial revival was essential. In imitation of Fascist Italy it set up INI (the National Institute of Industry), a state holding company intended to provide the infrastructural basis for an industrial take-off and to help out private capital in vital sectors. But the industrial growth achieved in the '40s (by 1948 industrial production had reached 1929 levels) could not continue within the restrictive framework of autarky. Surrounded by tariff walls, enclosed in a domestic market with a limited purchasing power, incapable of importing the raw materials or capital goods to supply and modernize its industry, the economy was starved. Further recovery demanded imports, the abandonment of controls, and the integration of Spain into the world market. By 1956 the limitations of autarky were exposed. 'A moment had arrived in which the desire for industrialization must be reconciled with the conditions industrialization demanded.'[1]

II

The architects of the new economic policy which was to reconcile rapid industrial growth with its 'conditions' were the technocrats associated with the Catholic lay order, Opus Dei (see p. 145). After 1957, piecemeal, with interruptions and hesitations, they introduced the 'conditions': the creation in Spain of a market economy where prices would control the allocation of resources, and the integration of that market into the capitalist economy of the West. The Stabilization Plan of 1959, a drastic remedy for inflation and a severe deficit in the balance of trade taken from the recipe book of orthodox capitalism, would cure the

---

[1] L.A. Rojo in S. Paniker, *Conversaciones en Madrid* (1969), 159.

economy of its inherited impurities so that it would function as a modern, 'neo-capitalist' economy. Rapid growth would take care of all problems.

How far the Development Plans of the technocrats, lifted largely from French indicative planning, produced from 1963 on the economic miracle of the '60s, in which Spanish growth rates outpaced all capitalist economies other than the Japanese, must be open to question. It has been argued that the plans distorted a Spanish boom which was a mere reflection of the European boom; that the 'triumphalist' propaganda of the regime, pouring out statistics of growth, was not a proof of a prosperity based on 'Franco's peace', but merely reflected the inevitable spurt that industrialization brings to any backward economy.

The economy was refuelled from three sources: foreign loans, beginning with the U.S. loans of the '50s which came, in the words of the economist Sardá, like water to a desert; the foreign exchange earnings of the tourist trade; the remittances of Spaniards working abroad. Spain became the playground of Europe, its beaches and sunny days a valuable capital asset exploited to saturation point by package-tour agencies catering to middle-class tourists; it also became the service area of northern Europe, supplying workers to the factories of France and Germany. By 1973 there were half a million Spaniards working in Germany and a quarter of a million in France.

The Development Plans were the favourite targets of the left-wing opposition, since criticism of the economic performance of the regime was tolerated. The technocrats' faith in private enterprise as the motor of growth, it was held, reinforced the hold of a narrow financial oligarchy ensconced in the 'big seven' private banks. (Given the low level of self-financing and the weakness of the stock exchange, only the private banks could finance industrial growth; this they did successfully, becoming the most conspicuous feature of the economic landscape of Francoism.) The planners' concentration on aggregate growth, in spite of an ambitious programme of 'poles of development' imitated from French planning, increased the gap between the rich and the poor provinces: the existing industrial areas prospered at the expense of the backward regions.[2] By 1970, 70 per cent of Madrid homes possessed television sets, but only 11 per cent in the province of Soria. Nor did the plans, in spite of their declared intentions, redistribute income. 'The one thing that has not developed', observed Cardinal Herrera in 1965, 'is social justice.' To the technocrats the criticisms of what they regarded as the growing pains of industrialization were beside the point: rapid industrial growth was achieved; the wages and living standards of the working class rose.

[2] See H.W. Richardson, *Regional Development Policy and Planning in Spain* (1975), 111–40

III

The most striking consequence of growth was a massive exodus from the countryside to the cities. The rural areas with a high birth rate were drained to fill the cities where birth rates were low; from the 'desert' centre and the poor south emigrants flooded to the prosperous periphery and the 'industrial triangle' of the north-east. Madrid became a metropolis unique in Europe: a city surrounded by a demographic desert. By 1970, 1,600,000 Andalusians were living outside their native provinces— 712,000 in Barcelona alone. Settling in shacks on the outskirts of Barcelona, later in the new high-rise suburbs, these immigrants threatened to swamp native Catalans and their culture. The absorption of these quasi-literate immigrants became a main concern of Catalanists; only if they were 'catalanized' could Catalanism be presented as a majority movement.

The first wave of emigrants—landless labourers and subsistence farmers from depressed areas like eastern Andalusia—sought to escape intolerable poverty. The emigrants who went to Germany in the early '60s were forced out by the recession induced by the sharp cut-backs of the Stabilization Plan. The later waves, which emptied villages of all but the old, were often composed of seekers after social mobility. Returning from abroad with their savings they bought a bar, a small farm, a lorry. The migration to the cities was a natural consequence of industrialization. Without it there would have been no industrial take-off—as the regime recognized when it abandoned its efforts to stop the exodus from the land and the agrarian ideology that idealized the peasant farmer. Even so, industrial growth could not absorb the totality of the rural underemployed released by the mechanization of the latifundia or those who left their marginal farms, creating the deserted villages described by the Castilian novelist, Delibes. Emigration to Latin America had been the safety valve in the late nineteenth century; serious unemployment in the 1960s was avoided only by the new emigration to Europe.

Agriculture remained the weak link in the new economy, even if it was the savings from agriculture that in the early years financed the beginnings of industrial growth, and the export earnings of agriculture (especially from citrus fruit and the other products of the Levante) that provided initially a minimum of foreign exchange to finance the import of capital goods. Apart from the persistence of primitive techniques (the *noria*—with its earthenware jugs tied to a primitive wheel irrigating the fields—and the earth threshing floor could still be seen in the '40s and '50s) the twin curse remained the great estates and the dwarf farms.

The latifundia remained intact and indeed were consolidated by the agrarian bourgeoisie of the south. The radical Falangist notions of agrarian reform dissolved in a regime dominated by conservative interests. Agrarian reform, in the sense of the expropriation and redistribution of large estates, was replaced by ambitious schemes of 'colonization'. The *latifundista* found a new justification. Increasingly he saw himself fulfilling a useful social function as a profit-minded entrepreneur; he was no longer a parasitical absentee *rentier*.[3] He cut labour costs (and labour troubles) by mechanization as the combine harvester replaced the gangs of day labourers. A minor agrarian revolution came with the motor cultivator on the more prosperous small farms of the Levante.

It was the tiny fields of the poor dry lands, the *secano*—22 million fields of less than 2 hectares—that were the intractable problem. Here the regime's policy of *concentración parcelana* (concentration of fields) made some progress in producing a race of middling peasant farmers, so conspicuously absent in the past. By the mid-1970s 800,000 small farmers had left the land.

The governments's support of cereal farming—a necessity in the hungry '40s—had less happy long-term consequences. By favouring wheat with protection and guaranteed prices, land was kept in cereals, and the agricultural system could not respond to the new demand for meat and dairy products created by the relative affluence of the '60s. Hence what is called 'the crisis of traditional agriculture' as the traditional crops can find no market.

'Spain is different' ran the tourist slogan. This was true of the economy of the '40s when half the active population still laboured in the agrarian sector. By 1978 the rapid decline in the agrarian population to the level of France showed that the economic structure of Spain was no longer so different from that of her neighbours. Farmers felt themselves the Cinderellas of an economy committed to industrialization at all costs. Like their French counterparts they blocked roads with their tractors in impotent protest. 'The massive protest of the farmers' the Banco de Bilbao reported in 1976, 'is more justified than that of any other sector of society.' But since they were only producing 8 per cent of the G.N.P. and losing labour at the rate of 100,000 hands a year, their protest lacked muscle.

IV

The new economy, would, its progenitors hoped, produce a stable, satisfied society. With a per capita income of $2,000, argued López

---

[3] J. Martínez Alier, *La estabilidad del latifundismo en España* (1968), 336.

Rodó, the most prominent of the new technocrats and planners, social tensions would disappear; the satisfactions of a consumer society would, according to Fernández de la Mora, the ideologue of the regime in its later stages, induce apathy, a desirable condition of political health, for, as we shall see, the induction of apathy was the prime political objective of the Francoist political system.

How far were the prophecies of the planners and the sociology of Fernández de la Mora justified by events? The answer is complex. After the apathy produced by hardship, the sheer struggle for survival in the 1940s (when used toothbrushes were on sale and fountain pens could be bought on the instalment system, when patched clothes were passed on to younger children and food was scarce, in what the novelist Umbral calls the long winter of queues), the relative abundance of consumer goods in the '60s was attributed to the 'peace of Franco'. Satisfaction with this new state of comparative affluence led the former Falangist Ridruejo to argue that the regime enjoyed the support of the majority of Spaniards.

By the 1970s two developments had weakened this support: the consumer society of the '60s led inevitably to rising expectations, to a desire in the '70s not merely for the material comforts of the West but for the political freedom of systems consistently denounced, by a government-controlled press and TV, as degenerate democracies. A gap opened between an authoritarian political superstructure and its social base; the conflicts inherent in rapid industrial growth set off an internal contradiction between the ideology of the regime and the 'conditions' of industrialization. Whereas autarky and authoritarianism were a perfect fit, it was harder, though not impossible, to reconcile the modern economics of neo-capitalism and the denial of modern liberal political institutions.

Two movements show the development of protest: that of the students and that of the workers.

An industrial society demands a developed system of higher education. The universities expanded in the '60s; but rather than supplying docile administrators of neo-capitalism they bred a generation of student radicals. The early student leaders were a self-recruited élite, exploiting student 'trade union' demands and fighting the monopoly of the Falangist student union. By the '70s the student protest had become a mass protest. Its demands had become politicized and the universities dominated by a Marxist sub-culture. Police occupied campuses, professors were dismissed, students imprisoned. The universities were reformed in 1970: some of the early attempts at forcible religious and 'patriotic' indoctrination were replaced by an emphasis on technical education. But successive governments could not master a movement that was itself divided by the Byzantine feuds of the left. By the mid-1970s the student movement had become a protest against society in general, seeking to turn the university from its traditional role as a transmitter of culture into a field for social and sexual experiment. If student radicals did not succeed in abolishing the university, the legacy of Francoism was a mass university, adrift and with no sense of purpose.

The workers' protest was likewise a consequence of what Marxists would call the contradictions of the system.

The workers' unions were completely destroyed in 1939. In their place came the vertical syndicates which embraced both workers and employers and embodied Falangist ideals. The class struggle would be replaced by class co-operation under the 'hierarchical'—a favourite Falangist term—direction of the state. Strikes were illegal, unions representative of the workers were replaced by unions dominated by Falangist bureaucrats. The compensation given to the working class for the suppression of workers' unions was job security for the employed, just as farmers were given security of tenure—measures that did not please modernizing industrialists or landowners but did something to contain social protest.

Increasingly the official syndicates, 'bureaucratic mastodons', proved incapable of solving the labour problems of a modern industrial economy. The regime itself admitted collective bargaining and the election of shop stewards; the workers formed the representative but illegal Workers' Commissions (CC.OO) increasingly dominated by Communist militants. Employers who wished to modernize and make productivity deals, if such deals were to stick at the shop floor, negotiated with the *illegal* unions. The government cracked down on the CC.OO in the 1970s. But the damage was done: the official syndicates, embedded alike in the ideology and structure of the regime, were discredited. The Communist party, which had had no secure union base in pre-Franco Spain, as a result of the success of the CC.OO controlled the most powerful union in the post-Franco era.

V

With average incomes almost tripled in a decade, López Rodó could claim 'Never has so much been achieved in so short a time'. But if the aim of Francoism was 'social peace' induced by prosperity, this aim was only partially achieved. If the technocrats of Opus Dei hoped to forge an amalgam of authoritarianism, traditional Catholicism, and the world of Americanized business efficiency, they succeeded only for a short period. Spanish society of the late '60s and '70s was superficially stable, but disturbed by conflicts between the inherited mores and values of the middle class which serviced Francoism as it had serviced every previous regime (values derived largely from traditional Catholicism which emphasized austerity and abstinence) and those of a materialist, consumer society, a nation of 'tele addicts' worshipping the golden calf of all western societies: the car. Between 1960 and 1970 the number of cars per 1,000 persons rose from 9 to 70. If only 1 per cent of Spaniards had TV sets in 1960, by 1970 the TV audience embraced 90 per cent of the nation. 'Everybody is watching TV serials with open mouths,' the Catalan writer Josep Pla said in 1972, 'such is today's culture.'

In structural terms, Spanish society changed more rapidly between 1957 and 1978 than in the previous century. It was not merely that the conservative establishment of the 1940s—aristocrats, landowners, and financiers—lost *some* of its influence to the new breed of entrepreneurs who joined its ranks. The rapidly expanding service sector produced a new middle class, distinct from the 'traditional' middle class. Some sectors of this new middle class—bank clerks and the lower ranks of the civil service—adopted radical attitudes.[4] It was this service sector that gave women an alternative employment to domestic service. The Women's Sector of the Falange accepted the view of most churchmen that a woman's place was in the home; but an education in household management was resented by girls who wanted to become secretaries.

The more intimate effect of these changes is difficult to estimate. The society of the '60s and '70s exhibited symptoms of what Gino Germani calls superficial modernization; there was a clash between the old and the new values. Bank clerks who pressed for the nationalization of the banks supported religious education. Workers, increasingly militant and class-conscious, were as conservative as the ideologues of the regime and the more puritanical sectors of the Church as to the role of women in a modern society.

The clash between the old and the new values was particularly acute between generations. Parents lose authority in industrial societies. Opinion surveys revealed a complete alienation from the regime and its values amongst the urban educated middle-class youth, an alienation not shared by rural youth or the older generation.[5] An opinion survey in 1977 revealed that Spanish youth were as 'progressive' about abortion or birth control as any corresponding generation elsewhere. The traditional prolonged courtship, the *noviazgo*, is going out of fashion;[6] by the '70s 'free use of the body' was demanded as a right by progressives. Yet we

---

[4] Ciriaco de Vicente, *La lucha de los funcionarios en España* (1977), 185 ff.
[5] See J.R. Torregrosa, *La Juventud española* (1970).
[6] A. Ferrandiz and V. Verdú, *Noviazgo y matrimonio en la burguesía española* (1974).

must beware of exaggerating this 'progressive' culture; more Spanish adolescents live at home than in any other country.

Most important of all was the continued growth of the industrial proletariat, especially that concentrated in large factories like the SEAT car works in Barcelona, with 23,000 workers. As we have seen, that proletariat became increasingly militant as memories of the repression of the 1940s faded and as the Communist policy of 'entrism' (use by illegal unions of the electoral opportunities of the official syndicates) proved successful. There were few strikes before the '60s; afterwards, though strikes were mostly motivated by wage claims or labour grievances, they became more and more 'political'—a consequence of the regime's refusal to allow representative unions. Again it was a new generation of young workers who took up the militant traditions of their elders. In the election of 1975 the union offices were crowded 'with long-haired beardies'.[7]

VI

Spanish society had become, especially where the post-Civil War generation was concerned, an often uncomfortable mix of imported fashion—from the *yé yé* and mini-skirt championships of the 1950s, the Marxism and Maoism of the '60s, to punk rock and Nietzsche in the '70s—and the traditional Catholic values that were those of Francoism.

The Second Republic corresponded with a second golden age in Spanish intellectual life. Francoism failed in its efforts to impose a 'Francoist culture, that could match up to the liberal culture it persecuted and whose representatives were in exile. Francoist culture (compounded of Tridentine Catholicism and the remnants of a Falangist imperialism, which as we have seen found its ideal in the Spain of Philip II) was a poor thing that could not—in the long run—resist the influence of the Europe it was the ambition of the technocrats of Opus Dei to join. Once the New Order of Hitler was defeated, Francoism was an isolated anachronism. Intellectuals were repelled by its rhetoric; no writer of stature accepted the official ideology. The censorship could successfully prevent the emergence of an alternative culture; it could not impose that of the regime. The 'tremendist' novelists of the 1940s and early '50s drew a sordid picture of the society created by Franco's victory. While overt political criticism remained impossible, the 'social' poets, novelists, and dramatists of the '60s, though mauled by the censor and unreadable as some of their productions were, attacked the social injustices of Francoist

[7] Quoted I. Boix and M. Pujadas, *Conversaciones sindicales y dirigentes obreros* (1975), 30.

society; they were nearly all members of the clandestine Communist party. The young writers of the '70s (the *novísimos*) rejected the crude language and realism of the 'social' writers in favour of a return to surrealism and fantasy; but their commitment to the opposition was as strong as their rejection of social realism. As for economists, sociologists, and psychologists, most were influenced by Marxism or liberalism—the two ideologies Franco was determined to burn out of the Spanish soul and which filled the cultural vacuum left by the collapse of a Catholic, Falangist culture.

The difficulties of the regime in imposing its 'culture' and the consequences of its failure to do so are nowhere more apparent than in the cinema. With more cinema seats per capita than any other European country, the Spain of the '40s and '50s was a nation of cinema addicts. A financially weak and artistically impoverished local industry could not produce enough films embodying the puritanical, 'heroic' ethos of the regime to satisfy demand. Imported American and Italian films, though mutilated out of recognition by the censorship, were carriers of values incompatible with those of the regime. A socialist state can rely on a supply of films that sustain the dominant ideology; but Spain was part of the capitalist world. Thus screens showing Rita Hayworth were pelted with ink bottles by Falangists as a protest against the exhibition of a corroding libertarianism. The replacement of the cinema by government-controlled TV made the provision of innocuous entertainment an easier task.

Most Spaniards neither noticed the discrepancies between Hollywood and Madrid, nor read the works of 'social' literature. They were immersed in the culture of evasion: the music hall; football (in the hungry '40s Real Madrid built a huge stadium), where nationalism found expression in the supposed 'Spanish fury' of the leading (Basque!) players; 'photo novels'; anodyne radio serials which enjoyed an extraordinary vogue; 'kiosk literature'; finally TV. All societies possess their cultures of evasion; but in authoritarian systems based on political demobilization such a culture plays an important role. Once the fierce repression of the early Franco years weakened it combined with administrative persecution (e.g. the withdrawal of passports) and the protection of career prospects (hence the silence of many university professors) to keep the ordinary citizen a passive member of the new consumer society. With his TV set and Match of the Day (which he himself never missed) Franco asserted that most of his subjects had nothing to complain about.

VII

Francoism was more than one-man rule—important though that one man remained until his death. It was a political system that, to the outside world, appeared an immutable political monolith. Given the changes in society, it could not have survived without at least cosmetic changes and some attempt to incorporate the new forces within the system. The legitimacy of that system changed over time. The simple postwar Manichaean division between victors and vanquished which, as Churchill observed, excluded half of Spain from public life, never vanished. 'The struggle between Good and Evil', Franco declared in 1959 on the completion of the vast basilica and cross of the Valle de los Caídos, 'never ends no matter how great the victory. Anti-Spain was routed but it is not dead.' But the vision could not hold. The 'dictatorship of victory' became 'the dictatorship of development'. Franco showed himself less as a conquering general, more as the benevolent family patriarch.

The regime prided itself on its capacity for 'institutional perfection', on the evolution of a constitution *sui generis*, completed by the Organic Law of 1966. This constitution embodied the principles of 'organic democracy', as opposed to the artificial 'inorganic democracy' based on universal suffrage, the party system, and the responsibility of governments to an elected parliament. The Cortes, set up in 1942, represented not individual voters but the syndicates, various corporate bodies, and after 1967 the heads of families: these were the *cauces* (channels) through which society communicated with government. There was no secure guarantee of individual rights—freedom of political association remained illegal; exceptional jurisdictions—courts martial and the Tribunal of Public Order—dealt with political crimes. Based on 'unity of power', the constitution was highly centralized, reflecting the Nationalist detestation of any tinge of separatism. As Head of State until his death, Franco retained the all-important power to appoint and dismiss ministers. In what was legally a 'traditional and Catholic monarchy', the Caudillo would remain Head of State 'as long as the Lord gives me strength', with the right to nominate his successor.

In spite of the Fascist trimmings of the early years—the goose-step and the Fascist salute—Francoism was not a totalitarian regime. It was a conservative, Catholic, authoritarian system, its original corporatist features modified over time. It came to have none of the characteristics of a totalitarian state: no single party parallel to the state administration; after the early years, no successful attempt at mass mobilization. It rested on the apathy of the public, the partial satisfaction of the pressure groups *within* the regime, and the systematic exclusion from power of those who did not accept the Principles of the Movement (set out in the Law of 1958) and unconditional loyalty to the victor of the Civil War. To deny the legitimacy of that victory and to admit the vanquished would be, as the old-time Falangist Girón declared, to hand over Spain to 'pigs'.

The secret of Franco's power, as every commentator has emphasized, lay in his right to nominate and dismiss ministers (he remained his own Prime Minister until 1972). His political chemistry balanced and neutralized what Amando de Miguel has called the 'families' of the regime. None was permanently excluded from power; none allowed a monopoly of influence.

The oldest and most committed family was the 'integral Francoists', bred in the Civil War and sustaining the spirit of 'the Crusade': men like Franco's *alter ego*, Admiral Carrero Blanco, and his long-time Minister of the Interior and friend from his cadet days, General Alonso Vega.

The army itself remained a pillar of the regime. Though its direct participation in government varied over time, it always controlled three ministries. Of Franco's first 90 ministers, 30 were from the armed forces. Overloaded with officers, the army was badly paid ('double employment' remained a necessity for junior officers) and badly equipped. In the 1970s a group of democratic officers sought, by exploiting professional grievances—much as the *Junteros* had done in 1917 (see p. 84)—sought to wean the officer corps from its political anchor in Francoism in order to bring it into contact with 'the people'.[8] They were without influence. More important were the professional soldiers who rose to the top as the political generals bred in the mystique of the Crusade died or retired. They were to play an important part in the transition to democracy. By 1976 the army was divided between right-wingers, nostalgic for the order of Franco, and neutral professionals loyal to their commander-in-chief and Franco's heir, King Juan Carlos.

In 1939 the Falangists appeared the most powerful of the organized political families. But the attempts of committed Falangists to create a state founded on the Falange as a mass party were thwarted by the conservative monarchists, the real victors of the Civil War. Though Falangists appeared in all ministries, their influence declined. In Ricardo de la Cierva's phrase, the Falange was a 'paper tiger'. Its power base was in the official syndicates and to the end of the regime it manned the syndical bureaucracy; but even there the illegal unions undermined its power. As a political *organization* the Falange was absorbed into the wider conception of the Movement as the *communion* of all Spaniards, i.e. those Spaniards who accepted the legitimacy of the rising of 18 July and

---

[8] J. Infantes, *El ejército de Franco y Juan Carlos* (1976), 113.

of Franco's rule. The blue shirts of the party were replaced by the smart white uniforms of the Movement.

Throughout Franco's rule Falangist influence and the remnants of their social radicalism were opposed by the conservative monarchists; their quarrels were one of the few public manifestations of political life. In 1942, after a brawl between monarchists and Falangists, both Falangist and monarchist ministers were summarily sacked: the first exhibition of what were called 'Franco's judgements of Solomon'.

The monarchists were weakened by their internal divisions. They had supported Franco in the Civil War not merely as conservatives, but because they hoped he would be a Spanish General Monck. Though he declared Spain a monarchy in 1947, he had no intention of resigning as Head of State.

Carlists and Alfonsists now divided between those who became indistinguishable from integral Francoists, ready to accept a restoration at Franco's hands, at his convenience and on his conditions, and those who conceived of their restored monarch as an *alternative* to, rather than as a loyal successor and supporter of, Francoism. To a greater or lesser degree this latter brand of monarchist became part of the so-called 'democratic' (i.e. non-Communist) opposition, ready to seek reconciliation with the vanquished of 1939.

The Carlists represented to Franco a noble but archaic creed; except for those who accepted his own rule with enthusiasm they were cold-shouldered and the dynasty expelled. The Young Pretender, Carlos Hugo, turned a movement that had been a conservative rural protest into Carlist 'socialism'; it was resolutely opposed to the regime and its clashes with the traditional Carlists became an annual ritual.

It was the Alfonsine monarchists and their representative, Don Juan (son of Alfonso XIII), who obsessed Franco and his court. In 1945 Don Juan hoped to be restored by the victorious Allies as a constitutional monarch, a democratic alternative. Franco never forgave Don Juan and his 'gang' of aristocratic liberals and generals ready to mount drawing-room conspiracies and enter into fragile arrangements with the left opposition, nor did he cease to suspect the Pretender's rival court. In 1969 Franco decided to restore the monarchy in the person of the Pretender's son, Juan Carlos. Juan Carlos, who swore loyalty to the Principles of the Movement, would continue Francoism after Franco. This proved to be the Caudillo's most serious political and personal miscalculation.

The Catholics were, of course, more than a family: all Francoists were Catholics. It was the blessing of the Spanish Church in the early years that *alone* allowed the regime to appear as a legitimate concern: the

Concordat signed with the Vatican in 1953 gave Franco a degree of international respectability. The poet Carlos Barral, suffocated and nauseated by the religious hypocrisy of postwar bourgeois Barcelona, found in 'the return of the priests' the hallmark of early Francoism.

Two groups represented organized Catholicism: the ACNP (the National Catholic Association of Propagandists) and the Opus Dei. Both sought to capture the political, economic, intellectual and social élite for the Church. The Opus prided itself on its 'discretion' and was accused of being a 'holy Mafia', a 'white' Freemasonry particularly concerned with recruiting academic notables and business whizz kids. While the ACNP was influential in the early years—especially in the educational system—the men of the Opus were the technocrats of the 1960s, combining the language of devotion with that of Samuel Smiles. In the final years of the regime it was the turn of the ACNP to regain influence.

The most enduring family was composed of professionals—of civil servants (including university professors) who had won their rank by competitive examination (*oposiciones*). Franco ruthlessly destroyed the political creations of liberalism—'inorganic' representative democracy and the party system—but he respected its administrative traditions. The absorption of middle-class talents into the administration and the government helps to explain the durability of Francoism. An ambitious man could only make a career within the system.

Franco balanced these families in his ministries, keeping the political élite satisfied within the system. When a family minister overstepped the mark or upset the family balance he was slapped down. Serrano Suñer went in 1942 once his Falangist ambitions made him unacceptable to monarchist conservatives; Ruíz Giménez, a Catholic associated with ACNP, was summarily dismissed in 1956 as too liberal; Fraga Iribarne and his supporters shared the same fate in 1969. With age, Franco took less interest, apart from foreign affairs, in the direct formulation of policy, spending more and more time hunting and fishing. 'Spain is easy to govern,' he boasted. One of the less observed results of Franco's balancing act was that it produced weak governments, in the sense that, composed of competing families, they lacked the coherence to resist Franco himself. To this weakness was added the weakness of poverty. Spain, until the 1970s, was a poor economy. The effects of poverty on government spending were compounded by a regressive tax system based on indirect taxation and with a very high level of tax evasion by the rich. Thus the Falangists could never find the funds to finance their ambitious social welfare programme; they never wrested the Ministries of Finance and Economics from their conservative political enemies.

VIII

After the weakening of the mixture of 'national Catholicism', Falangism, and the bleak military authoritarianism of the immediately postwar years, the regime was confronted with the necessity of achieving respectability and acceptance in a postwar western Europe that was now, Portugal apart, composed of democracies. Had Hitler won the war, this necessity would not have arisen. To a certain extent respectability was achieved in 1953 with the Concordat and the *rapprochement* with the U.S., when the greatest democratic state accepted Franco as the 'sentinel of the West', the most reliable anti-Communist during the Cold War. But acceptance was never complete: in 1962 the EEC refused to consider Francoist Spain as a potential member of the Community.

Acceptability in the West was part of a wider problem: how could the regime modify itself to 'fit' a modern industrial society in Spain itself? There were those who maintained that the 'essence' of the regime must never be changed, since to alter one piece of the structure would imperil the whole. Admiral Carrero Blanco remarked that to offer change to a Spaniard was like offering a drink to a confirmed alcoholic. Others believed that some form of wider 'participation' was necessary, that the regime must be 'liberalized' from within. Thus in the early '60s the new generation of Falangists round Solís, an energetic Andalusian Minister of the Movement and proponent of what he called 'political development', hoped to monopolize 'the contrast of opinions' within the Movement. But Solís' schemes for wider 'participation' in 'associations' controlled by the Movement ran up against the absolute impossibility of admitting any form of genuine party life; the same fate overtook his plans for enlarging 'participation' in the official syndicates. To the end of his life Franco regarded political parties as responsible for the disaster of 1898 (which had robbed him of a career in the navy) and the decline into the 'chaos' and 'communism' of the Republic. 'If by the contrast of opinions somebody is seeking to establish political parties, let him know *that* will never return,' he warned in 1967. Nor did he like the consequences of Fraga's limited attempts, as Minister of Information and Tourism, to liberalize the press and cultural life in general.

From 1969 until Franco's death, as the committed Francoists dug themselves into their bunker, the reformist 'openers' (*aperturistas*) fought—in vain—for 'liberalization' as the only policy which would enable the Francoist élite to survive in a post-Franco era. It was the protagonists of this internal conflict who presided over what has been called the 'decomposition of Francoism'.

In spite of the Caudillo's boast in his later years, 'all is tied down, well tied down', those who took as their slogan 'after Franco the Institutions' (i.e. that there should be no political changes and that the institutions created by Francoism should be manned for ever by faithful Francoists) could not be unaware of the failure of those institutions to contain the growing conflicts and sustain support for the regime. 'Decomposition' was evident during the government of Admiral Carrero Blanco, apostle of *continuismo*—the continuation of the existing political system, by force if necessary. The paradox was that, in the political ice age of the early 1970s, the press was becoming a 'paper parliament'. Governmental reformists like Fraga, author of the Press Law of 1966, argued in 1971 that a modern society must have modern institutions. But reformism did not prosper; it perished as protest and terrorism mounted.

Students and workers apart, in two areas the regime was increasingly running into trouble. It was losing the committed support of the Church, and its rigid, doctrinaire centralism was creating mass disaffection in Catalonia and the Basque Provinces—particularly Guipúzcoa and Vizcaya.

The support of the Church of 'National Catholicism' was, as we have argued, vital in the early years of the regime. In return, secondary education, the relatively feeble state sector apart, was handed over to the Church—it was in the church *colegios* that the élite was educated—and the civil law was based on canon law: hence the prohibition of divorce, a 'conquest' of the lay Republic. The younger clergy, especially in the Basque Provinces and Catalonia, began in the '60s the move towards an oppositional Church, but they found no support from a hierarchy bred in the 'Church of the Crusade'. It was the dying off of the older generation of bishops, together with events outside Spain—the reforms of John XXIII and the Second Vatican Council—that modified the official attitude of the Spanish hierarchy. Its more perceptive members realized the dangers of tying the Church to a regime that might not outlast the death of the dictator. By the '70s Cardinal Tarancón was the *bête noire* of the integral Francoists and Franco himself was deeply disturbed by what, to him, was an ungrateful and incomprehensible desertion. His explanation, for this as for all other unpleasant changes, was Communist infiltration and the Masonic conspiracy.

The rising wave of protest in the regions that had enjoyed Statutes of Autonomy under the Republic was comprehensible in terms of the regime's suppression of regionalism. The public use of the Catalan language was at first forbidden in favour of the 'language of Empire'—Castilian. Once this policy was relaxed a Catalan cultural revival was the symbol of a national protest, a surrogate for political freedom. Supported by Catalan priests, by 1970 Catalanism had produced its own brand of protest pop and, in 1971, the Catalan Assembly co-ordinated a national opposition. This protest was no longer a bourgeois or petty bourgeois concern; it had the support of the parties of the left, as the elections of 1977 were to prove.

The revival of Basque nationalism was the most remarkable feature of Franco's later years. Lacking the cultural confidence of Catalanism, Basque nationalism had a rough edge. A splinter group of young activists rejected the exiled leadership of the conservative Catholic PNV and its relative moderation for the terrorism of ETA. The latter combined, with some difficulty, Marxism and nationalism. ETA always feared that killings and kidnappings would alienate local support, depriving the terrorist fish of water to swim in. Mass support was provided when indiscriminate police repression alienated the local population. The Burgos trials of Basque terrorists in 1970 were a severe crisis, when it seemed the regime, rather than the terrorists, was in the dock. In December 1973 ETA staged its greatest *coup*: the assassination of Admiral Carrero Blanco, his car blown over the roof of the church to which he had come to attend mass.

If the terrorists miscalculated the regime's reaction, they had nevertheless struck a stout blow against *continuismo* as represented by Carrero Blanco. From now until Franco's death the government was divided, prey to a continuous crisis of identity: on the one flank stood the *aperturistas*; on the other the men of the bunker. For the first time the internal opposition became a decisive force, and to understand its former weakness and its new role we must trace its evolution since the end of the Civil War.

IX

The intellectual and political representatives of the 'other Spain'—mainly Socialists and left Republicans—were in exile in France, Mexico, and Argentina, and increasingly out of touch with conditions in Spain. It was the Communist party that first realized the importance of the internal struggle: after supporting the abortive guerilla movements of the 1940s it became the proponent of a united opposition front and its members experts in 'entrism'—the infiltration of the official syndicates by the CC.OO. The party's influence—and in spite of divisions and heresy hunts it was the most significant oppositional group until the '70s—was partly the creation of the regime itself, which built up the party as *the* threat, not merely to the peace of Spain, but to western civilization as such. Communist prestige was enhanced by the party's influence in university circles and on intellectuals and writers. Its devoted cadres, often recruited and trained in prison, were familiar with clandestine operations. The Socialists committed a short-term tactical error in rejecting 'entrism'. It was not until 1972, when the young internal leadership captured the movement which had been controlled by elderly exiles, that the PSOE could start on a period of spectacular expansion.

The 'democratic' (i.e. non-Communist) opposition was composed of Christian Democrats (including a repentant Gil Robles on the right and the ex-minister Ruiz Giménez on the left), liberal monarchists, Socialists, Social Democrats, and Republican groups, and representatives of the Catalan and Basque (non-terrorist) opposition. It was more or less tolerated and its main organ, *Cuadernos para el diálogo*, edited by Ruiz Giménez, published attacks on the system by both Marxists and left-wing Christian Democrats. It was anti-Communist, thus perpetuating the feuds of the Civil War. This meant that the united front advocated by the Communists, in spite of their professions of democratic pluralism, met with opposition from democrats who could not believe the party had rejected its Stalinist past.

Carrero Blanco's successor, his Minister of the Interior, the colourless administrator Arias Navarro, was therefore faced by a vocal opposition (this was the *Blütezeit* of the new political review *Cambio 16*) when his own government was divided. Basque terrorism gave arguments to hard-liners (only repression could defeat terrorism), strengthening them against the *aperturistas*. Arias' first move surprised public opinion: in a remarkable speech of 12 February 1974 he seemed to promise a genuine 'opening' of the regime via the old nostrum of political association. 'Passive adherence' would be replaced by active 'participation'. Had this opening been pursued, the opposition might have been in a difficult position. Cowed by the angry cries from the bunker, the final text of Arias' Statute of Political Associations was so restrictive that it was rejected, not merely by the opposition but by the regime reformists.

On 20 November 1975 Franco died. How had this ordinary man, a career soldier with solid bourgeois tastes, imposed Francoism on a country that, by 1975, was increasingly like other western European nations? Repression, ferocious in the early years, remained till the end; but physical repression was less important than the apathy of the mass and the ambitions of the élite. But by 1975 the system was in evident decay: the Church was divided; the working class militant; the Catalans and Basques in open revolt or passive hostility. Above all the press had become a Fourth Estate. The ambitious might well think that to link their fortunes with a system that possessed only physical force was to run the risk of being on the losing side.

11 The Monarchy of Juan Carlos: The Transition to Democracy

King Juan Carlos, now a man of thirty-seven, had been appointed by Franco as the best guarantee for the continuity of the institutions and spirit of Francoism; his tall figure had appeared standing dutifully slightly behind the Caudillo on all important state occasions. Yet he was to be, in the words of his Foreign Minister, the 'motor of change', the essential institutional element in the peaceful transition from 'organic democracy' to 'democracy without adjectives'. In order to legitimize a new monarchy dubious in its origins, he played the only card that, in the view of liberal opinion, could save his throne: the card of a democratic, constitutional, and parliamentary monarchy.

Yet, apart from vague conciliatory pronouncements, his first action was scarcely an indication of any democratic intent. He appointed Arias Navarro as his first Prime Minister, with a new government which, while it included reformists like Fraga and Areilza, also included representative figures from the ranks of the loyal Francoists, who still manned such institutions as the Council of the Realm (which nominated the *terna*, or list of three candidates for the office of prime minister to the king) and the National Council of the Movement (which vetted political associations as acceptable to its 'ideology'), and who still sat in the Cortes.

It therefore seemed unlikely that 'the institutions' would ever accept what the opposition called 'democracy without adjectives', or that the opposition would ever accept the monarchy of Juan Carlos. The opposition was still divided between a Democratic Junta (formed in July 1974 and including the Communists and political mavericks like Calvo Serer, now a democratic monarchist pushing the claims of Don Juan) and the Platform of Democratic Convergence (formed in July 1975, including Socialists, Liberals, and left-wing Christian Democrats). Though divided and though it included minute 'taxi parties'—so called because all the party members could get into one car—the opposition was roughly united in its programme: a 'democratic rupture' (*ruptura democratica*) which entailed a provisional government, a constituent Cortes to decide on the future institutions (i.e. whether there was to be a monarchical constitution, most of the opposition parties being formally Republican or indifferent to the monarchy), full democratic freedoms, and a complete political amnesty.

A resolute programme of reform from above stood an outside chance of isolating from the public the opposition, which was increasingly vocal in a press enjoying a freedom unimaginable in the heyday of Francoism. This programme the government of Arias proved incapable of implementing. The Cabinet was deeply divided. Arias himself went in perpetual fear of outbursts from the bunker and proclaimed his Francoist faith in the Cabinet. The 'Spanish democracy' promised by Arias on 28 January was completely unacceptable to the opposition. There were severe clashes between police and demonstrators which eroded the democratic image of the Minister of the Interior, Fraga, once the hope of the reformists. On 28 April Arias, in a speech which mentioned Franco, 'the veteran captain' and 'provident legislator', seven times, outlined a system based on universal suffrage, but which retained features of the *ancien régime* that made it completely unacceptable to liberal opinion. Yet it was too liberal for the institutions manned by the old guard. The Francoist Cortes used a rash of terrorist outrages to reject the reform of the articles of the Penal Code which penalized party political activities. Arias' failure was total: he had won allies neither on the hard right nor the liberal left. To the King's relief he resigned on 1 July. With reformism apparently blocked by the 'institutions', there seemed now no alternative to the democratic break which threatened to plunge Spain into a period of unprecedented political uncertainty.

•

II

The King's choice for his new Prime Minister was Adolfo Suárez. A young, handsome forty-three, he was a former Civil Governor and TV director, still president of a political association committed to *continuismo* in its more moderate form. The political class had expected the appointment of the former Foreign Minister, Areilza, leader of the 'civilized right'. The new Prime Minister was greeted with dismay—'a mistake, a formidable mistake'. Yet it was Suárez, bred in Francoism and with a Cabinet which seemed to the opposition dominated by Catholics and bankers, who was, with the support of the King, to dismantle Francoism and install democracy, leading Spain, in June 1977, to its first general election in forty years.

The achievement of Suárez was to accomplish the programme of democratization 'from above', using the legal institutions of Francoism. The Francoist political class committed *hara-kiri* when it passed the Law of Political Reform (November 1977) which set up a two-chamber Cortes elected by universal suffrage. To the old lion of Falangism, Girón, this complete abandonment of 'organic democracy' was to hand victory on a plate to the enemies of the Civil War.

Suárez was now confronted with two difficulties: pressures on both right and left.

First he must keep the army from backing the resentments of the Francoist bunker, enraged at surrender, and making capital out of the continuance of ETA terrorism. (From the beginning it was the Basque problem—Guipúzcoa and Vizcaya were in a state of permanent political agitation that earned much sympathy from foreign TV commentators—which was the most formidable obstacle to peaceful change. In containing the right and keeping the army loyal to the government the support of the King, as commander-in-chief of the army, was critical, enabling the government to retire factious generals who regarded it as their duty to maintain the existing (i.e. Francoist) constitution. Without the King's support the process of democratization would have been extraordinarily difficult.

The government had taken a tough line on public order: it had inherited a police force trained to regard demonstrations and flag-waving as sedition, but whose loyalty it must retain. Would the opposition, critical of this, and of the government's failure, in a period of obsession with politics, to deal with a worsening economic situation, accept democracy as a gift from above? This was Suárez' second problem.

The opposition was now united (23 October). If it clung to its 'democratic break'—a constituent assembly and a provisional government—then Suárez' policy of the legal installation of democracy was doomed. If his plans were rejected by the totality of the democratic opposition they would lack credibility; on the other hand the opposition ran the danger of isolation and accusations of wilful obstructionism if public opinion backed Suárez. Both sides held strong hands; neither played its trump card.

Unlike Arias, Suárez was not afraid to establish informal contacts with opposition leaders; nor did he prevent what were still technically illegal parties organizing in public. In December the Socialist party under its new young leader, Felipe González, held its first congress in forty years in a smart Madrid hotel, with police protection and widespread publicity.

As Felipe González recognized, Suárez' reforms put the opposition 'in a ghetto', in danger of being 'dished' by a government whose reform programme was to be overwhelmingly backed in a referendum held in December 1976. In late November, therefore, the idea of a 'democratic rupture was dropped in favour of a 'negotiated rupture'. A committee of the democratic opposition opened negotiations with the government.

This meant that the Socialists, formally republicans, were ready to accept the monarchy provided that it was a democratic monarchy.

Only one problem remained: the legalization of the Communist party. The party's Secretary General, Santiago Carrillo, forced the government's hand by appearing in Madrid on 10 December 1976. Unless the party was legalized the democratic opposition, however much it might distrust the Communists, could not accept the Suárez reforms; if the Communists were legalized then the government could expect a sharp reaction from the army and the right. For a few days, in the most intense political crisis so far, the government's democracy from above was in peril. Finally Suárez braved the reaction of the army and the right and legalized the party on 9 April. The army issued a protest but swallowed the government's decision 'out of patriotism'. The opposition could now accept the Suárez reform on condition that the elections were 'clean' and that parties had fair access to TV.

The way was clear for the final step in the government and the King's programme for the legal and peaceful installation of democracy: the general election of June 1977. The election was peaceful and the turn-out high (80 per cent). The results showed that the electorate rejected both the extreme right and the extreme left. The results were a triumph alike for moderation *and* a desire for change.

The Prime Minister's own loose coalition of Christian Democrats, Liberals, and Social Democrats, the UCD (Union of the Democratic Centre), emerged as the strongest party with 34 per cent of the vote—partly a reflection of Suárez' own and his government's prestige, partly because the independent Christian Democrats were annihilated, leaving what in the jargon of the time was called the 'political space' of the centre to the UCD. The Socialists came second with 28 per cent, an astonishing triumph for the new leadership, made possible because many voters were convinced by the party's slogan, 'A vote for Socialism is a vote for liberty', and overlooked occasional Marxist utterances. The Communists, now preaching Eurocommunism and the virtues of democratic pluralism, won only 9 per cent of the vote. The six seats in the Cortes won by Tierno Galván's Popular Socialists were a tribute to their leader's record of opposition and perhaps to the prestige enjoyed by professors. Most surprising of all was the poor performance of Fraga's AP (Popular Alliance), which polled 8 per cent—less than the Communists. The AP was a conservative grouping headed by a bevy of Francoist notables; its failure showed that, at least for the moment, what journalists called 'sociological Francoism' (i.e. the persistence of interests created by Francoism) was powerless against the forces determined to reject the legacy of the past. As for the unreconstructed Francoists, they obtained a mere 4 per cent. One feature deserves especial emphasis: only those parties which supported regional autonomy won in the Basque Provinces and Catalonia.

Suárez formed a government of his own coalition party. It was left with three main tasks: solving the long-neglected economic crisis; the passing of the constitution; the solution of the regional problem, complicated as it was by the continuation of ETA terrorism. It tackled the first two issues by 'consensus politics', i.e. negotiated settlements among the major parties which were then ratified by the Cortes. One of the main proponents of what he called 'government Italian style' was the repentant Stalinist, Carrillo.

The first exercise in consensus with the opposition (including the unions) were the so-called Moncloa Pacts (October 1977), which were successful in holding wage demands in return for promises of social and economic reform (above all in the tax system) and thus reducing the rate of inflation. The constitution, which established a democratic, constitutional monarchy, was the first Spanish constitution which was not imposed by a party but represented a negotiated compromise among all the major parties. Given the fissiparous tendencies of Spanish parties and the ravages caused by ministerial crises in the constitutional monarchy and Second Republic, the constitution contains every mechanical device to ensure stable government. It provides for a settlement of the regional problem by a mechanism for granting Statutes of Autonomy. It abandoned Catholicism as the official, state religion and opened the way for divorce. It was therefore regarded by the hard-line bishops as 'Godless' and by the hard right, in spite of its recognition of free enterprise, as 'Marxist'.

The most serious problem for the new democracy is the old issue that has haunted Spanish politics since 1898: the reconciliation of the claims of the regions with 'the unity of Spain'. The Catalans, after tough negotiations in the long night sessions which constitute the preferred technique of Prime Minister Suárez, obtained a Statute of Autonomy which satisfied their minimum demands. Complicated by the special status of Navarre, whose privileges of self-government had been respected by Franco, the grant of autonomy for the remaining Basque Province (Guipúzcoa, Vizcaya and Alava) did not eliminate the terrorism of ETA which had brought the region to the verge of moral and economic collapse.

Terrorists, in a dictatorship, can claim to represent a suppressed general will; in a democratic system terrorism is the claim of a self-appointed moral and political élite to *override* the general will, expressed by the vote. It aims to 'de-stabilize' democracy by provoking a right-wing backlash supported by the armed forces who see their colleagues killed. There are signs (1979) that terrorism is partially successful. The Armed Police have staged a near-mutiny; a general has called the Minister of Defence, General Gutiérrez Mellado (who has played an all-important role, with the King, in keeping the army behind the government), a traitor. Terrorists have tried to threaten Spain's surest form of foreign exchange, the tourist trade, by planting bombs in Mediterranean tourist resorts.

The weekly magazine *Cambio 16* put the issue dramatically: if the government cannot master terrorism, then terrorism will destroy democracy. Herri Batasuna, the left-wing nationalist party that supports ETA, can still muster respectable electoral support; a sympathy for terrorists, a legacy of Francoist blanket repression, persists. Such misguided succour still provides ETA with what Mao called 'water for the fish to swim in'. With the nationalists of the moderate PNV in control of the Basque government there is a hope that the water will be drained away.

It is not only in those areas where there is a long tradition of regionalism, based on historic and linguistic claims, that the government is confronted with demands, under the new constitution, for the setting up of autonomous governments. The most surprising of these demands is voiced by the Andalusian 'nationalists' of the PSA (Andalusian Socialist Party) whose claim is only flimsily based on history and cultural identity. It is the claim of an underdeveloped region neglected by the central government, a species of nationalism that has affinities with Third World nationalisms. Its denial by the government could produce an explosive mixture of frustrated 'nationalism' and the economic discontents of a region with the heaviest unemployment in Spain. In general, negotiations with the regions complicate and confuse politics and the existence of strong regional parties weakens the major Spanish parties on whose strength the working of a democratic system depends.

The consensus politics whose great achievement was the Constitution of 1978 could not continue; but even when consensus was replaced by an Iberian version of party politics there remained a feeling that political issues were settled, in the Spanish phrase 'behind the curtains', by negotiations with a government still dominated by reconstructed Francoists — 'old dogs in new collars'. There seemed to have taken place a relapse into the political apathy characteristic of the *ancien régime* evidenced in a steady decline in electoral participation and in the phenomenon of *pasotismo* among the youth. The *pasotas* (so called from those who 'pass' at cards) reject *all* values and *all* culture. The graffiti on university walls are silent memorials to a past age of concern and political enthusiasms.

This feeling of disillusion with the performance of the new democracy is summed up in the now fashionable catchword *desencanto* or disenchantment.

In my view this feeling is based on a false perception of what democracy is about and what it can achieve as a problem-solving system. Above all, behind *desencanto* lies what might be called the psychology of great expectations falsified. This is particularly evident in the hopes, which cannot be fulfilled, that grants of regional self-government will 'solve' deep structural problems: the poverty of Galicia, the pool of unemployment in Andalusia.

In a certain sense there was, in 1977, a repetition of the euphoria which accompanied the arrival of the Second Republic in 1931. Spaniards expected the mere installation of democracy to solve every problem from structural unemployment to pollution and access to education. To take a serious example: since the undemocratic nature of the Francoist regime had effectively kept Spain out of the European Community, then the coming of a democratic regime would ensure automatic and immediate entry. This hope was not realized. Such expectations occur at all levels of social life. There is a fierce rivalry between the football clubs of Madrid and Barcelona—a rivalry which can erupt in unfortunate mutual accusations. Listen to the centre forward of Barcelona: 'I thought with political change all this would change. But it has not been like that.' Why should it be? Why should political change mitigate the enthusiasm of football fans?

Certainly there was an expectation that democracy would usher in a cultural renaissance. This has not taken place. In a capitalist democracy—and Spain is a capitalist democracy—culture is, as in other Western societies, a market commodity subject to the fluctuations in the economic climate and to the necessity of selling its goods. In 1976, political curiosity and economic conditions underwrote a massive stream of publications. Now publishing houses are in financial difficulties.

There is a more paradoxical source of cultural *desencanto*. Felipe González, the Socialist leader, observes that there was a *cultura de constatación a la dictadura*, a protest culture that could survive in the erratic tolerance of decaying Francoism. It was the protest content of literature which gave it its resonance and its excitement. This supportive ambience has disappeared with the freedom of expression guaranteed by the constitution; less in fashion, intellectuals, heirs of the old *progrés* of the sixties, can now be heard complaining 'We lived better under Franco.'

Behind all this lies a deeper problem. The changes in Spanish society have been so rapid that the political system is confronted with processes of adjustment that, in other Western societies, took place over half a century. These changes have been telescoped into a decade or so, and the attendant problems have been exacerbated by the laxness of Francoist governments. Pollution is a striking example. Through lack of effective legislation under Franco, the new government has to control levels of pollution in Bilbao and Madrid that are the highest in Europe. Spain is confronted with problems common to the West and, indeed, in some cases in an acute form—stagflation, structural unemployment and an energy bill which eats up a higher proportion of export earning than in any other nation in the world. All these problems are made more intractable when the time-scale of adjustment has been telescoped.

It is not merely that there have been rapid physical and structural changes in Spanish society. These have been accompanied by what one might call a moral revolution, a cultural shock evident in the generational clash between a youth addicted to 'progressive' attitudes and their parents bred in the traditional morality of the Francoist era.

It is at least arguable that a section of the middle classes welcomed the Second Republic in 1931 as a better safeguard for their interests than the discredited monarchy; and similarly that, in 1976, those same classes saw in a democratic system a better prospect for stability than decrepit Francoism. Will they, when their interests are threatened or perceived to be threatened, turn against the new democracy as they did in the days of the Second Republic?

The extreme right has been unable to make any impression on the electorate, and Blas Piñar and his odious followers are left with the quasi-violent exploitation of certain features of the new democracy which are common to other Western societies: vandalism, pornography in the street kiosks and in the cinemas, drug addiction, divorce laws and propaganda for legalized abortion. It is an old technique of the right, invented in 1868, to attribute what is regarded as a general societal collapse to the advent of democracy. Not merely are the traditional moral values of the upper middle classes outraged. Their economic interests are threatened. Francoism saw a prolonged tax holiday for the well-to-do. Democracy means taxation all round.

The reaction of the disillusioned right under the Second Republic took two forms. Firstly, to base a conservative party, ambiguous in its loyalty to the Republic, on the defence of a persecuted Church; secondly, to appeal to the army as the saviour of society. Neither of these options is open. Though conflictive issues remain (for instance abortion and the plight of Church education in an age of inflation), the UCD is a sufficient defence of conservative interests and the Church.

As to the army, though individual generals thunder against democracy it is not probable that the army *as an institution* will intervene in Spanish politics. There is the loyalty of their commander-in-chief, the King, to the democratic processes. While he understands the outrage of officers when their comrades are brutally assassinated by terrorists, he has made it abundantly clear to the army that, in his words, 'for the army to lose discipline [i.e. allegiance to the legal government], would mean the end of the army'.

Secondly, the army is imprisoned by its own political theory. It has always intervened with the claim that it represents the general will of the nation corrupted by a clique of selfish politicians. This assertion cannot at the moment be sustained. Moreover there is no alternative model of an anti-democratic political system of the right available as there was in the 1930s. A return to Francoism as such is, politically speaking, inconceivable.

There is, therefore, no immediate prospect of a massive and effective right-wing reaction backed by the army. The extra-parliamentary left makes a great deal of noise; but its sound and fury is backed neither by numbers nor strong organization. Spain is an effective democracy, and those who criticize Suárez and his party as old dogs in new collars can replace him and it at the next general election. While it is true that certain hangovers of Francoist legislation, expecially the powers of the army over freedom of expression, still persist, these too can be modified by the democratic process. Democracy is less about the content of democratic policies than a set of rules of the political game. Provided the rules are respected neither Spaniards themselves, nor foreign observers of Spain, should exploit *desencanto* so that it becomes a self-fulfilling prophecy. That would be a disservice to Spain and to Europe.

Select Bibliography

In the early years of Francoism propaganda emphasis on the glories of the Empire of the sixteenth century combined with a view that liberalism had bred the 'anti-Spain' defeated in the Civil War to inhibit the production of scholarly works on the nineteenth century. With the collapse of Francoism the nineteenth and twentieth centuries have become modish. The production of books to meet the new demand mounts daily. The following bibliography is highly selective and emphasizes recent Spanish studies and books in English.

I. GENERAL STUDIES

The general history of the period is treated in the following works: Xavier Tusell Gómez, *La España del siglo XX* (1975), and Ricardo de la Cierva, *Historia básica de la España actual* (1974), both with useful bibliographies. J.M. García Escudero, *Historia política de las dos Españas* (1975), and M. Tuñon de Lara, *La España del siglo XX* (1966), represent respectively Catholic and Marxist interpretations. R. Carr, *Spain 1808–1939* (1966), is still of some use. M. Martínez Cuadrado, *La burguesía conservadora* (1973), represents a more quantitative approach to political and social history.

The economic and, to a lesser extent, the social history of the period is receiving increasing attention from Spanish historians. Essential statistics are to be found in *Estadísticas básicas de España 1900–1970* (1975). J. Vicens Vives, *An Economic History of Spain* (1969), is the work of a great pioneer; for Catalonia see his *Industrials i Politics* (1950). The Catalan school has continued to produce important studies. J. Fontana's *La quiebra de la monarquía absoluta* (1971) sets the stage; his *Cambio económico y actitudes políticas en la España del siglo XIX* (1973) examines the links between economics and politics. J. Nadal, *El fracaso de la revolución industrial en España 1814–1913* (1975), and G. Tortella Casares, *Los orígenes del capitalismo en España* (1973), are concerned to explain Spain's failure to industrialize. S. Roldan et al., *La consolidación del capitalismo en España* (1973), is a useful account of the economic effects of the 1914–18 war in the Basque country and Catalonia. See also

J.A. Lacomba, *Introducción a la historia económica de la España contemporánea* (1969) and J. Sardá's fundamental work, *La política monetaria y las fluctuaciones de la economía española* (1949); for the demographic evolution, J. Nadal, *La población española. Siglos XVI al XX* (1971). Social history is less well served but there is a reliable introduction in J. Vicens Vives, *Historia social y económica de España y America* (1959), vol.v, pp. 21–469, and in J.M. Jover's *Política, diplomacia y humanismo popular* (1976), pp. 45–64 and 229–345.

Agrarian history, in the past neglected, is now attracting scientific studies. M. Artola, *Los Latifundios* (1979), is the best study of the history of the great Andalusian estates and is complemented by A. Bernal, *La propiedad de la tierra y las luchas agrarias andaluzas* (1974); see also R. Herr's essay in D. Spring *European Landed Élites in the Nineteenth Century* (1977). pp. 98–126. J. Martínez Alier's *La estabilidad del latifundismo* (1968) describes the changes in Andalusia in the 1960s; A. Balcells, *El problema agrari a Catalunya* (1968), the fate of the Catalan *rabassaires*. Two modern studies of changes in eastern and western Andalusia respectively are M. Siguán, *El medio rural en Andalucía oriental* (1972), and A. López Ontiveros, *Emigración, propriedad y paisaje en la campiña de Córdoba* (1974).

The history of Spanish labour movements is a growth industry. M. Tuñon de Lara, *El movimiento obrera en la historia de España* (1972), is a good introduction. A useful short summary of the Socialist movement (with some documents) is A. Padilla, *El movimiento socialista español* (1977); J.P. Fusi, *Política obrera en el País Vasco* (1975), is essential for an understanding of the PSOE. G.H. Meaker, *The Revolutionary Left in Spain 1914–1923* (1974), is a detailed study of a critical period. J. Díaz del Moral, *Historia de las agitaciones campesinas andaluzas* (new edn. 1973), remains the classic study of rural anarchism. A modern study is Clara E. Lida, *Anarquismo y Revolución en la España del XIX* (1972). A general history of the labour movement in Catalonia is contained in E. Giralt and A. Balcells, *Els moviments socials en Catalunya* (1967), a more detailed study is A. Balcells, *Trabajo y organización obrera en la Cataluña contemporánea 1900–1936* (1974). For the CNT see A. Balcells, *El Sindicalismo en Barcelona 1916–1923* (1965).

The role of the military has not attracted the attention it deserves. Stanley Payne, *Politics and the Military in Modern Spain* (1967), remains the standard work. The social origins of the officer corps are studied in J. Busquets, *El militar de carrera en España* (1971). The collected works of General Mola, *Obras Completas* (3 vols., 1940) remain the best insight into the military mind.

Catalanism has evoked an abundant literature. M. García Venero,

Historia del nacionalismo catalán (1944), was written in the Franco period; the most useful modern history is A. Balcells, *Catalunya contemporánea* (2 vols., 1974); J. Rossinyol, *Le problème national catalan* (1974), is enthusiastically pro-Catalan. Isidre Molas, *Lliga Catalana* (2 vols., 1972), provides a detailed description of the organization of the Lliga; J. Pabón, *Cambó* (3 vols., 1952–69), is essential reading, not merely on Catalan politics but on the Restoration in general. The relationship between nationalism and the bourgeoisie is examined in A. Jutglar, *Historia crítica de la burguesía a Catalunya* (1972), and Borja de Riquer, *Lliga regionalista: la burguesía catalana i el nacionalisme* (1977).

The literature on Basque nationalism is growing fast. The best general histories are J.M. Azoala, *Vascunia y su destino* (1976), and Stanley Payne, *Basque Nationalism* (1975). The ideology of the founding father Sabino de Arana is dissected in J.J. Solozábal, *El primer nacionalismo vasco* (1975). A left-wing view is given in 'Beltza', *El nacionalismo vasco 1876–1936* (1976). 'Valencianism' is studied in A. Cucó, *El valencianisme polític* (1971). For Galicia see M.R. Saurin de la Iglesia, *Apuntes y documentos para una historia de Galicia en el siglo XIX* (1977), and J.A. Durán, *Agrarismo y movilación campesina en el país gallego* (1977).

II. THE POLITICS OF THE RESTORATION

M. Fernández Almagro's studies, *Cánovas* (1972), *Historia política de la España contemporánea* (2 vols., 1959), and his *Historia política del reinado de Alfonso XIII* (1934), describe the political vicissitudes of Restoration politics. Javier Tusell, *Oligarquía y caciquismo en Andalucía* (1976), and J. Varela Ortega, *Los amigos políticos* (1977), are essential for understanding the mechanics of electoral management. M. Martínez Cuadrado, *Elecciones y partidos políticos* (1969), contains all election results between 1868 and 1931. M. Artola, *Partidos y programas políticos 1808–1936* (2 vols., 1974) is a history of the parties together with their programmes. L. Aguiló Lúcia, *Sociología electoral valenciana 1903–1923* (1976), is useful as a local study of Levante politics.

The crises of 1909 and 1917 are studied in detail in J. Connelly Ullman, *The Tragic Week* (1968), and J.A. Lacomba, *La crisis española de 1917* (1970). J. Benet, *Maragall y la Semana Trágica* (1966), is a moving study on the reactions of a great poet to the repression of 1909. A defence of Maura and a 'monarchist' criticism of Alfonso XIII was written by Maura's son and M. Fernández Almagro in *Por qué cayó Alfonso XIII* (1948). The Maurista version is criticized in C. Seco Serrano, *Alfonso XIII y la crisis de la Restauración* (1969).

For the problem of 'regenerationism' J. Romero Maura, *La Rosa de fuego* (1975), is excellent. Apart from a general background to the crisis of 1909, it contains a new interpretation of Lerroux whose later political career is described in O. Ruiz Manjón, *El partido Republicano Radical* (1976).

The essential work on the clerical issue in politics between 1889 and 1913 is J. Andrés Gallego, *La política religiosa en España* (1975). For the educational problem see V. Cacho Viu's excellent study, *La Institución Libre de Enseñanza* (1962), which must be read with M.D. Gómez Molleda, *Los reformadores de la España contemporánea* (1963). There is an outline history of Catholic unionism: J.N. García Nieto, *El sindicalismo cristiana en España* (1960). O. Alzaga, *La primera democracia cristiana en España* (1973), studies the attempt to create a Christian Democratic party 1922–3, and provides an illuminating sidelight on the collapse of the Restoration system. J. Tusell continues the history of Christian democracy until 1939 in *Historia de la democracia cristiana en España* (2 vols., 1974).

III. THE DICTATORSHIP AND THE SECOND REPUBLIC 1923–36

The best study of the dictatorship of Primo de Rivera remains G. Maura y Gamazo, *Bosquejo histórico de la Dictadura* (1936). The role of the PSOE has been recently examined by J. Andrés Gallego, *El Socialismo durante la Dictadura 1923–1930* (1977). For the dictator's economic adventures see J. Velarde Fuertes, *Política económica de la Dictadura* (1973); but nothing replaces the apologia of Primo's Finance Minister José Calvo Sotelo, *Mis servicios al estado* (new ed. 1974). A detailed account of the collapse of the monarchy and the coming of the Republic is contained in Schlomo Ben-Ami, *The Origins of the Second Republic in Spain* (1978).

The literature on the Second Republic is extensive and I have concentrated on a few works in English. Gerald Brenan's *The Spanish Labyrinth* (1964) remains the best introduction, and G. Jackson, *The Spanish Republic and the Civil War* (1967), the most useful general history; Stanley Payne, *The Spanish Revolution* (1970), is a hard-hitting criticism of the left. E.E. Malefakis, *Agrarian Reform and Peasant Revolution in Spain* (1970), is a definitive history of the all-important agrarian issue. Paul Preston's *The Coming of the Spanish Civil War* (1979) and Richard Robinson's *The Origins of Franco's Spain: Right, Republic and Revolution 1931–36* (1970) are contrasting interpretations of the roles of the CEDA and PSOE. An important study of the party system is S. Varela, *Partidos y parlamento en la Segunda República* (1978); a general history, C. Seco Serrano, *Historia de España: Epoca Contemporánea* (1962), vol. vi.

Two essential apologias by participants are J.M. Gil Robles, *No fue posible la paz* (1968), and J. Chapaprieta, *La Paz fue posible* (1971). M.

Blinkhorn, *Carlism and Crisis in Spain 1931–36* (1975), is an excellent study of the right. The attitude of the Catholic Church is revealed in the correspondence of Cardinal Vidal i Barraquer, *Esglesia i Estat durant la Segona República Espanyola* (2 vols., 1971), scrupulously edited by M. Batllori and V.M. Arbeloa. For the 1936 elections see J. Tusell, *Las elecciones del Frente Popular* (1971), and Santos Juliá, *Orígenes del Frente Popular en España 1934–6* (1979); Ian Gibson, *The Death of García Lorca* (1975), is important for the atmosphere of July 1936.

IV. THE CIVIL WAR

If the bibliography of the Republic is large, that of the Civil War is unmanageable. Again I give the main works in English. Hugh Thomas, *The Spanish Civil War* (new ed. 1977) remains the most complete account. R. Carr, *The Spanish Tragedy* (1978), is analytical rather than chronological. Burnett Bolleten's earlier study on the role of the Communist party has been re-issued as *The Spanish Revolution* (1979). D. Catell's *Communism and the Spanish Civil War* (1955) remains useful. Ronald Fraser's *The Blood of Spain* (1979) is an oral history of the war, concentrating on the proletarian parties. There is a massive history of the Popular Army: R. Salas Larrazábal, *Historia del Ejército Popular de la República* (4 vols., 1974) to be complemented by the studies of J.M. Martínez Bande. For the role of the CNT see J. Peirats, *La CNT y la revolución española* (1971), and for the POUM the many works of V. Alba (a former POUM militant), especially *El Marxismo en España* (1970) and *Historia del POUM* (2 vols., 1974). For the origins of German intervention, see A. Viñas, *La Alemania nazi y el 18 Julio* (1974), and for the British attitude, J. Edwards, *The British Government and the Spanish Civil War 1936–1939* (1979). Italian intervention is fully described in J.F. Coverdale, *Italian Intervention in the Spanish Civil War* (1975). Among the host of eye-witness accounts the best are H.E. Kaminski, *Ceux de Barcelone* (1937), George Orwell's classic *Homage to Catalonia* (1938), and F. Borkenau, *The Spanish Cockpit* (1937). For the Basque campaign there is a sympathetic account in G.L. Steer, *The Tree of Guernika* (1938). H. Southworth's *The Day Guernica Died* (1977) is a definitive account of the bombing of Guernica. V. Ramos, *La Guerra Civil en la provincia de Alicante* (3 vols., 1972) is an ill-ordered but revealing description of the war at the local level.

Collectivization is defended in N. Chomsky, *American Power and the New Mandarins* (1939), pp. 62–129. Alberto Pérez Baró, *Trenta meses de colectivisme a Catalunya* (1970), considers the legislation and its effects on reality; J. Bricall, *Política económica de la Generalidad* (1970), gives production figures. On agrarian collectives see R. Fraser, op.cit., pp. 347

ff., and H. Thomas in R. Carr, ed., *The Republic and the Civil War in Spain* (1971). For the dilemmas of the CNT see C.M. Lorenzo, *Les anarchistes espagnols et le pouvoir* (1961).

For the politics of Nationalist Spain, M. García Venero, *Falange en la Guerra de España* (1967), and M. Hedilla's *Testimonio* (1972), together give the Falangist version of unification. Stanley Payne, *Falange* (1961), is a history of the movement; both R. Serrano Suñer, *Entre el silencio y la propaganda* (1979), and Dionisio Ridruejo, *Casi unas memorias* (1976), are the memoirs of disillusioned enthusiasts. The general atmosphere is described in R. Abella, *La vida cotidiana durante la guerra civil*, i (1973), and J. del Burgo, *Conspiración y guerra civil* (1970).

V. FRANCOISM

There are three English biographies of Franco: by George Hills (1971), J.W.D. Trythall (1970), and Brian Crozier (1967). A prejudiced if vivid portrait emerges from *Mis conversaciones privadas con Franco* (1976), by Lt. Gen. Francisco Franco Salgado-Araujo; for the views of Spaniards on Franco and his regime see J.M. Gironella and R. Borràs, *100 Españoles y Franco* (1979). Franco's political utterances have been arranged thematically in *Pensamiento político de Franco*, ed. A. del Río Cisneros (2 vols., 1975).

The Franco period and the transition to democracy with emphasis on the social and economic transformations is treated in R. Carr and J.P. Fusi, *Spain: Dictatorship to Democracy* (1979); R. de la Cierva's *Historia del Franquismo* (1975) provides a detailed history. R. Tamames, *La República: La era de Franco* (1973), is a remarkable instance of criticism of the regime while it still existed. The institutions of Francoism are dissected in K.N. Medhurst, *Government in Spain: The Executive at Work* (1973) and J. Amodia, *Franco's political legacy* (1977).

A. López Piña and E. Aranguren's *La cultura política de la España de Franco* (1970) is a penetrating summary of recent work. For the opposition see X. Tusell, *La oposición democrática al Franquismo* (1977), Guy Hermet, *The Communists in Spain* (1974), and P. Preston, ed., *Spain in Crisis* (1976). For ETA, from the inside, see 'Ortzi', *Historia de Euzkadi: el nacionalismo vasco y ETA* (1975), and J. Aguirre, *Operation Ogro* (1975). There is a useful account of the Arias Navarro ministry in J. Oneto, *Arias entre dos crisis* (1975), and an account by his Foreign Minister J. M. de Areilza, *Diario de un ministro de la Monarquía* (1977).

J.M. Maravall has written two important works on student and working-class opposition, *El desarollo económico y la clase obrera* (1970) and *Dictatorship and Political Dissent* (1978). J. Amsden describes the working of the official trade unions in *Collective Bargaining and Class*

Struggle in Spain (1972). C.W. Anderson, *The Political Economy of Modern Spain* (1970), and J. Clavera, J.M. Esteban, et al., *Capitalismo español* (2 vols., 1973), discuss the changes in economic policy. The postwar atmosphere is re-created in R. Abella, *Por el imperio hacia Dios* (1979).

For hostile accounts of Catholic attitudes to Franco see A. Sáez Alba, *La ACNP y el caso de 'El correo de Andalucía'* (1974), and Daniel Artigues, *El Opus Dei en España* (1968).

For the changes in Spanish society under Franco see A. de Miguel, *Manual de Estructura social de España* (1974), and his *Sociología del Franquismo* (1975); Carlos Moya, *El poder económico en España* (n.d.), is a suggestive analysis of the economic élite and V. Pérez Díaz, *Pueblos y clases sociales en el campo español* (1974), of the rural scene. There is a great deal of raw information in *La España de los años 70*, ed. M. Fraga; in *Informe sociológico sobre la situación social de España*, published by the FOESSA foundation in 1970, and in *Comentario sociológico. Estructura social de España*, published in 1978 by the Cajas de Ahorros. For an illuminating study of some aspects of modernization see Ronald Fraser, *The Pueblo* (1973).

Index